GENDER, SMALL-SCALE INDUSTRY
AND DEVELOPMENT POLICIES

GENDER, SMALL-SCALE INDUSTRY AND DEVELOPMENT POLICY

Edited by I.S.A. BAUD and G.A. de BRUIJNE

IT PUBLICATIONS 1993

Intermediate Technology Publications
103/105 Southampton Row, London WC1B 4HH, UK

© IT Publications 1993

A CIP catalogue record for this book is available from the British Library

ISBN 1 85339 152 2 (Hbk)
     1 85339 156 5 (Pbk)

Typeset by Inforum, Rowlands Castle, Hants, printed by SRP, Exeter

Contents

About the Authors   vii

Acronyms   x

Part I — Perspectives on the role of small-scale industries in third world development

1 *Introduction*   Gender aspects of small-scale industry
   and development policy   3
   ISA BAUD

2 Small-scale industry's contribution to economic
   development   16
   ROGER TESZLER

3 Subcontracting — the incorporation of small
   producers in dynamic industrial networks   35
   PETER KNORRINGA and HERMINE WEIJLAND

4 The labour process under amoebic capitalism — a case
   study of the garment industry in a south Indian town   47
   PAMELA CAWTHORNE

Part II — Gender aspects and policy experiences in small-scale industries

5 Gender aspects of industrialization in India and Mexico   79
   ISA BAUD

6 Gender inequality — labour market and household
   influences   97
   INES SMYTH

7 Women in small-scale industries — some lessons from
   Africa   109
   MARILYN CARR

8 Women's organizations and subcontracting — a case
   study from India   116
   MIRA SAVARA

Part III — Case study — the footwear industry

9 Recent trends in the world footwear industry   131
   FERENC SCHMEL

10 Developments in the Indian leather and
    leather-products industry   151
    K. SESHAGIRI RAO

11 Small-scale units in the Agra leather footwear industry   170
    J. GEORGE WAARDENBURG
12 Women outworkers in the Neapolitan leather trade   187
    VICTORIA GODDARD

Notes   200
References   206

About the authors

Isa Baud (Dr) is associate professor at the University of Amsterdam. Her area of interest is women's labour during industrial development, with a focus on small-scale industry. Currently she is involved in a research project on women's labour in small-scale industry (footwear), considering the impact of technological change on women workers, with a view to developing strategies to maintain women's position within the industry when such changes occur. Recent publications include *Forms of Production and Women's Labour: Gender Aspects of Industrialization in India and Mexico* (1991), and (with C. Andersen) *Women in Development Cooperation: Europe's Unfinished Business* (1987).

Marilyn Carr (Dr) is currently Senior Advisor on Technology and Small Enterprise Development with the United Nations Development Fund for Women (UNIFEM). Previously, she was Chief Economist with the Intermediate Technology Development Group (ITDG) in the UK. She has written several books on small-scale industry and appropriate technology including *Blacksmith, Baker, Roofing-sheet Maker; Employment for Rural Women in Developing Countries; The AT Reader; Theory and Practice in Appropriate Technology*, and *The Barefoot Book; Economically Appropriate Services for the Rural Poor.*

Pamela Cawthorne (Dr) has recently completed her doctoral thesis on the knitwear industry in Southern India and is a member of the Development Policy and Practice Group at the Open University in Milton Keynes. She has lived and worked many years abroad including posts at UNIDO and UNRWA. Prior to research work in India she also worked for OXFAM in the United Kingdom. Current interests include small-scale industry developments in Europe and in India, and the history of the hosiery and knitwear industry.

Victoria Goddard (Dr) is an Argentine anthropologist who has carried out research in Naples, Southern Italy on outwork and small enterprises, focusing particularly on questions relating to women, work, and sexuality. She is Lecturer in the Department of Anthropology and Community Studies, Goldsmith College, University of London and at the Department of Anthropology and American History at the University of Barcelona.

Peter Knorringa (MA) is a development economist, working at the Free University of Amsterdam on issues of industrial networks, specifically focusing on forward linkage — such as direct marketing and subcontracting relations. His fieldwork experience is in India and Indonesia.

Mira Savara (Dr) is a research consultant working mainly in the field of 'women in the informal sector'. Since 1985 she has been co-ordinating a project on women in food processing, and has recently concluded a project on women's organizations in the informal sector in Bombay. Her publications include (with J. Everett) *Institutional Credit as a Strategy toward Self-reliance for Petty Commodity Producers in India: A Critical Evaluation*, in Singh and Kelles-Viitanen, *Invisible Hands, Women in Home-based Production* (1987).

Ferenc Schmel (Dr) obtained an MA degree in Mechanical Engineering at Kiev University, and wrote a dissertation on computer-aided design. He has a long experience as a footwear technology researcher, and has worked in numerous developing countries as an UNIDO expert. He is Industrial Development Officer at the United Nations Industrial Development Organization (UNIDO) in Vienna. He has published fourteen books in Hungary, and papers in various international technical journals. Recent fields of interest include application of artificial intelligence and expert systems in industrial training and production control.

K. Seshagiri Rao (MA) is an economist of long standing, specializing in the economics and marketing of leather and the leather-products industry. He has headed the Economics Research Division of the Central Leather Research Institute in Madras for almost thirty years, and served as FAO consultant in Nigeria in the 1970s. Projects carried out under his guidance include market research to assess export prospects for India's leather and leather products in Europe, the American continent and selected Asian countries. He has served on various national committees on leather and allied industries, and has brought out more than eighty publications.

Ines Smyth (Dr) has a PhD in Social Anthropology from University College London. Currently she is Senior Lecturer at the Institute of Social Studies, the Hague, where she occupies the post of Teaching Convenor of the Population and Development Programme. Her main fields of academic interest are rural industrialisation, women's work in small-scale industries, and gender issues in the context of population theories and policies. Her most recent publications are: (with Loes Keysers) 'Family Planning: More than Fertility Control?', in *Peripherie*, Vol.36, No.9, 1989; 'Collective Efficiency and Selective Benefits' in *Labour and Society*, Vol.3, No.3, 1991; and 'The Family Planning Programme in Indonesia: A success story for women?' in *Development and Choice*, Oct. 1991.

Roger Teszler (Dr) is a development economist and senior staff member with the Department of Agricultural and Development Economics of the University of Amsterdam. He is one of the authors of the UNDP/

Netherlands/ILO/UNIDO study on 'Rural Small Industrial Enterprise' (RSIE, 1988), and has carried out research and evaluation studies for donor and international agencies on small-scale industry in a number of African and Latin American countries. His main research interests include the policy framework for small-scale enterprise development in times of economic crisis and the significance of small industry for regional development.

J. George Waardenburg (Prof.) is professor at the Centre for Development Planning from the Erasmus University in Rotterdam. His main research interest is the development of small scale and rural industries in Asia, in particular India and China. Additional fields of interests include (inter)regional planning, mixed and changing economic systems, and international scientific cooperation. A recent publication is (with W.L.M. Adriaansen and S.T.H. Storm), *Forty Years of Experience in Development Theory and Practice*, in W.L.M. Adriaansen and J.G. Waardenburg (eds), *Development in a Dual World Economy*, (1989).

Hermine Weijland (Dr) is senior lecturer in Development Economics at the Free University, Amsterdam. She has specialized in income distribution and rural industrialization and is currently doing research on rural non-farm activities in Central Java, Indonesia. Recent publications include an article on 'Dual Production and Marketing of Vegetables in Swaziland: a case of marginalization of Female Traders' (with H. Sandee), and Research Memoranda on *Cottage Industry in Indonesia* and the *Urban Bias of Rural Industry* (Free University, Amsterdam).

Acronyms

Benelux	Belgium, the Netherlands, Luxembourg
BPS	Indonesian Central Statistics Office
C&F	cost and freight
CIF	cost, insurance, freight
CIM	computer integrated (footwear) manufacture
CITU	Centre of India Trade Unions
CPI	Communist Party of India
CPI(M)	Communist Party of India (Marxist)
crore	ten million
DEMATT	Development of Malawi Traders Trust
ECU	European Currency Unit
EEC	European Economic Community
ESI	Employees' State Insurance
FOB	Freight on Board
IDPAD	Indo-Dutch Programme on Alternatives to Development
INDEFUND	Investment and Development Fund of Malawi
lakh	one hundred thousand
MUSCCO	Malawi Union of Savers and Credit Co-operatives
PF	Provident Fund
Rs.	Indian rupees
RIIC	Rural Industries Innovation Centre
SADCC	Southern African Development Co-ordination Conference
SATRA	a UK organization for industry research and statistics of the footwear industry
SEDCO	Small Enterprise Development Organization
SEDOM	Small Enterprise Development Organization, Malawi
SIDO	Small Industries Development Organization
SSE	small-scale enterprise
SSI	small-scale industry
UPLDMC	Uttar Pradesh Leather Development and Marketing Organization
UNDP	United Nations Development Programme
UNIDO	United Nations Industrial Development Organization

PART I

Perspectives on the role of small-scale industries in third world development

1 Introduction — gender aspects of small-scale industry and development policy

ISA BAUD

The contributions small-scale industries can make to the development process in many developing countries have received increased attention in recent years. Not only have a large number of academic studies been carried out in this area[1], but also numerous international and national development agencies have been active in designing, implementing and evaluating programmes for this type of industry[2].

Attention has also been focused on a second area — women's employment outside large-scale factory production, a heterogeneous sector including trading and services, as well as small-scale industries[3]. Such studies have been carried out within the framework of 'gender and development' studies, and have indicated that women are often a major part of the workforce in small-scale production[4] and the associated domestic outwork. Equally, their contributions are little acknowledged, and sometimes are even denied outright.

Given the interest in the 1990s of various donor countries in increasing the employment and production role of small-scale industries in the development process[5], it is important to develop a context in which women's contributions to this production are not inadvertently missed. In this volume, an attempt is made to present an analysis that brings together a gender perspective on small-scale industries with the perspective commonly used by economists, which stresses the contribution of small-scale industries to higher employment and wider distribution of production, without looking explicitly at the social groups involved.

In order to reach this goal, the first two parts of the book are concerned with the following issues:

o the role of small-scale industrial units in the development process;
o the (changing) gender division of labour in such industries, and the ways women combine employment with their reproductive tasks and 'community' roles; and
o the lessons to be learned from development programmes directed

The contributions to this volume were first presented at a seminar on 'Women in Small Scale Industry and Development Policy' held in the autumn of 1989 in Noordwijkerhout, hosted by the Institute of Human Geography of the University of Amsterdam, co-organized by Anneke van Luijken of the Industrial Restructuring Education Network for Europe (IRENE), with financial contributions by the Directorate General of International Development Cooperation of the Netherlands.

towards women in small-scale industries, or, in wider terms, the so-called 'informal sector'.

In the third part of the book, the issues raised are considered within the footwear Industry. It is used as an example of an expanding agro-industry[6] within developing countries, about which little is known (both from the enterprise side and in terms of women's employment)[7].

Basic Concepts

Women's employment and reproductive work

Employment is usually defined by economists as the exchange of labour for cash or kind. This leaves out various types of productive work to which women contribute heavily. A wider concept of employment includes non-market or subsistence production, unpaid work that contributes to family based production, and work in putting-out systems (Grown and Sebstadt, 1989). In this volume, all these aspects are included in the term employment. Women's reproductive work includes all activities directed at their maintenance activities for the daily and future well-being of the current and next generations (usually within the context of the family/household) (Barrett, 1980). Although women's reproductive work is not focused on specially in this volume, it has to be taken into account as part of women's total work burden.

Small-scale and micro-industries

Definitions of small-scale and micro-industries are plentiful and vary widely (Liedholm and Mead, 1987). For the purpose of this study, the term 'small-scale industries' includes both small-scale and micro-enterprises. The former usually are defined according to an employment criterion as having ten to fifty, and the latter zero to ten, employees. However, this criterion alone raises a fair number of questions. The statistics usually collected leave unclear whether 'employment' indicates the occupational status of the person involved, i.e. whether it concerns full or part-time employment, a direct employer-employee relationship or an indirect one (putting-out work), the degree of casualness of the work, or whether all productive contributions, including unpaid family labour, are counted.

Therefore, when using 'employment' as a criterion for distinguishing types of small-scale and micro-enterprises, it is necessary to indicate the types of labour recruited by the enterprise. Aside from the entrepreneurs themselves, labour categories include: (1) short-term wage work, (2) casual wage workers, (3) disguised wage workers and (4) unpaid family labour. People working in a situation intermediate between employee and entrepreneur include (1) dependent producers and (2) self-employed people (Baud, Chapter 5).

4

Teszler (see Chapter 2), confronting the same problem, proposes a combination of other criteria for classifying such industries. This would help to identify the strengths and weaknesses of the various types of enterprises, and differences in their reactions to policy stimuli. The criteria he uses in addition to number of employees are first the level of technology, and second the type of entrepreneurship. On the basis of sub-divisions using these criteria, he gives three categories of micro-enterprises: individual self-employment, group self-employment, and home-based enterprises (cottage enterprises). There are two categories of small enterprise: those using traditional technology, but switching over to modern technologies; and those using modern technology.

This differentiated classification is a great improvement on existing definitions, as it indicates the variability in the internal characteristics of the enterprises concerned. However, as described by Teszler, the first two types of micro-enterprises concern producers who may have a set of tools and skills, but very little visible 'enterprise' (in contrast to a great deal of entrepreneurship). Thus, two more areas need to be defined to present a complete picture of the environment in which such producers work — the marketing linkages of the enterprise and the socio-economic goals toward which producers strive.

Industrial networks
The external relations of micro- and small-scale enterprises are often serious sources of constraints on growth. External relations include financing systems, relations with raw material and technology suppliers, marketing channels and subcontracting arrangements (Schmitz, 1982). From the point of view of micro- and small-scale producers, the extent to which they can influence external relations is very important. To gain more insight into that process, the concept of industrial networks is used[8].

An industrial network is a group of traders and producers who carry out a complete marketing and production cycle for a particular set of final products, designed for a specific market segment (Knorringa and Weijland; Chapter 3). The authors emphasize that within such a network, the conditions for small producers are set from the demand side. The demands determine to a large extent their vulnerability as enterprise and the extent and security of the employment created.

Links within an industrial network are often laid down to an important extent by subcontracting arrangements. This is a process in which a contractor places an order with a subcontractor to manufacture all or part of a final product, which the contractor then markets as his own. Arrangements can be classified under two main headings: commercial subcontracting and industrial subcontracting (Knorringa, 1988). In the former situation, the contractor does not participate in the production process, but only takes care of marketing and financing. Industrial contractors use subcontractors for the execution of specific tasks within their own production processes. In fact, long chains of subcontractors are possible (Beneria and Roldan, 1987; Pineda-Ofreneo, 1982).

Employment and economic goals

What implications do such subcontracting arrangements have for the economic and employment goals of the small-scale and micro-producers involved?

The economic goals of the various categories of producers involved are linked to the income level of the person and his/her immediate social group, and they influence the 'employment' strategies used. 'For the poorest, survival is the main goal; the poorest women strive to generate income to purchase food, shelter, and clothing.' (Grown and Sebstadt, 1989) Among those whose basic survival is assured, security of income may become the economic goal; rather than maximum income, a regular source of income is desired. Finally, for those who have gained a degree of security, economic growth may become the goal.

Chambers (1990) expands this discussion to include non-economic aspects in this series of goals. At the level of survival, the methods used by people to obtain an income include splitting up families (e.g. for labour migration), taking children out of school for work, reciprocal exchanges with poor relatives and neighbours, and patron-client relations. Security entails 'the ability to meet contingencies without further impoverishment' (ibid.). The third goal is self-respect, that is, independence from humiliating social relations enforced by poverty and powerlessness.

These distinct types of socio-economic goals indicate the perspectives from which people participate in employment — for the survival and benefit of themselves or the social group of which they form a part and for which they take partial responsibility. Incorporating such perspectives — differentiated by gender, age, and social group — should enable future policymakers to better direct their efforts by fitting them to particular groups of people.

Small-Scale Industries in Economic Development

The first theme is the role of small-scale industries in the larger development process. As we are concerned about women's employment in these industries, employment effects in particular should be kept in mind. The following issues are considered: (a) the contribution of small versus large industries, (b) the linkages between large and small industries, and (c) characteristics of employment in small industries.

The last forty years have shown that large-scale industrial development has not led to an integrated industrial structure, capable of providing employment for a major share of a country's domestic population, except under specific circumstances.

It is clear that small-scale industries do not form a substitute for large-scale industrial units. Given the large number of people looking for employment, and the labour-intensive character of most small-scale and micro-enterprises, they do form a very necessary complement. Based on the results of an extensive inter-country survey (UNDP/Neth/ILO/UNIDO, 1988), Teszler, in Chapter 2, indicates that the role of small-scale and micro-enterprises differs with the phase of development. In high- and middle-income, and newly industrializing countries, small modern enterprises are important, and micro-enterprises based on traditional technology tend to die out. In low-income countries, however, small industries using traditional and/or modernizing types of technology form the backbone for industrial development. In countries with an important agricultural sector, this should serve as a growth pole for rural small-scale enterprises.

Overall, Teszler sees the direction of structural change in industry as tending toward 1) the disappearance of the smallest enterprises, and 2) a reorientation of larger small-scale enterprises towards national and international markets.

The linkages between large-scale and small–scale industries have been viewed alternately as exploitative or as benign: exploitative, as they constrain the growth possibilities of small enterprises, and lead to a form of dependent capitalism (Harriss, 1982; Moser, 1978); benign, in terms of spreading employment and income effects to a wider range of people (UNIDO, 1985). Other authors have made a distinction between the external relations of small enterprises, in which dependence on the large-scale sector is extensive, and internal relations (technology and labour) in which dependence is much less (Harriss, 1982; Baud, Chapter 5).

Knorringa and Weijland (Chapter 3) develop a more explicit model of the environment of small-scale enterprises (conceptualized as industrial networks) in order to assess both positive and negative effects of linkages. By looking at the various forms of subcontracting which take place, they consider more explicitly the factors and processes which influence the extent of small scale industries' independence. There has been a substantial increase in the amount of subcontracting by large firms in a number of large developing countries (e.g. India, Indonesia, the Philippines) in the late seventies and eighties. This trend has been linked to the liberalization of industrial policies in favour of industrial exports, and has occurred in situations where labour legislation is not backed up by strong regulations and enforcement.

The extent to which small producers can set conditions within the industrial network varies: the most favourable situation is that of the specialized subcontractor with a scarce skill or machine. Nevertheless, the authors

7

suggest that, even for more vulnerable groups such as 'homebound' workers, it may initially represent an improvement over their previous position. The question remains how long initial improvements retain their importance for such groups of producers in terms of their 'goals'.

Employment within small-scale industries is much more heterogeneous and structured than was acknowledged in early studies of small industries[9]. Labour-market segmentation also occurs in these industries, and only some social groups enjoy the 'easy access' to small-scale and micro-enterprise employment usually assumed to apply. A number of studies have shown that segmentation occurs along caste, ethnic, regional, gender, and occupational lines (Holmström, 1985; Breman, 1990; de la Peña and Escobar, 1986); and that it involves power struggles between groups of working people and enterprise owners/managers (Cawthorne, Chapter 4; Harriss, 1982; Kalpagam, 1981).

The characteristics of the labour process within small-scale and micro-industries also undergo changes as they expand. Pamela Cawthorne has gone into this process (see Chapter 4) for an expanding labour-intensive industry in India — the hosiery industry — with an export market orientation. She indicates that capital accumulation is taking place and becoming concentrated in fewer hands, without a concomitant centralization of the production process. This process is characterized as exhibiting a de-centralized work organization, using casual labour. The categories of labour used vary. Wage-workers are largely recruited on the basis of piece-rates and work very long hours. A large group of hidden workers exist: women working at home and children (both at home and in workshops) working as 'helpers' or 'apprentices'.

In terms of job skills, a general process of skill acquisition has occurred among the working people involved. This is also emphasized by Schmitz, who indicates that access to new skills is much more important in developing countries than a process of de-skilling (1985).

The extent of labour mobility is still largely uncharted. It includes horizontal shifts between similar jobs, upward mobility towards better jobs, and downward mobility in terms of earnings and job security. Although labour mobility has been regarded as positive, this very much depends on the type of mobility under discussion. A number of authors have stressed that many people (particularly in casual forms of labour) strive for security rather than mobility (Breman, 1989; Chambers, 1984; Holmström, 1984). This points back to the discussion of socio-economic goals mentioned at the begining of this chapter.

Gender Aspects of Employment in Small-Scale Industries

The second theme concerns gender aspects of employment in small-scale and micro-industries. First, the gender composition of employment in small-scale and micro-industry and how it is affected by various changes in the internal and external circumstances of the enterprise is covered; secondly, gender aspects are considered from the point of view of how women combine productive and reproductive tasks at the family/household level.

The first point comes back immediately to the issues discussed in the previous section on employment. At a global level, women's participation in industry has increased (UNIDO, 1985). However, gender differences in labour market segmentation are extensive. Women's access to employment in agro-industrial sectors is relatively great (Baud, 1991; Banerjee, 1990), whereas research tends to indicate that other small-scale industrial sectors are less open to women than to men (Roelofs, 1987; Carr, Chapter 8). As entrepreneurs, women tend to take up activities that require little capital and to build on existing skills (Chen, 1989; Carr, Chapter 8). As workers, women are recruited more extensively than men into the more casual forms of labour; short-term wage labour, disguised wage work and especially unpaid family labour (Rutten, 1990).

At the level of the labour process, women and men are usually recruited for different operations; there is a clear gender segregation. This makes comparisons of wage levels and workloads very difficult. Changes in technology and work organization occur throughout an industrial branch; and changes in large-scale production affect small-scale and micro-enterprises fairly directly. Baud shows that when new technology is introduced in large enterprises, women's employment within the firm can be either increased or decreased. If the work content of jobs becomes more complex, women are usually edged out. If it is simplified, women are recruited more extensively.

External effects can also be seen in the linkages between large and small scale enterprises. When introducing new technology, large companies exhibit a propensity for subcontracting production out and using more casual forms of labour. This leads to a greater emphasis on women's employment in the most casual labour categories (the casualization hypothesis; see Banerjee, 1990; Rao and Husain, 1990).

Women also acquire different types of job skills than men, and in a different manner. In Chapter 5, a clear gender difference in the channels used to acquire new skills is indicated; women have less access to formal channels that provide comprehensive skills training; they use family or neighbourhood channels to obtain skills training informally. Goddard (Chapter 11) demonstrates that girls acquire skills training within existing social networks of working women, rather than through the sort of apprenticeship systems that exist for boys.

The question of labour mobility is very important to women working in small-scale and micro-industries. A major goal of the majority of these women is security (Baud, Chapter 5). For women working as wage workers in small-scale units, this can be linked to good personal relationships with

9

the owner of the unit; for women working as domestic outworkers (micro-entrepreneurs) security is sought by spreading risks and taking work from as many different middle(wo)men as possible.

These findings suggest that it is difficult to conclude that change in women's employment in small-scale industries is one-directional, as is often assumed when using the 'marginalization thesis' regarding women's employment. One needs to assess the effects of, first, trends in the industrial sector as a whole and how these affect total production; second, the way linkages between large- and small-scale enterprises affect the latter with respect to employment creation; and third, how the introduction of new technology and work organization affects the division of jobs between men, women and children.

The ways women combine their productive and reproductive work has various facets: the poverty level of the household, the division of labour and authority within it, life cycle patterns, and cultural patterns. On the basis of a study in West Javan villages, Smyth (see Chapter 6) indicates that household responsibilities pose constraints during several phases of women's lives. She shows that limitations on educational opportunities due to early marriages are a main factor determining women's concentration in low paid economic activities. Also, a woman's access to employment before marriage is restricted by social pressures concerning her marriageability; after marriage, social restrictions are relaxed, but the level of responsibility for home duties limits the range of productive employment.

A somewhat different life-cycle pattern is reported from Mexico by de la Rocha (1986). She found the heaviest work burden for women in the early period of marriage, when care for small children must be combined with employment by both spouses. In a later phase, with older children also earning income, the woman's need to earn an income diminishes, lightening her double burden.

Women's combined workload can also vary seasonally according to the economic needs of the household, and the labour available within it. Rutten (1990) has illustrated this in the Philippines, where women combine artisanal activities with household work to supply income in particular periods when other sources of income are low (due to the agricultural cycle). It is interesting that men will take over household tasks in such periods, in order to allow women to earn cash income.

Intervention Programmes for Women in Small-Scale Industries

The third theme concerns the experiences to date of intervention programmes designed to reach women working in small-scale industries. Two questions are of concern: how do different types of organizations vary in their outreach to women in small-scale industries, and what kinds of strategies are most effective in improving women's positions at work?

Organizations which carry out programmes for women in small-scale and micro-industries include government programmes, banks, national support agencies, NGOs, women's organizations, and trade unions. In this volume, the experiences of African national agencies giving support to small-scale entrepreneurs in the SADCC countries is recounted by Carr (Chapter 7) and those of several women's organizations in Bombay by Savara (Chapter 8). In Africa, the agencies had great difficulty reaching women entrepreneurs, who formed only a small percentage of the total number of clients. This was due to problems both from the side of the agency, and from that of the women themselves. A solution currently being tried out is the creation of women's desks within the agencies.

In India, local women's organizations in Bombay creating income-earning activities for poor women had no difficulty in reaching these women (Savara, Chapter 8). The organizations operated as intermediaries, obtaining orders as subcontractors to create employment. However, they were often squeezed out by competitors with less idealistic motives, who were willing to pay their employees lower wages; in the end, the conditions offered by the women's organizations were similarly exploitative.

These two examples illustrate the relative strengths and weaknesses of different types of organizations. Women's organizations are better able to reach poor women, but thus far have lacked the economic knowledge and power to protect their clients. National agencies can in principle offer better support services, but have difficulty reaching the poorer women entrepreneurs.

The types of strategies used by different organizations vary. National agencies often provide credit, but only for investment purposes. Several problems occur regularly in this type of support system. Making credit available for investment only overlooks the problems many small producers have in obtaining working capital (Everett and Savara, 1986; Baud, 1991). For women particularly, it also disregards the need for consumption as well as productive credit (Grown and Sebstadt, 1989; Everett and Savara, 1986). What has been shown in the SADCC countries may be true more generally; namely, organizations found it difficult to make loans small enough to attract women entrepreneurs. Others found lending difficult due to women's lack of collateral. A solution to the latter problem was the introduction of hire-purchase schemes for new equipment (Chapter 7); group loans are used in the Asian region (Ahmed, n.d.).

A second strategy is skills and management training. In the SADCC countries, possibilities for skills training were restricted by women's lack of awareness of such programmes and their lack of time. Such programmes needed to be organized around women's existing time schedules. Some experiences indicate that bringing training as close as possible to the trainee's usual place of work is an important aspect for both men and women (Carr, 1989). That this applies even more strongly to women with double responsibilities is obvious.

11

The support services most needed by women, however, may need to be differentiated according to their labour category. Until now, interventions have been geared mainly towards the entrepreneur; be she small-scale or micro-entrepreneur. As Carr suggests, what women entrepreneurs need from national agencies is better access to credit, plus business and technical skills training.

The women casual wage workers in Savara's study, however, would benefit more from another package of strategies. She concludes that three elements are necessary to strengthen the position of women casual wage workers: a legal framework covering the context of this type of employment, mass organizations which in addition to considering grass-roots problems also look at the macro-context, and technical and economic support for women's organizations.

Women domestic outworkers — otherwise called micro-entrepreneurs — need a package of support strategies that address problems including credit with exorbitant interest rates, harassment by officials, and marketing channels (Chen, 1989).

Unpaid family workers present particular problems — since they do not earn money wages, interventions could be directed towards the constraints they face in terms of time and energy. Labour-saving devices — adapted to household-level usage — might provide a possible solution for this group of women.

Women in the Footwear Industry

The issues raised in the previous sections are here applied to the leather footwear industry. This sector is an interesting case because it, together with the clothing and textile sector, is a major employer of women. In contrast to the latter industries, very little research has been done on this sector, particularly on the question of how rapid technological developments, together with a process of relocation to developing countries, are affecting women's position in the industry.

World trends in the footwear industry show a steady decline in production for a number of industrialized countries, and an increase in production and exports for a number of developing countries (Schmel, Chapter 9). Companies in industrialized countries are increasingly making use of production in low wage labour countries, retaining mainly marketing and product design activities.

In many developing countries, a small-scale industry structure predominates, coupled to a labour-intensive production process (Peattie, 1982; Waardenburg, 1988). Women are employed mainly in low-grade operations rather than skilled jobs. Overall, technological changes have occurred in the materials used (a shift from leather to non-leather materials), and a certain amount of mechanization has occurred (a conveyor-belt system of production). More specifically in industrialized countries, the most recent trends include automation and flexible production lines. Schmel suggests that in developing countries, it is essential for small scale industries to establish co-operation in marketing and technological developments, to maintain a degree of independence from the multinational footwear companies.

One of the developing countries with an expanding footwear industry is India. Rao (Chapter 10) in a national-level overview of the industry, shows how upgrading of the raw materials in the leather tanning industry over the past ten to fifteen years is now paying off in the expansion of production of higher value-added products.

Production units in the industry generally come under the 'small-scale sector', but still vary widely in size, products, and market segment. In contrast to those producing for the domestic market, export production units are not limited in size. Subcontracting orders or parts of the production process is extensive in major centers of production, such as Agra and the Madras area. Currently, an extensive research project is underway on the extent of women's employment in the industry; preliminary results indicate widespread use of casual forms of women's labour, such as short-term wage work in factories and workshops, paid and unpaid homework from middlemen, and small scale production[10].

Waardenburg (see Chapter 11) goes into employment generation in greater depth, analyzing the different types of small-scale production units within the industry in Agra, India. The classification of units is based on the primary market channel used: either exporters and ancillaries, government and regional suppliers, or local suppliers.

Subcontracting arrangements are extensive in Agra, and occur for various reasons: specialization among producers, the need to increase capacity, and to save on costs. Subcontracting also occurs in employment relations: (a) 'independent workers' hire other workers and unpaid family labour, (b) contract workers obtain 'helpers', and (c) subcontractors put work out to women homeworkers. The author describes the increasingly low piece-rates paid for such casual forms of labour, and the vulnerability of the people involved.

Finally, women have been incorporated in this industry in a very decentralized pattern in industrialized countries as well. A prevalent type of labour relation in the Italian footwear industry is that of domestic outwork, performed by women and children. Victoria Goddard (Chapter 12) sketches the implications of this type of employment pattern for women in the Neapolitan shoe industry.

From a household perspective, domestic outwork is a crucial option for maintaining income levels in a situation where secure and adequately paid employment is generally lacking. The problem is compounded by social relations within the household, where the main responsibility for household tasks rests on women's shoulders.

13

Skills training for these jobs occurs outside formal training institutions, and is linked to informal networks among outworkers. Locally, it is considered an alternative to formal education. The self-esteem of the workers is also closely bound up with the extent to which they have been able to build up work skills and the quality of the product they make.

A few women are able to make the leap from domestic outworker to small entrepreneur. This possibility is limited, however, to those producers with the highest and most scarce skills, and who make up only a tiny minority of all women workers.

Conclusion

The contributions to this volume suggest that existing models need to be expanded in several respects. Small-scale enterprises appear to be more heterogeneous in their characteristics, with the larger types of small-scale enterprise having greater viability in the long run than smaller ones. Furthermore, in terms of policy, there is a need to improve the demand situation for these enterprises by creating a more 'enabling' environment, rather than focusing attention exclusively on the supply-side situation.

There is greater diversity in the goals pursued by the entrepreneurs involved than previously thought — the poorest showing a mainly survivalist attitude, those with slightly higher incomes oriented towards stability, and only those with a certain stability being oriented toward growth. Also, it must not be forgotten that where ethnic or caste factors help determine the economic sector in which one works, self-respect within a certain occupation is another (non-economic) goal which may be held by entrepreneurs.

Women participate in numerous ways in small-scale industries — not only as entrepreneurs but also in various forms of casual and unpaid labour and 'family management'. The recognition for their contribution decreases as the type of labour relation becomes more casual. This variety in working situations makes it necessary to specify more clearly the differential distribution of 'benefits' from employment in small-scale industries in future models, and to indicate which types of employment or entrepreneurship are avenues of development for women, and which are dead-ends.

Intervention programmes for women also need a more differentiated package approach which is in tune with the way specific groups of women participate in such industries, and is related to the problems they experience. Entrepreneurs may be served best by credit programmes to which women have sufficient access (as a pre-condition) and which takes into account their special conditions, combined with skill and management training. Women domestic outworkers need a package of support measures to provide alternative forms of credit (for both production and consumption), improved marketing channels, and less harassment by local officials.

14

Women casual workers could, therefore, be better served by a legal framework covering this type of employment, combined with women's organizations which provide sufficient economic and technical support, and have a good working knowledge of the national economic context. Finally, unpaid family workers initially need measures directed towards saving their time and energy — labour-saving devices in productive and reproductive tasks.

Taking the aspects mentioned above into account, it is clear that future development policy designed to address gender issues in the area of small-scale enterprises should be specific in its target groups and strategies at the project level, and market-oriented and enabling at the national and international level. The following chapters are a first step in the direction of an approach in which gender and economic aspects are combined. The hope is that a more balanced perspective on development will evolve.

2 Small-scale industry's contribution to economic development

ROGER TESZLER

The triumph of the twentieth century is that it has purged itself of certainty. The Economist

Economic development is a combination of economic growth and structural change. As such, the process of development is far from harmonious; it suffers from many imbalances which do not seem capable of redress by planned intervention. Indeed, imbalance as such has been considered a good thing (Perroux, 1955; Hirschman, 1958) to be stimulated on its own merits: in due course the spread of forward and backward linkages will stimulate other economic activities, and hence consolidate the process of economic growth and development[1].

Industry plays a key role in this process. However, due to the narrow definition used for 'industry', i.e. modern manufacturing (sometimes even further limited to large scale manufacturing only), many potentially important forward and backward linkages have been neglected. Although predicted imbalances did occur, in most cases they failed to act as effective stimuli to the process of national development, since the beneficial spread effects of the linkages seeped away to foreign enterprise and markets.

The neglect of small businesses is an important case in point. Attention to this category of economic activity has often been restricted to the promotion of a separate or alternative process of (especially social) development. Within this narrow framework, the focus has been on the position of particularly underprivileged target groups. The long-term perspective for special protective measures towards such groups tends to become somewhat hazy, thus keeping their development apart from the mainstream (or, still worse, stimulating no development whatsoever) and neglecting the potential for linkages.

In this chapter an attempt is made to review some of the strong points of small enterprise from the point of view of development, as well as some of the ways these could be made to contribute more effectively to the overall development process. This does not mean neglecting the problems which small businessmen and women face when dealing with the powerful forces

The chapter draws heavily on contributions to The Hague workshop, 'Small Scale Enterprise Development, in Search of New Dutch Approaches' (6–7 March, 1989). References to the presentations at this workshop have been omitted.

Words such as 'entrepreneur', 'his', and 'businessman' have been used as collective forms, indicating both men and women. Where specific references to men or women are intended this is always made explicit.

of the free market economy. That aspect of small enterprise development is covered in a brief critical review of the policies and institutions involved.

Although the main argument is that development policy and practice, until fairly recently, have failed to integrate the development of small enterprises in larger development strategies, it is worth reflecting on whether the attempts to redress this past mistake have not led to 'overkill': sometimes pushing forward small enterprise as *the* solution to the problem of underdevelopment. That is a too singular focus on the role for small enterprise; small enterprise may well later be seen as something which must be used more carefully for it has the potential to hinder rather than foster the development process, if not used appropriately.

Industrialization and Development: a process of structural change

Of the many definitions constructed in an attempt to capture the essence of development, the most promising seem to be those that focus on growth with change, rather than on growth alone. Such change becomes visible in new economic and social structures in which self-sufficiency (individual or group) is gradually replaced by specialized economic activity and dependence on the market. Specialization, in turn, leads to increased production, which in turn requires markets for the sale of agricultural produce and purchase of necessary goods and services, which are no longer made at home.

Much of this specialization is in the form of industry, and industry has increasingly become dominated by modern manufacturing to such an extent that the words 'developed' and 'industrialized' are now often used as synonyms.

Industrially developed countries tend to have:

○ a highly diversified industrial structure, including a broad range in sizes of factories and goods produced;
○ a strong network of functional linkages throughout the economy (national as well as international);
○ good infrastructural systems and communication networks, which allow industrial activity to spread beyond the geographic boundaries of major urban areas.

In developing countries, these characteristics are less prevalent and industrial development is less pronounced. Industrial development in the 101 developing countries with a population of one million or more (World Development Report, 1988) by and large has not yielded impressive results. What significant industrial development has occurred in the Third World (where approximately one sixth of the world's manufacturing now takes place — a share which is still growing) is concentrated in the dozen or so countries that are loosely labelled newly industrialized countries (NICs).

17

The NICs tend to combine one or more of the following characteristics: first, an industrialization policy of export-led growth, with its roots in an expanding world economy (Taiwan, Korea, Singapore in the early sixties). Following similar policies in times of economic recession does not work, as a number of mainly Latin American countries found out a decade later. The future looks somewhat brighter for such policies in the present wave of global economic expansion, as exemplified by Thailand, Malaysia, Indonesia, and the Philippines (the so-called second-generation NICs). Second, a large domestic market (India, Indonesia, Brazil, Mexico) where, even with modest average income levels, the sheer volume of purchasing power is sufficient to generate effective demand. This in turn stimulates economies of scale in manufacturing. Third, specific conditions such as political stability and a tradition of little or no government intervention (except for specific assistance to industry); or legislation granting privileges for free zone processing for export. Hong Kong has long been characterized by free market conditions favouring international trade in general and industrial exports in particular. Attempts have been made to create such conditions in other small countries such as Mauritius or in certain areas of large countries (e.g. the Maquiladoras of Northern Mexico).

Except in the most advanced NICs, the undoubtedly often spectacular results achieved by industrialization often have had only limited impact (in some cases even negative impact) on the overall development process. The picture for most developing countries can be summed up as follows:

o a number of developing countries, in particular in Asia, Latin America, and the Caribbean, have succeeded in achieving a limited industrial breakthrough. For some of these countries (e.g. Colombia, Chile, Pakistan, Egypt) this may well imply being on course for NIC status;
o smaller, low income countries — mostly found in Sub-Saharan Africa — on the other hand, would appear to have little hope of achieving any significant and sustainable industrial breakthrough in the near future;
o an intermediate category of countries, for example, Kenya and Zimbabwe in Africa, appear to be in the process of consolidating an incipient process of change in their economic structure.

In most developing countries where modern manufacturing does occur, it often has remained an enclave, having few positive effects (spread or trickle-down) on the rest of the economy. In spatial terms, such industrial enclaves contrast sharply with the abject poverty surrounding them; from a functional point of view the linkages of modern industry to international businesses and markets often outweigh their lack of domestic impact. Major sectors of the domestic economy remain beyond the reach of these spread effects, although negative backwash effects are all too easily felt. However, from the point of view of national development, it makes bad economic sense to leave major sources of income and growth of a country

18

untapped. In that respect, small enterprises, regardless of the sector they belong to (agriculture, industry, or services) play an all too important role in the economy, if only as a fall-back option, for those people who fail to reap any benefits from modern large-scale manufacturing. For the 'least developed' countries, small enterprises may indeed be the only sustainable approach to structural change.

Development, however, does not restrict change to industry and urban areas. Changes which accompany development in rural areas are equally spectacular, in many respects:

1. rural self-sufficiency gradually gives way to specialized agricultural production (creating economies of scale and market dependence);
2. non-agricultural activities outgrow the farm; they tend to become concentrated in small market centres and district towns; and
3. the initially clear-cut dividing line between city and countryside is replaced by something resembling an urban-rural continuum.

This process of agricultural specialization lies at the heart of one of the major disequilibria of the development process: a shortage of employment possibilities for existing supplies of labour. Modern (large scale) manufacturing is not the answer to this problem. Its high degree of capital intensity results in a limited demand, mainly for highly skilled labour. The existing supply of labour tends to lack these skills, as well as the attitudes required for industrial work. Here again, society finds an answer of sorts to this lack of effective employment opportunities, by resorting to a broad variety of small-scale activities.

To sum up, modern manufacturing structures of any significance are not only beyond the reach of most developing countries (high cost, poor access to major world markets); they also fail to provide adequate solutions to the problems of unemployment, and their impact on the rest of the economy is often more negative than positive.

That a development strategy based on the growth of modern manufacturing has led to disappointing results can be traced to a lack of integration with the rest of the economy. When this became clear, the result was a continuous search not for complementary measures, in an attempt to remedy apparent deficiencies, but for alternative 'keystones'. After concepts such as 'human resources', 'agriculture' and 'international trade' (to name but a few), 'small-scale enterprise', and the 'informal sector' were discovered. Each of these concepts then proceeded through the various stages of the development product cycle (incubation, selected application, mass application, rejection, etc.). Small and especially micro-enterprise has now become the umpteenth in the long series of development fads, mainly for the following reasons:

○ large enterprise, whether plantation, manufacturing plant, or large

19

business, has failed to stimulate a wide-ranging development process to the extent fondly imagined possible at one time by development theorists and planners;

o the untapped pools of unemployed labour formed due to the disequilibrating forces of the development process have no social security system to fall back on, and hence must attempt to survive by searching for alternative sources of income. For all practical purposes, this primarily means self-employment;

o the labour-intensive nature of most small-scale enterprise implies that good use will be made of available factors of production (much labour in combination with little capital).

Research sponsored by USAID and the World Bank has indicated that[2] industrial employment increases with the growth of average income; industrial production and employment are largely concentrated in smaller firms; the role of the smallest of the small firms (including self-employment) decreases with development; and that increases in disposable income tend to lead to a more than proportionate increase in the demand for small enterprise products — larger and more frequent purchases.

These findings, in turn, have made it clear that modernization in general, and modern manufacturing in particular, are not able to correct disequilibria in employment stemming from the process of development; corrective measures as a part of planned intervention processes have been inadequate because they have failed to recognize the integrated nature of the development process. Instead they concentrate on separate solutions. The struggle for economic survival is a desperate, but not necessarily insignificant contribution to the development process; it provides some correction to the previously mentioned distortions. Many forms of small enterprise emerge from the struggle for survival (however, many also disappear, whether quickly or slowly).

If small enterprise acts as a corrective measure, it may well be worthwhile stimulating such compensatory trends, using policy and institutional interventions. The potential for such interventions is examined below.

Disaggregating the Classification of Small Business; small-scale enterprise and small-scale industry (SSE and SSI)

The term 'small-scale business' covers a multitude of activities; it also comes in various shapes and sizes: it can differ considerably between countries, within a country between regions or from urban to rural areas. Each of the many guises of small business differs in development potential. Different forms will not necessarily be susceptible to the same types of outside intervention; some may even resist any outside intervention whatsoever.

In this chapter, the term 'small-scale enterprise' denotes all small business no matter what economic activity is carried out. Small-scale industry refers more specifically to transformation and processing activities, as well as to the making, servicing, and repairing of tools and equipment. In actual practice these dividing lines are usually not clear-cut. Therefore, many authors prefer to refer to SSE rather than to SSI. On the other hand, manufacturing or industry in general is purported to have more spread-effects than trade and related services, because its ability to add value usually surpasses that of tertiary sector activities. For the purposes of this paper, however, there is no need to differentiate small-scale industry from small-scale enterprise.

Small-scale enterprise (SSE) can be defined in relative terms (as opposed to medium- and large-scale enterprise); but such definitions-by-default would seem to create rather than to solve problems because they remain meaningless as long as the other categories are not defined first. On the other hand, a definition in more absolute or positive terms may leave less to be defined (in the present case only one category, instead of three), but requires more precise definition. The fact that as far back as 1975 more than fifty definitions were being used for SSE, even before it had become really popular in development circles, is indicative of the lack of agreement on the definition of SSE (Auciello, 1975 cited in Liedholm and Mead, 1987).

The approach to definition adopted here is based on three criteria:

○ size of enterprise (for all its drawbacks, there seems no way to avoid this aspect);
○ level of technology applied;
○ type of entrepreneurship.

Broadly, SSEs can be divided into two categories of size: small and micro. The dividing line between the two categories of SSEs, as well as between SSEs and other types of enterprise, remains highly specific per country and over time (Colombia, for example, changed all its definitions in 1983).

The most frequently used criteria refer to items such as number of people employed, total wage bill, turnover volume, etc. Each of these leaves something to be desired, even when the necessary information can be obtained (often this is not possible). Employment data in many cases fail to distinguish between full and part-time employment. Thus existing and available data on labour and employment provide the shakiest of foundations for even a summary estimate of the degree of capital intensity of small-scale manufacturing; similarly, they fail to consider the implications of short-term wage work, casual labour, unpaid family labour, apprentices etc. Sizeable portions of the wage bill are paid out cash in hand and turnover tends to be a closely guarded secret (in the smaller SSEs often even from the entrepreneur).

21

The limited extent to which consensus has been reached on classification of SSEs by size is reflected in broad agreement that micro-enterprises employ no more than ten people, and small enterprises fewer than fifty. Sometimes the upper limits are put at five for micro and twenty-five for small enterprises.

Any attempt to adjust employment numbers according to country size or level of development will increase the relevance but diminish the comparability of the data. It should be recognised, however, that the smallest enterprises in each country share common characteristics with similar firms in any other country; inter-country comparison of common characteristics and experiences may well make more sense for development than taking refuge in numbers.

Thus far, all that has been ascertained is the hardly surprising conclusion that micro-enterprises are smaller than small enterprises. The hypothesis of this paper being that it is unlikely that all SSEs respond to their economic environment and to development policy in the same way, a somewhat more sophisticated classification of small enterprise is required.

Supplementary criteria are needed to obtain a better perspective on the strengths and limitations of the various types of SSEs. The classification may be refined by taking into consideration differences in the levels of technology applied. The following classification is suggested using this criterion (UNIDO, 1979):

1. traditional technology, such as still used widely in handicraft and cottage activities;
2. modernizing technology, where changes have been introduced in the production process. These are often related to a change in sources of energy, and with a resulting increase in scale. A classic case of modernizing technology is the replacement of the handloom by the powerloom, a change-over that has gathered momentum in Pakistan, India and Bangladesh in particular;
3. modern technology, where the only major difference from modern large-scale manufacturing is one of plant size. Or maybe not even that; cases are known, in India among others, of larger firms being broken up on purpose into a number of units small enough to qualify as suppliers under SSE government reservation schemes.

Each of these three levels of technology could occur in micro- as well as small enterprises. The general trend is, however, as expected, for modernization of technology to go hand in hand with enterprise size. Modern technology is seldom found in micro-enterprises (a recent and notable exception is the pirating and production of computer software); and if the 'larger' small firm still employs traditional technology, this is due often to the way in which the enterprise is organized, such as co-operative organization of a number of small producers into a larger unit. Here the same

22

technology that characterized the previously independent small operations may still be applied, with co-operative activities being limited to specific issues such as location, purchasing (including credit), and marketing.

Using technology as an additional yardstick does clarify some aspects, but it does not help to grasp the essence of small enterprise. The addition of the third criterion mentioned, type of entrepreneurship, is helpful.

Basically, there seem to be three types of SSE entrepreneurship:

o highly mobile survivalist self-employment;
o co-operative arrangements among micro-entrepreneurs;
o well established, specialized SSEs.

Self-employment is usually the 'domain' of the poorest of the poor, who, because they lack the resources (personal savings and/or those of relatives or friends) to establish a durable form of enterprise are forced to eke out a minimal living with the barest of means. The aim of such activities is simply to allow the entrepreneur to survive physically. The continuous worry of having to keep one's head above water makes any thought of lasting economic betterment or development totally illusory. One may even question whether this type of self-employment has any entrepreneurial characteristics at all, or if it would be better to consider such activities as inevitable proxies for a (non-existent or malfunctioning) system of social security. Often various family members must have recourse to self-employment to scrape together sufficient income to cover the bare necessities of the family. Many self-employment activities are mobile (such as hawking, with or without a fixed route) and are subject to sudden change, depending on the opportunities available.

It is also possible for specific groups to pool some (e.g. marketing), or even all, of their activities in some form of co-operative in order to improve their livelihood and social status. In this case, self-employment becomes more structured and regulated. Whereas single-person self-employment tends to fade away in the course of the development process as people find more stable employment in other types of enterprise, group self-employment is more tenacious[3]. It can be instrumental in improving the welfare of the participants, their families, and their communities. This approach is often adopted for assisting specific and underprivileged target groups who are the victims of long-standing discrimination or social neglect.

The third category of SSE entrepreneurship refers to micro-enterprise proper, as opposed to self-employment. Whereas, in the latter, entrepreneurship would appear to be little more than a euphemism for lack of employment in the former, the micro-entrepreneur seems to be the backbone of the industrial structure of many developing countries, especially if the category is extended to include firms employing up to ten persons. Most such firms tend to be located at home and to involve intensive family participation. The entrepreneur works along with the others and cannot limit his activities to management tasks.[4]

Here women entrepreneurs have an important role: they supplement the wage income of the male family members by processing (such as foodstuffs) or transforming (e.g. textiles) activities. Retail trade (often village or neighbourhood store) and services (like food stalls) are also possible. Often a variety of activities is carried out simultaneously because it is unclear to the entrepreneur where her comparative advantage lies. This is different from a self-employed person, who must try to grab any work she or he can get.

If, however, the entrepreneur has managed to carve out a niche in the market due to special skills, know-how, or experience (or probably all three), the chances are that the firm will be a small-scale rather than a micro-enterprise. Such an establishment may continue to rely on traditional technologies (especially if it is involved in the production of traditional or artistic goods), but it may also have succeeded in linking up with large enterprises via some kind of subcontracting arrangement. In most cases the latter require the introduction of more modern equipment, because of the standardization required for inputs into large industry. The entrepreneur will have become a manager, who can devote much time to purchasing and marketing; he will also have someone he trusts to look after the firm when he is away. Some of these small entrepreneurs, individual owners of one or two pieces of machinery or equipment, have been known to pool their resources into a medium sized production unit. Former President of the National Federation of Small Industries, Maximo San Roman, is known to have been the pushing power behind such a combination of small metal-working establishments in Lima.

The combination of the three criteria discussed (size, technology, and entrepreneurship) results in the following classification of SSEs:

Micro-enterprise:
1. individual self-employment;
2. collective or group self-employment;
3. home based enterprises employing fewer than ten people (cottage industry).

Small-enterprise:
1. SSEs using traditional technologies, but increasingly switching over to modern technologies;
2. SSEs using modern technologies and increasingly linking up with the rest of the economy in general and large industry in particular.

In adding this classification to the burdensome load of those already in existence, I have been guided by considerations of policy formulation rather than availability of statistical data. Perhaps attempts could be made to gather information in developing countries with a view to formulating

24

and implementing development policy. As far as SSE is concerned, the late Dudley Seers' lament of twenty years ago that the wrong data are being collected has remained unheeded[5].

The five categories of SSEs given above should not be seen as a continuum of development from 'rags-to-riches'. As noted, there is little chance for the self-employed to progress, except by finding employment in larger SSEs. Similarly, when micro-entrepreneurs fall on hard times they may well end up as self-employed 'survivalists'. Only successful SSEs, using modern technology stand a chance of growing, because in this case the barrier is merely one of scale, instead of the far more daunting one of attitude. Given the assumption that most SSEs are the self-employed entrepreneur 'micro' variety, and that only a small number will be modern SSEs, this should not come as any great surprise.

It is worth bearing in mind that one of the essential characteristics of SSE is that it occurs entirely within the private sector. Attempts by the public sector to become actively involved in this sector have run into difficulties as soon as such participation went beyond financing or capital ownership. The fact that most SSE entrepreneurs like to go it alone, furthermore, makes co-operative or collective SSEs non-starters except in cases where collaboration holds out tangible rewards. The following combinations are possibilities:

o co-operatives for specific activities such as buying in bulk, leasing equipment, obtaining credit, and marketing. In such cases, individual producers retain their own identity, but work together when this suits their purposes;
o a looser arrangement, in which SSE associations are formed based on a common trade or a common location;
o co-operatives formed by specific groups who find other means of economic and social development all but denied to them (minorities from an emancipatory, social, or religious point of view).
o the pooling of equipment in order to achieve a stronger market presence.

I have refrained from getting involved in the informal sector debate. However, some observations on the organization of economic activities point are in order here. Informality appears to stem from the inability of formal structures to cope with reality, primarily in two related ways: first, modern large-scale enterprise, whether in the agricultural, industrial, or service sector, is capital intensive; as such, it is unable to absorb the rapidly-growing population of most developing countries; second, public-sector institutions in most developing countries have been geared to the needs of large and modern enterprises, because these are purported to be the harbingers of economic growth and development. The primary outreach to large segments of the population consists of providing low-paid public-sector jobs. Often as a result, these public institutions lose their effectiveness and fall victim to the temptations of bureaucracy and corruption. Services constrained by the public sector (transport and public utilities) tend to suffer a similar fate.

The result has been informality by default, on an ever-increasing scale. De Soto's studies and observations on retail trade and transport in Lima are unique mainly because of the impact they have had on the outside world (de Soto, 1987)[6]. The populations of many bankrupt African countries survive only because of their informal sector activities. Such activities are found primarily at the micro-enterprise level. Informal larger SSEs are less common, except in cases where the ineffectiveness of the public sector has reached truly disastrous proportions.

Further reflection of the ineffectiveness of the public sector can be observed in the blossoming of non-governmental organizations (NGOs) as the paramount institutions working to enhance SSE development. The significance of NGOs for SSE development is reviewed later.

To round off this discussion, brief mention must be made of existing labour relations, both within SSEs and between SSEs and other participants in the economic process.

The self-employed survivalist is at the beck and call of practically everybody. Street hawkers may seem to be independent, but in many instances they are heavily indebted to their suppliers, and those hawking perishables often do not have the right to return the unsold wares. Micro-producers are often dependent on larger producers or retailers, who will not fail to pay the least that the traffic will bear. Although in theory this can be considered a type of subcontracting, for practical purposes it is nothing more than outwork. In turn, within such micro-enterprises, workers (often family members or apprentices) are badly underpaid, and must work in sweatshop conditions. The 'entrepreneur' is no more than first among equals.

Collective self-employment probably constitutes the most durable form of self-employment, due to the strong motivation of the participants, although the strain of labour relations between equals may sap the entrepreneurial strength of the undertaking. This type of SSE may also find itself at the mercy of powerful customers (such as large retail stores and their middlemen).

Conditions of work, especially in micro-enterprises, are among the worst imaginable. The organization of employed labour here would appear to be an unattainable luxury; living standards achieved by most of the self-employed entrepreneurs (and even those of some of the more established businessmen and women) barely allow for economic survival. Costs can only be kept low by employing apprentices (who often have to pay for the privilege) and unpaid family labour.

In the end, the quality of working conditions in small enterprises will depend on the possibility of getting labour unions involved. This is often

26

far from easy, because the entrepreneur can always fall back on casual contract labour, which does not require social security payments. Recent studies show that in such circumstances women tend to work under the worst conditions (Baud, 1991).

The Significance of Small-Scale Enterprise for Economic and Social Development

The five point classification described is an attempt to provide a framework for an analysis of the significance of SSEs for economic and social development. In applying such a classification, factors such as the level of development and the size and economic structure of a country must be considered. A few over-generalized examples may be given to illustrate the significance of this argument:

o high middle-income developing countries and NICs tend to have a reasonably well-developed industrial structure; small modern enterprise has an important role to play, and there is a tendency for micro-enterprise to die out, except among certain special interest groups;
o in low-income countries in general, effective demand will not be sufficient to warrant large-scale manufacturing (unless the total domestic market is large, as in China and India); here small industry, traditional as well as modern, should form the backbone for structural change;
o in countries with an important agricultural sector, this should be seen as the magnet or growth pole, serving to stimulate rural small industrial enterprise by linking it directly to increases in agricultural income (UNDP *et al.*, 1988).

In general terms, self-employment and other enterprise aimed merely at survival will tend to disappear. Efforts to facilitate the formalization of the informal sector are evident in a number of countries (e.g. Colombia, Kenya, Peru) as an answer to the ineffective complexities of bureaucracy and in belated recognition of the important role of informal-sector entrepreneurs as a vital part of the economy.

The development of a country has important implications for its industrial structure. Industry, and in particular manufacturing, changes during the process of development because of changes in effective demand, but industry can also be seen as one of the major stimuli for the development process (Griffin, 1989). These changes can have important implications for SSEs:

o individual self-employment will tend to be absorbed into other enterprises as wage or contract labour;
o traditional technologies will be modernized (even in the handicraft sector);

27

o the linkages between small enterprise and the rest of the economy will be strengthened.

This process of structural change is not so much a process of graduation, with small enterprise becoming larger; it is more the disappearance of the smallest of small enterprises and reorientation of larger SSEs. Most newly formed SSEs will then be of this larger type. The result is a stronger manufacturing structure and to some extent a correction of the disequilibria caused by the development process.

This prognosis is based on the strong and weak points of SSEs. Each of the five types of SSE has an important role to play at some time in the development process, but there is no reason to assume that this role is the same over time. The roles of the various types of SSE can be derived from a review of strengths and weaknesses.

Some of the major strong points of SSEs include:

1. The ability of SSEs to absorb large amounts of labour: this is the direct result of the labour-intensive approach most SSEs (except for the modern ones referred to above as Category B2) use in their activities. Except for certain handicrafts, most labour can be relatively unskilled; what training is required is usually provided 'on the job'; indeed, the SSE entrepreneur will tend to prefer providing his own on the job training — this is the only way of ensuring that the labourers have the exact knowledge required and have not been 'spoilt' by external, formal specialist training. Here it is worth remembering that self-employment is inherently a very labour-intensive way of scraping together a living.

2. Whereas the location of large enterprise is determined by the availability of locational amenities (economies of agglomeration, the availability of high-tech essential services and person to person contact with other entrepreneurs, central government and foreign enterprise, and finance), most SSEs are far more footloose. They can flourish in non-metropolitan areas, as long as the basic condition of an adequate effective demand is met. This target is easier to reach for SSEs because of their modest output volumes. Given the high labour absorption capacity of SSEs, this implies that they can assist in stemming the flow of rural-urban migration, at least to the most overcrowded cities. Hence any policy aimed at stimulating the geographical spread of industry will have a greater chance of success if directed specifically at SSEs.

3. The labour-intensive SSE activities entail not only considerable capacity for absorbing labour; they are also often considered more efficient from the point of view of development because in principle they use more of the abundant production factor 'labour', and less of the far scarcer factor 'capital'. A number of studies on India in particular have pointed out, however, that the efficiency of capital usage is lower in small than in large industry, overall as well as within a given industry[7]. While these

observations undoubtedly are correct *in abstracto*, the implied criticism appears to exaggerate the homogeneity of similar goods produced by large and small industry, at the cost of neglecting the market segmentation that arises from differences in income, and hence variations in effective demand between sectors of the population. (see also the following point).

4. SSEs produce simple implements and consumer goods (processed foods, clothing, household utensils, wooden furniture, and farm implements). The quality of these products does not generally compare well with the trade marked output of modern large enterprise; however, their relatively low price brings them within the financial reach of large segments of the population. All except modern small enterprises make use of existing artisan traditions and knowledge for such production. In India's Second Five Year Plan (1956-1961), the Minister of Planning, P.C. Mahalanobis, pursued a dualistic industrialization policy, with capital goods and basic goods (e.g. refining of minerals) concentrated in the public sector, and consumer goods considered as the domain of SSEs. This reservation policy in due course proved ineffective, because the ensuing industrial structure remained unbalanced, with few medium-sized firms (the same or slightly bigger than the B2 category used in this paper); these often proved to be among the most efficient and labour-intensive factory types, as measured by total factor productivity (Nanjundan, in 'Small Enterprises, New Approaches' 1989). Furthermore, SSEs can also be important producers of non-consumer goods (ox-carts, coffee decorticators, etc.).

5. SSEs tend to use only locally-available materials; hence this type of enterprise is less dependent on imports than large-scale manufacturing. The conclusion to be drawn is that stimulating the development of SSEs generally has little adverse effect on a country's trade balance.

6. SSEs have the added advantage that their small size and simple management structure makes it relatively easy for them to react quickly to changes in demand according to fashion trends (clothing, footwear etc.). In situations of declining income and crisis, on the other hand, SSEs can produce cheap substitutes for products previously supplied by large enterprise or through imports.

This brief selection of SSE strengths may suggest they are the answer to the developer's prayer. However, a number of serious drawbacks go some way toward bringing back any undue euphoria to more normal proportions. Some of the major weaknesses of SSEs can be summed up as follows:

First, most SSE production is relatively inefficient; many firms are overcapitalized in terms of output. Restructuring of industrial manufacturing into a number of fewer but larger units could lead to an overall increase in capital productivity (the critique by Little *et al.*, referred to in[7]).

Second, the risk in producing cheap goods for the masses is mainly one of inferior quality. This is not necessarily a disadvantage, as long as replacement does not overtax meager personal incomes. However, there is considerable scope for quality improvement with many SSE-produced goods which does not entail a sharp price increase.

Third, most SSEs suffer from a weak management structure. Clear-cut divisions of labour are rarely found in micro-enterprises; if they do exist they certainly do not apply to the entrepreneur, who does a bit of everything and is unwilling to delegate authority. (In most cases there is nobody to delegate to!) This tendency is slightly less in the larger SSEs, which are usually no longer located in the home of the entrepreneur.

Fourth, working conditions in SSEs are among the worst imaginable, even admitting that means to bring about any significant improvement in this state of affairs are not readily available. All micro-enterprise and most small enterprise is unorganized; external pressures to improve conditions have only rarely led to any success.

Fifth, since many SSEs operate outside legal structures, they do not have to keep accounts. This not only leaves them at the mercy of the tax collector's caprice; it can also lead to delayed recognition of signals which indicate things are going seriously wrong. Many SSEs do not consider organization and administration serious problems, and outside attempts to remedy this situation are not usually welcomed[8].

Sixth, small enterprise has no economic clout; the individual entrepreneur is not able to exert any influence on his markets, cannot compete with the aggressive marketing tactics of large enterprise and has no effective means of resisting government pressures.

This review is not intended to be exhaustive; however, it demonstrates that SSEs are key players in the development process, where they have strong and weak points (just as do others). In this context, self-employment must be seen as a transitional activity; it will be given up as soon as more rewarding opportunities are available, because its weaknesses outweigh its strong points. To a lesser extent this is probably true for many micro-enterprises and small traditional firms.

Only group self-employment and modern small enterprise seem to have a more lasting role in the process of development; the former because of the strong motivation guiding it, and the latter because it fits in well with a developed industrial structure. However, the unfortunate facts that successful development is still relatively rare, and that economic crises and structural adjustment programmes are increasingly leaving their mark on many developing countries, unwaveringly point towards the conclusion that individual self-employment, micro-enterprise, and small traditional enterprise will remain important parts of the economic life of many developing countries for a long time to come.

Can SSEs be Assisted so as to Improve their Contribution to Economic and Social Development?

Given the potential of SSEs to contribute to the development process by helping the otherwise unemployed to survive, by providing cheap consumer goods for mass consumption, and by forging a link which is often missing in existing industrial structures, it is still necessary to consider whether and how this role can be enhanced.

The extent to which any intervention will prove effective depends primarily on the outlook of the SSE entrepreneur. Most SSE entrepreneurs are loners who:

○ repair and design their own equipment;
○ as micro-entrepreneurs operate at least partially within the household;
○ prefer to train their own labour force;
○ finance fixed assets as well as working capital out of personal savings, or those of relatives and friends;
○ do not have a positive attitude towards outside intervention, if only because of unhappy past experiences with tax collectors and other public sector 'busybodies';
○ are not very good at delegating authority and responsibilities within the SSE;
○ have a firmly-fixed perception of their problems (which is often correct), and are willing to accept outside help only if it will solve precisely these problems.

In order to survive, and if possible, grow, the entrepreneur must have a forceful personality. This is undoubtedly a prerequisite for the growth of a firm, but may not be so good for labour relations and working conditions. The characteristics listed are especially typical of the informal micro entrepreneur; they tend to soften somewhat as the enterprise grows and becomes formalized.

Not least because of disappointing results achieved by attempting direct assistance to SSEs and because of the scarcity of public-sector means imposed by structural adjustment programmes, increasing confidence is being placed in policies aimed at improving the economic and social environment in which such firms operate: in other words, increasing effective demand for SSE products.

Sidestepping the crucial issue of whether and to what extent policies can bring about changes in the economic and social environment, it is possible to envisage two basic scenarios in which effective demand for SSE products and services would be enhanced:

1. increasing disposable income within broad segments of the population (demand side income effect);
2. decreasing income, leading to demand substitution of higher-priced

31

goods produced by large-scale industry, or derived from imports by SSEs of products of lower price and quality (demand side substitution effect).

These effects occur in diametrically opposed situations. Apart from illustrating the flexibility of SSE as a development concept, it may be theorized that increases in demand side income effect will mainly benefit small enterprises, and that increases in demand side substitution effect will lead to increased activity at the micro-enterprise level. The following argument will concentrate on the income effect alternative.

Policies aimed at increasing effective demand for SSE products and the broad development of SSEs will focus on:

o Stimulating income increases; in rural areas this can best be achieved through the development of agriculture, by:
  – getting the prices for agricultural produce 'right';
  – stemming unfair competition from subsidized food imports;
  – removing major disequilibria in rural income distribution (via land reforms such as carried out in Japan, Korea, and Taiwan).
  In urban areas no comparably clear-cut leading sector emerges; however, the existence of a large market potential may be considered a stimulus not found in rural areas.
o Eliminating bias of existing institutions against smaller economic units. Thus, banks usually are not willing to lend out money to SSEs because of a (supposed) lack of collateral; small loans are relatively expensive to administer and therefore can only be extended in return for higher rates of interest. Special guarantee funds can help to remove such barriers against SSEs.
o Improving physical (roads, transport, public utilities) and social infrastructure (educational and health facilities). These of course benefit the entire economy, but by no means can be provided by small enterprise (large firms can have their own schools and hospital services or at least see to it that their employees can afford to use existing facilities).

Policies aimed at bringing about, maintaining or improving such environmental factors will be extremely beneficial to the development of SSEs and the integration of the various actors and sectors of the economy into a close-knit and developed structure.

The demand side approach to SSE development has a number of clear advantages:

o it offers far better coverage than any institution could ever hope to achieve;
o it does not discriminate against any enterprise;
o it leaves the self-esteem of the entrepreneur intact and does not meddle in his affairs.

No other type of assistance can hope to achieve such results. Demand-side policies are to be considered preconditions for other types of (supply-side) intervention; the latter can in no way be seen as a substitute for the former. This 'substitute' approach was characteristic of many early attempts to foster the development of SSEs; it often led to SSEs being shielded from the harshness of economic life behind the supposedly safe walls of industrial estates and other such institutions. In general, any successes were at great expense per client; most efforts, however, have turned out to be costly failures.

The supply side approach tends to focus on an institutional approach to SSE development. A wide range of (often subsidized) facilities and services, of which the average SSE is imagined to be in dire need, are offered. But the limits set by budget ceilings and the availability of extension staff are such that only a small number of SSEs are reached effectively, even by the best of such institutions.

For supply side intervention to be effective, the institutions involved should:

o have good local outreach and acceptance (establishing a confidential working relationship will sorely tax even the most competent and patient extension officer);
o have the authority to take the necessary decisions at the local level. This is especially important for rural small enterprise, because many SSE institutions are found in urban areas (thus helping to maintain the myth that micro-enterprise is a typically urban phenomenon).

Among the institutions that best fulfil these conditions of outreach, acceptance and local authority, particular mention must be made of:

o non-governmental organizations (NGOs), which often operate only at the local level;
o associations of small enterprises. These are probably the best catalysts for channelling support to SSEs, because they are founded by the small enterprises themselves, enjoy their confidence, and hence are well aware of the problems faced and the solutions required.

NGOs and small enterprise associations are particularly important to the development of micro and informal enterprise. The larger varieties of SSEs have usually built up a more solid reputation, have easier access to formal institutions, and are more susceptible to external advice and counselling.

In this context it should be observed, finally, that NGOs and small enterprise associations are often in need of external assistance to increase their professional and managerial capacities. Assistance from donors, international agencies and private voluntary organizations (PVOs) from developed countries can prove quite effective.

Conclusion

This brief review of potential contributions of the various types of SSEs to the development process has attempted to demonstrate that different categories of SSEs have different roles to play in this process, and that their relevance depends on specific circumstances. In more general terms it can be argued that the strength of micro-enterprise lies in providing an outlet for large segments of the economically-active population of a country, which would otherwise be trapped in the imbalances accompanying development.

Self-employment is then an answer out of despair to the severe shortage of formal-employment possibilities and to the absence of effective social security systems. The economic crises which have led to large-scale adoption of structural adjustment programmes have given self-employment a new burst of life and postponed its demise. Self-employment in a co-operative or group form is often practiced by people who for a variety of reasons are barred from more formal activities; as such it has a more lasting role, because there is no reason to believe that discrimination will end with the coming of development.

Micro-enterprise in general, as well as most larger small enterprises that apply traditional technologies, will also lose much of their importance where (or rather, if) development proves to be sustainable.

Small modern enterprise will become increasingly important within the industrial structure of more developed countries, strengthening inter-industry linkages and thus making more efficient use of a country's resources, of which its labour force is undoubtedly the most important. In smaller least developed countries, such as most Sub-Saharan countries in Africa, modern small industry may well be the axis of the industrialization process, in turn stimulating ancillary activities.

The process of small enterprise development is best aided and abetted by an economic and social environment that favours its expansion, i.e. that promotes effective demand for the products of SSEs among large sectors of the population. In such circumstances, specific institutional intervention may be highly effective. This action must not be used alone, however; as a substitute for demand side policies, it fails disastrously. All this implies that SSE in its various guises will be an instrument of development for a long time to come, and that its importance is too great to be left to the whims of development fashions.

3 Subcontracting — the incorporation of small producers in dynamic industrial networks

PETER KNORRINGA and HERMINE WEIJLAND

Industrial Networks and Subcontracting

The industrial sector can be seen as a complex constellation of product branches, within which distinct products are produced for various market segments and their specific buyers. In this context, an industrial network is made up of a group of traders and producers who form a complete marketing and production cycle for a particular set of final products, destined for specific market segments. Such networks can be identified by looking for high degrees of specialization and contractually fixed linkages.

Industrial networks adjust to manipulated or spontaneous changes in demand and supply. Markets are in a constant state of flux in developing economies, with producers and traders connected to increasing numbers and varieties of consumers. The emerging market structure is therefore increasingly segmented. Industrial producers and traders serve these increasingly diverse clients by increasing the variety and complexity of production and marketing. They also face external changes in technology and consequently, they are continually adapting.

In most Asian economies, the industrial sector includes a large number of very small and isolated producers who traditionally have sold their products to local customers. In a developing industrial environment, with a growing number of large- and medium-sized modern enterprises and broadening market channels, these small producers are often incorporated into larger networks through various means: regular or incidental market contacts, wage work, or subcontracting with larger firms. Larger enterprises, on the other hand, face various 'make or buy' decisions, which are not confined to these extremes (i.e. making a product or carrying out a process within the firm versus buying it on the open market). Subcontracting is one option on a continuum of possible decisions (Mead, 1984).

In a subcontracting relation the contractor places an order with a subcontractor to manufacture or process all or part of a final product, which the contractor then markets as his own. Such a subcontracting relationship starts with a contract, written or verbal, setting out the precise specifications of the order (Knorringa, 1988). Subcontracting can be distinguished from a normal market purchase by the exact specifications given, which are made to suit the particular identity of the contractor. Such a contract therefore differs from a routine buy-decision involving a readily available or standardized item. On

The authors are greatly indebted to Henk Kox for his valuable comments.

the other hand, it is unlike a make-decision, since production does not take place within the contracting firm.

Subcontracting arrangements can be divided into two main categories: commercial versus industrial subcontracting. In commercial subcontracting, also referred to as putting-out, the contractor does not participate in the actual production process, but takes care of marketing and usually also financing. The contractor usually specializes in a specific product range, and organizes production by establishing contracts with selected enterprises or individuals, who then are committed to work according to fixed specifications. Often the subcontractors are organized such that each completes only a part of the whole production cycle. Thus they form a chain of complementary producers, with the contractor as the central linchpin. The finished products are then marketed under the name of the commercial contractor.

Industrial contractors, as distinct from commercial contractors, use subcontractors for the execution of specific tasks within their own production processes. The fixed tasks are usually labour or skill-intensive, and may include the following activities (Nagaraj, 1984; Panini, 1978):

○ undertaking a distinct phase of the production cycle (e.g. casting a crude model for a metal product);
○ assembly of components produced by the contractor (as in the electronics industry);
○ production of components for the contractor's product (as in the car industry);
○ job work, or handling part of a distinct phase (e.g. cutting metal or stitching specific parts of garments);
○ labour-jobs, performed by subcontractors within the firm of the contractor (e.g. repair and maintenance).

The rationale and implications of subcontracting for small producers in Asia are addressed, within the wider context of networks. Analysis of the dynamics of the wider industrial environment is followed here by a demonstration of how and why small producers are incorporated in specific types of industrial networks, the margins within which particular producers must work and barriers to entry. An intervention policy for improving the position of certain vulnerable categories of producers in particular branches does not necessarily require direct intervention at the level of the small producers themselves. It might be more effective to intervene in industrial networks at other levels, where the conditions for participation are set.

The Structure of Networks

Formation of networks is seen as led primarily by demand forces. Demand patterns change with population growth, higher standards of living, changes in taste and improved communications. Leading entrepreneurs within marketing and production networks react to these changes; they expand, improve products, differentiate, and specialize. Leading entrepreneurs direct 'their' networks to specific buyers with special preferences and characteristics, such as various categories of households, individuals requiring particular standards and qualities of consumer goods, firms requiring special machines, or professional groups requiring special equipment.

The variation and continuous changes in demand results in a dynamic market segmentation. Any market segment may be served by a number of competing networks, each performing the range of activities needed to complete an entire marketing and production cycle. Competition may extend to other market segments, and in particular to those offering similar goods. Networks may vary in strength and structure; there may also be such variation among the networks serving the same market segment. Nevertheless, it may turn out that, as a rule, each market segment tends to have one dominant type of network at a particular moment. However, because of the changes in demand on the one hand, and changes in technology, input markets, state regulations, and the social norms and values involved in exchange relationships on the other hand, this dominance is unstable. Leading entrepreneurs are continually adapting their internal and external organization, so that new networks form and old networks disintegrate simultaneously.

An industrial network contains a complete marketing and production cycle, consisting of a number of phases. To start with, producers need access to relevant information on existing or potential demand. Although marketing know-how is very important, few producers have this strategic information. Only after identifying the market situation can initiatives be taken to fulfil a specific part of the demand for a given market segment. After a particular market segment has been selected, product specifications can be determined. These preliminary phases set the boundary conditions for the organization of production: procurement of a workplace, provision of energy and water, installation of machinery and equipment, purchases of raw materials, and recruitment of a work-force. Organization and execution of physical production come next, followed by trading and transport of products. This involves detailed price setting, promotion and distribution.

All of these activities could be undertaken within one plant or production unit, but this is often not feasible or not efficient. When the product is large, complex, and has a lengthy production time, financing in particular is a serious problem. Usually it is also inefficient to undertake the entire production process, because certain production phases require a much higher capacity installation than the market for the final product can bear. Such a phase can be performed more cheaply by a specialized unit that supplies several units producing different products, but requiring the same

37

intermediary product or process. There may also be production phases that can be more efficiently executed on a much smaller scale by many small enterprises, working with more labour-intensive technologies, lower wages and without labour union influence. Large, integrated enterprises may also suffer from inefficiencies, due to lack of specialized information and skills, absence of a sufficiently large and cheap local labour force, or distant location of bulky inputs. Due to these problems in the organization of marketing and production, networks often consist of many participants, each specializing in only one (or a few) of the activities which make up the total marketing and production cycle.

The network structures that emerge differ according to the complexity of the product and the production process and the type of relations between actors within a specific network. Among the relationships which may occur are:

○ tradesmen buying from tradesmen;
○ tradesmen buying from small producers;
○ tradesmen buying from big producers;
○ small producers buying from small producers;
○ big producers buying from big producers;
○ big producers buying from small producers;
○ big producers buying from tradesmen.

A network may consist of only one of these elements, but usually more than one element is present. For example, the traditional carpet industry in Pakistan still includes many hybrid networks of small independent cottage weavers, who sell their crude, hand-woven mats directly to consumers on the local market. However, the same carpet industry also includes long-term, complex commercial networks: large wholesale trading houses, which sell to retail shops in large cities all over the world, and who own factories that grade and finish large quantities of finely knotted rugs woven in sub-contracted workshops all over Pakistan. The trading houses also control spinning factories, which produce high quality thread for the weavers, and employ a large number of middlemen to bring wool to the weavers' cottages and to collect the woven products.

The wooden-toy industry offers another traditional example. Trade houses usually place orders with middlemen, who approach workshops in villages where wood industries cluster. The toys are shaped with lathes in small workshops, and then taken home to be painted by children.

A more modern example is the football industry. Large multinational producers of sports articles subcontract to factories in Asia to punch and paint football segments, which are then given to local (male) home-based workers to be threaded together. The flat balls are collected, transported overseas, and finally inflated in the mother factory, where they are also imprinted with their famous brand name.

The most modern example of a sophisticated industrial network is the Japanese automobile industry. Here production includes so many levels of subcontracting that most enterprises involved are both contractors and subcontractors. Five levels have been officially recognized, but the lowest of these often subcontracts informally to household industries (Annavajhula, 1989).

Network Actors and Contract Relations

Actors in the various networks include trading and production enterprises, individual decision-makers, and groups of individuals participating in a common activity. Large and small enterprises, household industries, and individual home-based workers may all be actors within a given network, carrying out specific tasks. On a lower level labourers can be seen as actors within enterprises; the same holds for unpaid family workers in household industries. Actors may even participate in several networks at the same time, but within a particular network they have a certain rank. They are interrelated through production and trade contracts, which restrict their behaviour.

The decision making power of most actors is limited by contractual commitments to traders and/or big firms. Leading oligopolistic firms, such as the international carpet trading houses mentioned above, or multinational producers of sports articles, dominate their networks and incorporate smaller traders and producers through commercial or industrial subcontracting. Within their networks they may create commercial or industrial sub-networks with the help of middlemen, who are responsible for delivery and production of a distinct intermediate product. Nevertheless, there is often room for smaller, independent but subordinate networks in the cheaper niches of the market. Middlemen and master artisans function as leading actors within such market segments. Examples of such relationships can be found throughout metal-working, furniture making and tailoring, or, more generally, in all branches of production where work can still be done efficiently on a small scale.

Leading actors have superior access to relevant information and resources; therefore their decisions carry the most weight. When operating in oligopolistic markets with high entry barriers, they dominate the production scene. They determine product specifications and prices, in accord with the intended market segments. They also decide whether or not to use subcontractors, and they shape the linkages within their specific networks as far as possible, given the competition from adjacent networks. Using their dominant position, they maximize gains and minimize risks, with the bounds set by prevailing norms and values. In this context they survey the alternatives within the make-or-buy continuum to identify phases of the production process that can be separated out, choose certain options, select 'suitable' actors, and incorporate them into their networks.

39

The Cost of Incorporation and Specialization

In the manufacturing sector, internal economies of scale are ubiquitous and inexhaustible, thus, in theory, plants for homogeneous products will never reach their technically optimum size (Weijland, 1982). Economies of scale derive from: (1) plant size, (2) differences in equipment, (3) specialization of labour, and (4) the availability of lower prices for large quantities of raw materials and utilities (Haldi & Whitcomb, 1967). According to empirical studies, the most important sources of economies of scale are indivisibility of machinery and division of labour (Pratten *et al.*, 1965). Indivisibility of machinery occurs most frequently in processing plants; thus they have a relatively large optimum technical scale and tend to expand continually (e.g. the chemical industry, steel mills, oil refineries). Division of labour, on the other hand, is more often a characteristic of complicated products with numerous technically-separable production phases (such as automobiles or electronics). One might expect that manufacturing of such complicated products would also tend to be concentrated in ever-larger plants. This has generally been the case, but drastic improvements in communication have made contracting production phases and specific jobs out to specialized units an attractive alternative. The reasons for this tendency toward disintegration have already been given: lack of financing, inefficient use of available capacity, lack of cheap labour, lack of special information or skills, high transport costs for raw materials, and management problems.

However, according to current organization theory (see Langlois, 1988), there are limits to specialization and the accompanying disintegration of marketing and production. Even though there may be technical advantages for a large production unit in contracting-out part of its production or marketing activities, such a tendency toward specialization brings with it a number of managerial problems. These occur before the make or buy decision has been made in favour of subcontracting, as well as after. First, a firm must weigh the risks of buying or contracting-out a specific marketing or production activity, versus internal implementation. Certain products and processes are difficult to test for quality; the more complicated and expensive its products, the more a firm may wish to control all phases of production. For such products the risk of the firm is great, even when the entire production process is integrated and ruled by bureaucratic control. Therefore, instead of deciding to leave production to outsiders (in order to increase efficiency), a firm may choose to focus on quality, integrate production within its own organization, and encourage socialization and common norm setting within the strategic phases of its production process, as is characteristic of a 'clan' type of organization (Ouchi, 1980).

Nevertheless, numerous standardized (parts of) products and processes can be easily tested, which therefore can be contracted-out and monitored at relatively low cost. Many such goods can be produced on a small scale, and are quite suitable for contracting out to small units with labour-intensive production technologies. When the contractor can choose among a large number of willing subcontractors with equal qualifications, preference is given to persons from the contractor's own social network, so that a certain degree of social control can be exerted. Suitable parties must also be found to do the marketing or production, complementing the firm's own activities. Contracts must be designed to specify the goods and the terms of delivery. Also, after the contract is agreed upon, monitoring its execution may require a great effort (Williamson, 1981). Naturally, each party concerned initially tries to get a better deal, and this raises the problem of opportunistic behaviour. The worst manifestation of opportunism is the 'hold-up' situation, in which one party takes advantage of the other's dependence on large physical or human investments, which have been made in order to execute the contract (Alchian and Woodward, 1988). The more specific investments one party has made, the larger the scope for blackmail by the other, who can threaten to cut inputs, raise prices, lower payments or reduce quality.

The greater the competition among potential suppliers, the less risk the contractor runs that orders will not be executed correctly. Here the threat of giving no further contracts acts to ensure the compliance of subcontractors. On the other side, subcontractors are better off when more firms are interested in buying; they then have alternative outlets and can shift towards the firm offering the most favourable conditions.

The Rationale of Subcontracting

Subcontracting can satisfy the need of traders and producers to reap the gains of specialization and low cost production, while at the same time preserving a high degree of control over the production process.

Services may be demanded from various categories of subcontractors:

o Large specialized firms producing components, to the specifications of contractors;
o Medium-scale industries specializing in one industrial activity;
o Small-scale modern industries;
o Small-scale traditional industries;
o Household industries;
o Home based workers.

Evidently, contract relationships will tend to be more equal and reciprocal among producers of similar technological status, who both also have other contract options.

The subcontracted production can be controlled by fixing standards for inputs and equipment used. When dealing with small producers, inputs and equipment are often provided by the contractor. Further control is exerted

41

by offering advance payment for production and/or credit for buying special machinery and equipment. In this way the contractor can manoeuvre himself into a 'hold-up' position, so that the subcontractor becomes entirely dependent and has no possibility of shifting to a contractor who pays more.

Nevertheless, subcontracting may offer an improvement over the original situation of a small producer; therefore they are often quite willing to accept such a contract. The most eager are homebound producers such as married women, young girls, and handicapped or aged people, who may be seen as the solid base for the supply of subcontractors. In addition, there are other categories; many traditional small entrepreneurs have joined the category of subcontractors. Particularly in rural areas, where labour absorption in agriculture is low, traditional crafts outmoded, and financial resources depleted, many workers are willing to enter production arrangements that hardly differ from casual labour contracts.

One of the main advantages of subcontracting arrangements for subordinate producers is that it can compensate for fluctuations in their traditionally seasonal income patterns and reduce their entrepreneurial risks. This may facilitate their entry into another, more risky line of production that otherwise they would not have dared to attempt.

Subcontracting becomes more attractive when it includes steady contracts, advances, and a supply of raw materials, machinery and equipment. Some contractors even offer training courses and share technological know-how. These beneficial arrangements, however, are usually reserved for relations with those higher up in the network, where subcontractors possess some specialized knowledge or skill. If a contractor is to make such efforts, however, he must be sure of his investments in his subcontractors. This means he will need a test period to judge the potential capabilities of subcontractors. It is plausible that the better subcontracting arrangements are made only with well-known producers, working in production clusters where traders and producers have regular contacts.

Policy Recommendations

Current trends in industrial organization indicate that subcontracting will gain in importance as long as macro-economic policies remain as favourable as they are now in most Asian countries. Subcontracting arrangements have been mushrooming, particularly where international trade policies have been liberalized in favour of industrial exports, and where labour policies lack strong regulations regarding wages and working conditions, so that subcontracted workers can be paid very low wages. In such cases subcontracting lowers costs and raises competitiveness for many standardized or traditional export goods. In Indonesia, subcontracting has been encouraged by currency devaluation to such a level that several East Asian oriented trade houses are now moving their labour-intensive, subcontracting-based industries towards that country. The effects of this move can already be observed in West Java, particularly in the Jakarta district. These experiences lead to the conclusion that a country such as Indonesia can increase employment through subcontracting, via liberal policies on trade, production and labour. Such a policy will encourage leading trading houses and production firms to establish networks in densely populated areas with a prevalence of traditional entrepreneurship and underemployed household labour.

The question, however, is whether one would want to support such a free process of incorporation; and, if not, whether instruments are available to regulate it. If intervention seems desirable, network analysis can contribute to the formulation of adequate policies and the selection of effective instruments. The network approach gives priority to those types of intervention which aim to strengthen the whole chain of economic activities and improve network relationships, rather than dealing with the problems of the weaker actors in isolation. The entire network may be in need of support due to stagnating demand, weak marketing channels, or, more generally, to the failure of network leaders to innovate regarding products and market outlets. Thus networks can be strengthened by policies that widen their market segments and raise the revenues within networks. Such policies give scope for network expansion and improvements in the situation of all actors. Whether these benefits accrue to the lower network levels depends on the relationships between the various levels. These relationships vary according to scale and technology differences and the resulting differences in competitive power between and within networks. Structural distortions arise when leaders exert monopsonistic or oligopolistic power. This power can be affected by various measures in the fields of macro- and sectoral policy.

On the one hand, changing the structure and increasing the strength of networks may be more effective in improving the position of the weaker actors than taking direct measures to improve the productive capacity of a single category of small producers. On the other hand, instead of strengthening existing networks and attempting to curb their distortions, policies may encourage the creation of alternative, competing networks by organizing new leading units for marketing and/or production, either as private or state enterprises, or as co-operatives.

Subcontracting malpractice can be countered in several ways. In India, alternative public networks for the organization of production and marketing have been created. State corporations for small-scale and household industries have been established, which erected mini-estates to house small enterprises and home-workers, set up marketing channels, and provided the necessary raw materials for manufacturing. These corporations serve numerous small producers who traditionally depended on traders and

43

masters. However, evaluations of this programme suggest that such broad, direct, and centralized intervention is not manageable. The services offered are either too few or too many. The few stronger, better-served producers within the corporations claim they would be better off if they could work under the traditional system of masters and middlemen, while the majority of producers complain that to survive they need much stronger and broader support than the corporations are able to provide. The main problems of such large public networks are their weaknesses in marketing, provision of low-cost housing and inputs, and selection of capable producers. Most of these activities would be more efficient if decentralized or left to private initiative.

Another option is to leave the most strategic phases of production of the network in private hands, but to encourage — e.g. via subsidies — the development of fair network relationships. This approach has been tested in ancillarization programmes. Ancillarization involves a long-term agreement in which the ancillary unit functions almost as a department of the parent enterprise. Ideally, the parent buys a large portion of the ancillary's output over an extended period at a fair price, and also gives support in the form of technical know-how and training (UNIDO, 1985). Potential parent firms are attracted by tax-holidays and/or credit facilities, which serve to compensate for the set-up costs of subcontracting arrangements with the ancillaries. These costs include training of potential ancillaries, and a risk premium for the initial contract period. In principle, such subsidies could be extended to traders, to reduce the cost to them of contracting-out and encourage them to give more financial support to subcontractors.

One of the problems of subsidized networks is that the leaders are quite willing to receive subsidies, but not to incorporate and train those who are most in need of technological upgrading. Freely elected ancillaries are logically not the 'most deserving'. In Indonesia, programmes therefore oblige large firms to adopt specific vulnerable categories of small producers. This method can be successful in branches where the technological gap between the parties is not too wide. Otherwise parent firms tend to consider the imposed relationship to be a social obligation and disguised tax. Therefore it might be better policy to levy such a tax on a broader scale, and invest it in infrastructural services for small producers and networks in which they can get better options.

The mentioned experiences suggest that policies should aim at improving the subcontracting environment, rather than creating alternative public networks, or forcing subcontracting relationships upon network leaders. This indirect network approach may include various measures to stimulate the formation of new private networks or to strengthen existing networks and improve their structures. Government support of technologies that facilitate disintegration of production and increase subcontracting can spur the formation of new networks. Credit facilities can be developed in ways

44

that encourage large, leading enterprises to curb their investment in specialization, and direct the separable, labour-intensive phases of production towards subcontractors. A more drastic way to create linkages between large and small enterprises is to set limits on the scale of production in the branches where subcontracting is feasible. Such a policy, however, usually leads to sub-optimal organization of production.

In order to strengthen existing networks in which many small producers are incorporated, policies can be directed towards raising the demand for products that are suited for production by large subcontracting networks. For this reason, export promotion of traditional or labour-intensive products has been widely practised. Income and expenditure policies can also be used to increase demand.

A different but complementary method is the use of policies aimed at changing power structures within networks and strengthening the bargaining power of small subcontracting enterprises and home-based workers. More equitable contract terms for small producers can be achieved by increasing the number of competing contractors. Monopolistic situations can be curbed by liberalizing trade policies that abolish licensing schemes and terminating subsidies for large enterprises. Another way to make more competing traders and producers accessible to scattered small producers is to improve transportation and communication, so that small producers receive more offers and better information on markets for their products.

In addition to the above network level policies, actor-oriented support is needed to improve the technical know-how and production capacity of the weaker actors in the network. The technological capacity of small producers and workers can be raised by improving their general knowledge, technical skills, and access to information and financing. According to recent studies in this field, local institutions tend to be more effective than centralized ones, and partial support is to be preferred over comprehensive approaches (UNDP et al., 1988). Evidently small producers are served most efficiently by local agents who know the specific problems of local enterprises and how to deal with them. Local agents, who are in daily contact with small enterprises, should be key informants for small entrepreneurs. Their functioning is greatly enhanced by trade organizations, which can take care of further dissemination of information and basic training.

However, such a decentralized actor- and problem-oriented approach is effective only for well-established enterprises. At the lowest levels of networks, the most vulnerable group of home-based workers is hardly identifiable, as the poorest producers tend to take up various jobs at the same time, and frequently interrupt their lines of production. Changes in their economic environment and personal situation often make them shift to other activities which might be more profitable or better suited to their condition. This instability affects their willingness to invest time in private trade organizations, and hampers effective, specialized support. Consequently these poor producers tend to be the least informed and most exploited. On the other hand, they also are the fastest to quit, as their industrial investments are so minimal that they can easily accept any other job. Therefore, it might be better policy not to give special support for the producers at the fringes of the networks, but serve them indirectly through broad infrastructural improvements which increase their local economic opportunities or raise their economic mobility. This policy might be the most effective for the strengthening of the position of the lower level producers.

4 The labour process under amoebic capitalism — a case study of the garment industry in a south Indian town

PAMELA CAWTHORNE

The cotton knitwear industry in India is characterized by its sectoral divisions (that is, according to the type of raw material used to produce the fabric: cotton, wool, and synthetics); by its spatial concentration in particular localities within India (see Figure 4.1), and by the reservation of 'hosiery' production for the small-scale sector. Empirical research on this industry in the town of Tiruppur, Tamil Nadu acted as a vehicle for investigation of processes of economic and social change under conditions of economic growth and accumulation. Change has been fuelled primarily by opportunities during the eighties to gain access to export markets.

The labour process, as a concept, draws attention firstly to a discussion which centres on what happens to workers as economic change takes place: how it affects work and what workers themselves do about it[1]. Secondly, the concept points out what managers or owners do: what kinds of strategies they use to run 'their' businesses. Thus, both empirical information related to conditions of work and a more general view of the labour process are discussed. Jobs, skills, and hierarchies in the division of labour, as well as general conditions of work — the length of the working day, and low wages — are included.

All these phenomena are structured and affected by the formal and spatial splitting of firms under single ownership or partnerships and by the splitting of the production process (job work). That is, as ownership and capital become more concentrated, production is being decentralized into separate units. I use the metaphorical term *amoebic capitalism* to conceptualize this process. Like all metaphorical expressions, it cannot capture this process exactly. But it has enabled me to think more clearly about the way production is organized in this industry. In India there is a specific Government-set limit on the capital investment of a firm which wishes to remain legitimately within the small-scale sector (in 1989 Rs.35 million lakhs). While very few firms actually come close to this limit, this is in part because the limit acts as a disincentive to vertical integration of production

This chapter is based on doctoral research (Cawthorne, 1990) entitled 'Amoebic Capitalism as a Form of Accumulation: The Case of the Cotton Knitwear Industry in a South Indian Town.' It was first presented as a paper at a workshop on 'Development change in the labour process in the Third World and advanced capitalist countries' held at the Institute of Social Studies, The Hague 14–15 April, 1989.

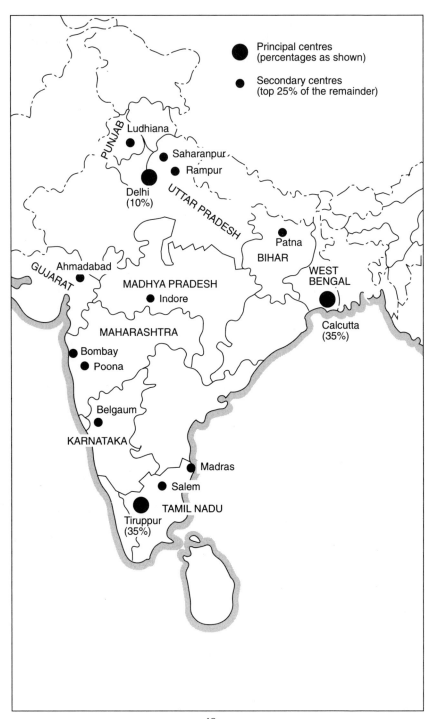

Principal centres
(percentages as shown)

Secondary centres
(top 25% of the remainder)

PUNJAB
Ludhiana

Saharanpur
Rampur

Delhi
(10%)

UTTAR PRADESH

Patna
BIHAR

WEST
BENGAL

GUJARAT
Ahmadabad

MADHYA PRADESH
Indore

Calcutta
(35%)

MAHARASHTRA

Bombay
Poona

Belgaum

KARNATAKA

Madras
Salem

TAMIL NADU

Tiruppur
(35%)

processes (Figure 4.2 illustrates the processes that constitute the cotton knitting industry in Tiruppur). However, a second consideration has also encouraged the division of firms into separate production units: if they employ more than ten workers (with power), or more than twenty workers (without power), they come within the ambit of the Factories Inspectorate.

Tiruppur and the Knitting Industry

Tiruppur is, by whatever criteria, quite unremarkable on first acquaintance. It is a dusty, bustling little town, lying in a hot, flat plain, with neither the hills nor forests to relieve it that make Coimbatore (the second largest town in the state of Tamil Nadu) seem less oppressive. It lies almost due east (approximately fifty kilometres) from Coimbatore, on the main railway line to Madras, and is well connected by road to Coimbatore and nearby market towns such as Avanashi and Erode. The latter is also a thriving small-scale town (an outlet for a considerable quantity of knitted garments made by small-scale producers in Tiruppur, many of whom have found ways of smuggling goods to market in Erode, thus avoiding the payment of sales taxes). Erode also has a large and expanding powerloom-weaving sector, and much of the woven cloth used in knitted garments in Tiruppur is made on powerlooms in Erode.

In many ways, Tiruppur seems to straddle two centuries. Arriving there is like stepping back into the nineteenth century while remaining in the late twentieth[2]. Workshops of petty commodity producers and their child 'helpers' jostle factories employing thousands of people, for the town as a whole is a hive of 'textile-related' industrial activity. Handloom weavers producing cloth using techniques known for a thousand years or more coexist with ginning and spinning mills using highly sophisticated technologies and employing thousand or more people in each factory. The powerloom sector uses machines designed a hundred years ago. They clack loudly and dangerously back and forth, jammed together in rows, fifty or more to a room. Skinny 'machine tenders' (for that is all they are) re-link broken yarn and check the machines. They move deftly between the machines with just inches to spare. Knitting workshops contain rooms full of (by contrast) pleasantly quiet revolving knitting machines. These are based on a more recent design, but nevertheless have remained basically unchanged for forty years. Then there are making-up factories, with rows of (male) sewing machinists, tiny workshops with only a couple of sewing machines, and all sizes of workshops in between. Bleaching and dyeing works ring the town;

Figure 4.1 (opposite) *Centres of concentration for cotton knitwear production*

Source: Rao (1985) Status of Indian Hosiery Industry, paper presented at XIXth Knitting Congress in Delhi

49

these have recently been joined by screen printers in well laid out factories. Sequins are sewn into T-shirts in women's homes, and other kinds of decorative work (e.g. embroidery) is performed on a classic subcontracting basis. There are also workshops where groups of women unravel scraps of material to make yarn for cleaning machinery. This was the only example I found of women in business for themselves, but, ironically, they described their income (loosely translated) as 'pin money': 'Our men are earning good money in this industry. We are lucky. We can do this to bring in a little bit more money.'

Older women, although bent and grey, tended to work in the mill sector (see Table 4.1). (Manager Somanur Mill, Coimbatore: 'They are still fast, and they don't have children any more. Also we can pay them less.') Everywhere, too, child 'helpers' were illegally employed in large numbers, across all sizes of firms in the knitting industry and in the powerloom workshops. Tiruppur has the feel of a 'boom town', and the boom has undeniably come about from the recent and rapid expansion in the demand for garments made of cotton knitted fabric. There is currently a fashion boom in Western Europe and North America for all kinds of cotton knitted clothes.

Table 4.1 shows the distribution of industries using Factories Inspectorate Lists. Fifty-six per cent of all factories are in the knitting industry, but when all textile-related sectors are taken together, 84 per cent of 'factory' industry in Tiruppur is textile related. Small-scale industrial-unit registrations (with the Directorate of Industries and Commerce) reveal a distribution that is even more highly concentrated spatially. Of total small-scale industrial-unit registrations for textiles and textile products (codes 23 and 26), over 80 per cent of the units are in Tiruppur[3].

Although, as Table 4.1 shows, the ginning and spinning mills employ the largest number of people per workplace, (and do not employ children below the legal minimum age of fourteen) the production of cotton knitted cloth, and the increasingly diversified kinds of garments made from it, dominate the town economically. Tiruppur supplies local and all-India markets with *banians* (the Indian word for vests and T-shirts) and underpants. In addition, well-known European retailers (C&A Modes and the French Connection, to name the two encountered directly) and large Indian merchant capitalists with numerous agents were placing orders in Tiruppur, and have opened up access to export markets for a diverse range of outerwear garments made from cotton knitted fabric[4]. As in any urban area in India, this dense industrial activity is interwoven with numerous other kinds of petty (often 'service-type') economic activity: teashops, godowns, barbers, repair shops of various kinds (cycles, sewing machines), flour grinding, metalworking workshops, general stores, three-wheeler drivers, and so on. Much of this activity profits from the growth of the knitting industry. There are also direct backward and forward industrial-

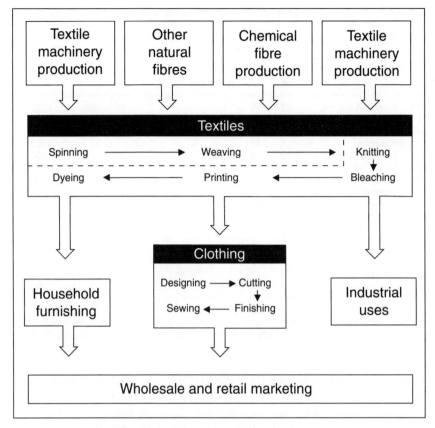

Textile machinery production	Other natural fibres	Chemical fibre production	Textile machinery production

Textiles

Spinning → Weaving → Knitting

Dyeing ← Printing ← Bleaching

Clothing

Designing → Cutting ↓

Sewing ← Finishing

Household furnishing		Industrial uses

Wholesale and retail marketing

Figure 4.2   *The place of cotton knitting and cotton knitwear in the textile industry as a whole*

linkage spin-offs both locally and further afield. These include thread suppliers (including the large multinational, Madura Coates, formed by a merger with JNP Coates UK, Madura Mills, and Harvey (UK) Ltd) and small, medium, and large firms (both in Tiruppur and other nearby towns) supplying elastic, buttons, clothing labels, packing materials (primarily cardboard and polythene) and chemicals and dyes (large Indian companies in Bombay and Delhi). The circular knitting machines are nearly all supplied by firms in the North (in or near Ludhiana), although there is one machine supplier in Tiruppur and another was just setting up in Coimbatore in 1987. Sewing machinery is all Japanese made, but second-hand machinery is easily obtainable.

Tiruppur is a higgledy-piggledy conglomeration of new versus old, bustle versus stasis, peeling dereliction versus glossy bank facades, filthy tent encampments of 'gipsies' and 'cheris'[5] versus modern, brightly-painted

Table 4.1   Distribution of Registered Factory Industry in Tiruppur, 1986

Code	Industry	Size of factories by category						Total	Total employed
		20–49	50–99	100–199	200–499	500–1000	1000+		
20/2	Rice and Oil	22	25	1				48	1790
22	Tobacco	1						1	20
23	Ginning	4	10	17	23	1		55	6860
23	Spinning	8	10	7	5		7	37	9360
23	Dyeing/bleaching	10	9	3				22	950
23	Powerloom	2						2	40
23	Labels, cone-rewinding, sizing	10	3					13	350
26	Knitting	151	89	9	3	2		254	9970
27	Timber	2						2	40
28	Printing	3						3	60
30	Polythene	2						2	40
33	Metal rolling	6	1					7	170
34	Engineering	2	2					4	140
40	Electricity		1					1	50
97	Bus transport	1	2					3	120
	Totals	224	152	37	31	3	7	454	29960

Source: Factories Inspectorate Lists for Palladam Taluk, Tiruppur Minicipality, 1986.

'breeze-block' constructions for industrial use and private housing, tumbledown buildings in the 'old' part of the town, and two well-laid out industrial estates, one built by the Small Scale Industries Development Corporation, SIDCO, and the other (the LRG estate) privately owned and set up as a Trust. The railway and the river Noyyal (a filthy trickle of dye-stained water, often, if implausibly, given as one of the main reasons for the location of the knitting industry[6] — neatly dissect the town and separate the new (north of the railway) from the old. In many ways, Tiruppur combines sights, sounds, and smells typical in any urban area of India. India writes its contradictions large and plain for all to see.

Tiruppu is a Tamil word meaning spinning, but Tiruppur has long been a centre for handloom weaving as well as selling raw cotton. The mill sector of the textile industry in Tamil Nadu has both a colonial and post-Independence history of successful if uneven economic development (Sreenivasan, 1984; Murphy, 1981; Baker, 1984). Also, like many other states in India, it has witnessed recent and rapid growth of a powerloom-weaving sector (Mazumdar, 1984). Mills in the south, however, are predominantly spinning mills, and the industry is very heavily concentrated in and around Coimbatore (Mackie, 1981). These mills produce varied kinds of yarn, including the 'hosiery yarn' cones used for the manufacture of cotton knitted garments (T-shirts, or banians)[7].

Historically, knitting is a much more recently-developed industry than weaving and spinning; in India there is no historical equivalent of the European framework knitting industry. Primarily, this has been related to the lack, until very recently, of a domestic market for knitted garments. Even woollen garments were woven; widespread use of cotton knitted underwear is a relatively recent development.

The first knitting machine was brought to Tiruppur in 1940. Both capital and labour constraints are minimal in the knitting industry (the reasons for this are explained below), and many of the workers in the industry are 'first-generation' industrial labour. Capital has been mostly generated within the area (the result of rapid accumulation within the industry). There was only one instance, in 1986–7, of a large, privately owned company, (Crystal Knitters) being set up by a mill-owning group based in Coimbatore and Tiruppur. State Banks provision of relatively easy access to credit has assisted the expansionary process[8].

The two other main centres for cotton knitted garments, Calcutta and Delhi, are older centres. Knitting machines were in use in Calcutta at the turn of the century. More recently, Ludhiana, in the Punjab (better known for its production of wool garments and textile machinery), has begun to produce cotton knitted garments. This was not difficult, since the vast majority of all circular knitting machinery produced in India is manufactured there (by the Punjab Machinery Co.). Capitalist owners in Tiruppur were bitter about this (competition in, and potential loss of, North Indian markets, which are threatened by Ludhiana's development) and blamed it on strike action, particularly in 1984. But smaller centres all over India are developing this industry in response to both 'ease of entry' and increasing demand, both in the home markets and abroad, for these kinds of garments.

Job Work from a 'Labour Process' Perspective: fragmentation of the workforce and indirect control

One of the most prominent characteristics of the knitting industry is a divided production process (with job work as a facilitating form of organization). As noted, I have termed this 'amoebic capitalism'. By the end of 1986, this phenomenon, under conditions of expansion, had given rise to:

(a)   a small number of large (in a very few cases vertically integrated) firms producing garments increasingly, and now in many cases, exclusively, for export markets;

(b)   a much larger number of medium-sized firms primarily making garments for sale in out of state Indian markets, but increasingly combining production of garments for the Indian market with that for the export market. In the latter case, a number of these medium-sized

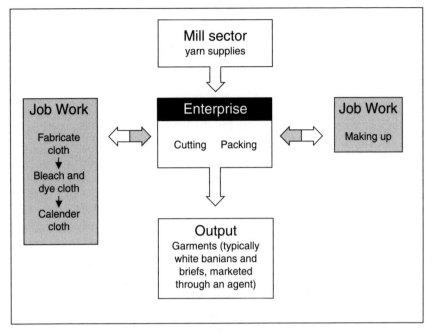

Figure 4.3   *Job work and the cutting firm*

NB: such an enterprise requires working capital only to buy raw materials, and access to (rented) premises with a cutting table; the latter requires an investment of approximately Rs.500.

firms make such garments as 'job work' for larger firms, who obtain orders from foreign buyers;

(c)   a still larger (but unknown number) of very small-scale petty commodity producers making garments to be sold in small-scale localized markets, sold for the most part to agents acting on behalf of small-scale wholesalers and retailers[9].

None of this was apparent from any of the secondary sources consulted. Designation of the sector as 'small scale' means that firms which are expanding can simply register additional, spatially separate 'units of production' (despite their common ownership). This gives the somewhat distorted impression of that the industry is composed solely of small-scale and medium-sized individual firms.

'Job work' is a way of organizing production which allows expansion without vertical integration of the production process. It acts as one mechanism to facilitate accumulation. Tiruppur entrepreneurs use this term to describe interactive networks between and also within enterprises. These networks connect specialist firms: those in fabrication, finishing and making-up. But 'job work' is also used in some cases to describe divisions

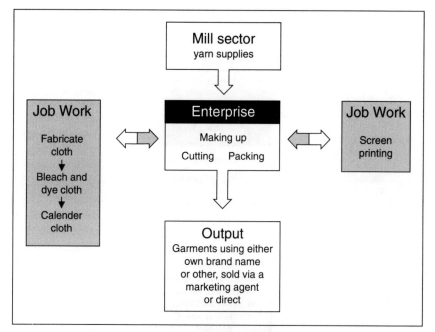

Figure 4.4 *Job work and the making-up firm*

NB: such an enterprise might own, but is more likely to rent premises, and would require a minimum capital investment of approximately Rs.4000 total. This would include one 'power table' with four seats (1 over-lock, 1 chain-lock, 1 lable-stitching machine and 1 rib-cutting machine — a maximum approximate investment of Rs.2000, buying second-hand machines; plus one hydraulic/mechanical press — approximately Rs.1000 and one cutting table with irons — approximately Rs.1000.

of labour within enterprises. In the latter case, an owner often employs a 'job-work contractor' for each unit. This person is a kind of production manager, who is also responsible for employing labour for a particular 'job'. Such an organizational system within the firm then parallels the process divisions found in the industry as a whole, and is identical to older forms of 'inside contracting' (Lazonick, 1979; Samuel, 1977; Mead, 1984).

On one hand, therefore, job work enables smaller firms to specialize in different parts of the production process, yet still be in a position to sell a finished commodity. On the other hand, it means that larger firms do not need to vertically integrate production processes in order to expand production, and can keep capital investments to a minimum. In other words, capital accumulation is taking place, and is becoming more concentrated, but without centralization of production processes.

Figures 4.3, 4.4, and 4.5 show how individual capitalists — petty, medium-sized, and large — can use job work to exert control over crucial stages of the production process. All three variations in the type of firm are

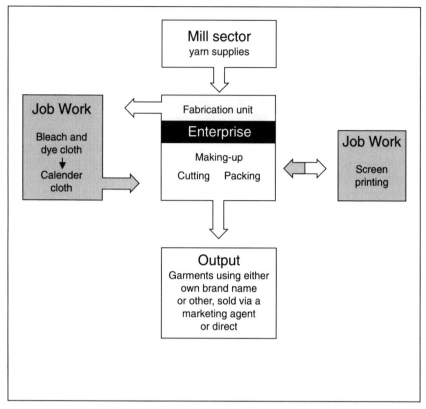

Figure 4.5 *Job work and the combined firm*

NB: such an enterprise would require a minimum fixed capital investment of approximately Rs.1 lakh (representing 5 second-hand knitting machines, costing approximately Rs.20,000 each, five machines covering various diameters being about the smallest economically viable number; and a further Rs.4000–10,000 for a power table, hydraulic press and cutting table.

instances of exerting technical control, because buying yarn (hence ensuring its quality) is crucial. Secondly, controlling the cutting of garments allows wastage of cloth to be minimized.

Job work can thus be conceptualized as: more or less vertical integration of the production process under single ownership, but also as a networking system which benefits small-scale owners. Figure 4.3 illustrates the most extensive case of job work as networking; Figure 4.4, more direct control of the labour force, but still with limited vertical integration; and Figure 4.5, more direct control of the labour force, combined with more vertical integration. Yet even in the last case, where a firm combines both making-up and fabrication (and in a very few cases bleaching and dyeing also), this extended control may be offset by the use of 'inside contracting' systems.

56

That is, many of the owners of the larger firms in Tiruppur were seeking to evade direct control of their workforces in two ways: (1) through the use of 'inside contracting' within their own firms and (2) through the use of 'job work' in which other firms specialize in parts of the production process.

Do you mean indirect employment? Yes, I create lots of other jobs because I am getting the orders. That's how the job work system works here. I don't want to employ any more than one hundred workers myself, and I haven't expanded beyond this point for the last ten years. It's because of all the labour disputes. I'm buying land in Coimbatore . . . so if things get very bad here I can move my business. (Owner of Leela, interviewed November, 1986).

Thus, many large firms set up individual 'units of production' and place a 'job-working contractor' in charge of production and hiring. The owner/manager of the 'parent' firm then concentrates his (since they are all, without exception, male) attention on marketing and sales. Balasubramaniam owns one of the largest firms producing garments for the Indian domestic market. This firm now includes seven separate production units, three fabrication units and four making-up units. His brother owns a bleaching and dyeing factory. 'This is good, it means that I didn't have to worry about investing in these areas myself — it's an expensive operation if you have to buy modern dyeing equipment.' (Balasubramaniam, owner of Jay Jay).

I used to run it all like one factory – employ all the labour. But since just before the strike [1984] I have another system. I have a general manager whose main task is to deal with all the distribution and co-ordination aspects of work between and with all the separate units. He buys the yarn* and gives it out to the fabricating units. The rolls of cloth are returned and stored here [the SIDCO estate premises] and my offices are here. I do all the marketing now and get the orders [from Agents] and I make all the necessary contacts. A list of requirements is drawn up from the order obtained, and passed to my managers [he has two assistants]. Now, in each of the units is a 'subcontractor'. His main job is to take care of hiring labour required for a particular job and to organize production for that job. He's responsible for quality and he will lose part of his money if there are defects. This system works well. The subcontractors were some of my best and most long-standing workers. I call them 'managers' now and they are very happy . . . I have a leasing system for the machinery. The subcontractor leases a number of machines* from me and then sub-leases six machines to each worker[10].

As a firm expands and accumulates, various factors interact and affect the

---

* Both working capital and machinery are provided/owned by Balasubramaniam.

57

form it takes. The two most significant factors which emerged from field-work research were: those related to decisions about, first, how far to increase capital investment (expand capacity); and second, as the quotations above show, how much increased responsibility to take on for an expanded labour force (and whether to do that directly, or employ someone else as an 'inside contractor'). In both cases, job work allows capital investment and direct involvement with labour to be minimized.

In the sample group of firms, there was only one case of a large firm which intended to integrate as many of the production processes as was consistent with the owner's prospects of accumulation.

> I want to be like the spinning mills here. That is my ambition. Then I will have all the stages as one operation — calendering, bleaching, dyeing, etc. This way, I have much better managerial control than otherwise. I don't believe in subcontracting work . . . labour problems are there. It doesn't matter whether you try to keep your production units small scale or not, whether you split them up or not. With a large factory you know exactly what is going on. (Kandaswamy, Okey Textiles).

All other large firms in the sample group (eight in all) had adopted strategies which were more or less explicitly aimed at evading the responsibility inherent in large workforces. They all had three or more spatially-separate units of production (one had nine and another ten separate units). Here is the owner of Leela, currently one of the largest of the knitting firms, and one of the first to make garments for export markets. His response is typical of many others. When asked if a rapid expansion in demand had led to any pressure on his capacity, he said that using the job-work system enabled him to deal with all the extra work.

> When necessary, I will get the stitching done by other enterprises, but we will always check, iron, and pack the garments to control the quality here. I have made fairly permanent arrangements with twelve other enterprises who always carry out work for me. [However, none of them are solely dependent on him[11].] These other firms are mostly much smaller making-up firms, and sometimes, for some jobs, I supply machinery plus a supervisor employed by me to control the overall production. These people need to be watched, because they don't have the experience. Yes, I use other people's [that is, the workers in these smaller firms] labour. This way, I can avoid the problem of labour control here at my place. (Author's comment, transcript of interview with Gangadharan, owner of Leela).

Gangadharan was explicit in saying he wanted to avoid employing a labour force much larger than approximately one hundred, and therefore had not expanded his own enterprise much beyond this point, largely due to the various labour disputes of the last ten years. Part of the reason for

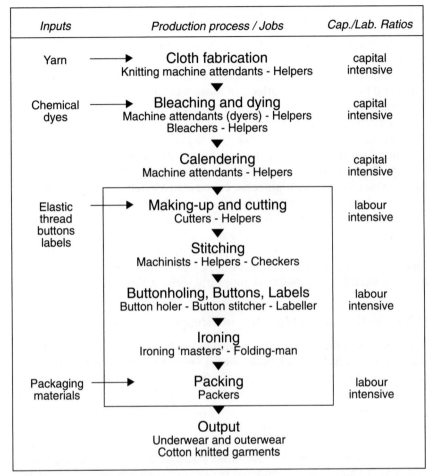

Inputs	Production process / Jobs	Cap./Lab. Ratios
Yarn ⟶	**Cloth fabrication** Knitting machine attendants - Helpers	capital intensive
Chemical ⟶ dyes	**Bleaching and dying** Machine attendants (dyers) - Helpers Bleachers - Helpers	capital intensive
	Calendering Machine attendants - Helpers	capital intensive
Elastic ⟶ thread buttons labels	**Making-up and cutting** Cutters - Helpers	labour intensive
	Stitching Machinists - Helpers - Checkers	
	Buttonholing, Buttons, Labels Button holer - Button stitcher - Labeller	labour intensive
	Ironing Ironing 'masters' - Folding-man	
Packaging ⟶ materials	**Packing** Packers	labour intensive
	Output Underwear and outerwear Cotton knitted garments	

Figure 4.6   *The production process and the division of labour in the cotton knitting industry*

acquiring land in Coimbatore was his intention to move his business there if 'things got very bad in Tiruppur'. He has no intention of altering his present arrangements, and sees his future prospects as intimately tied up with continued access to export markets.

Where the firms are smaller — the making-up firms, for example, shown in Figure 4.6 — their control over the labour process is considerably less than for the larger firms which combine cloth fabrication with making up (and, in a few cases, dyeing and bleaching as well). But such firms appear (from the sample group) to be most concerned with avoiding the extra capital cost of acquiring the knitting machinery needed to fabricate cloth, rather than avoiding employing larger numbers of workers. There was one case of such a small-scale making-up firm with an 'inside contractor'; however, he also worked as a machinist. But this firm had only recently started, and was something of an exception to other similar-sized firms in other respects also.

The fact that workers in this industry have managed to some extent to transcend the fragmenting effects of these ways of organizing production is testimony to the courage and determination of both workers and union representatives (reputedly an atypically honourable group of people). Less dramatically, the extent to which this industry is spatially concentrated, together with the rapidity of its expansion, also makes for consciousness raising. These factors appear to have overcome the fragmentation of work-forces which comes with amoebic expansion. Certainly it was highly un-usual in India for piece-rated workers to have achieved concessions regarding the payment of dearness allowances (compensation for infla-tion). One of the most significant factors here was the much increased rates of profit on exported garments. Export markets are currently acting as a kind of 'vent for surplus', and it is unlikely that the cotton knitted garment industry would be expanding significantly without those markets.

Labour in the Knitting Industry in Tiruppur

The concept of the labour process also prompts questions about the way in which workers (sellers of labour power) are organized for production, and the things that capitalists (buyers of labour power and owners of capital equipment and plant) do to achieve this organization. In the Braverman and post-Braverman debates on the labour process, many questions focus on the kinds of skills (leaving aside the difficulties with this word for now) necessary to the individual tasks and the overall jobs which are performed. Related questions are how these jobs and tasks come to be devised and organized, and how the hierarchies considered necessary to achieve the owner's objec-tives of efficient production and the generation of profits come into being. There are also questions where that is happening, about the effects of intro-ducing ever-more sophisticated machines into the production process. Such a trend is not yet evident in the knitting industry in Tiruppur. I have only limited data about labour, so only some aspects of such questions can ad-dressed in the paragraphs below. In particular, I will describe the jobs that exist in the knitting industry and their associated skill categories.

In Tiruppur, conceptual boundaries normally taken for granted tend to blur. Many workers think of themselves as potential petty capitalists, or have achieved this status. Such owners are classic 'petty commodity pro-ducers', exploiting their own labour power. Such people have combined a range of (often first-generation acquired) industrial skills, in many cases gained from experience across divisions of labour such as cutting, machin-ing, and ironing as a part of making up.

At the same time, there is also a class of owners who can be clearly identified as 'industrial capitalists' (as opposed to merchants or financiers). These people have a very different 'class' background from petty workers cum owners, and are for the most part well educated.

On the other side of the divide, militant workers, who belong to active and successful communist party-affiliated unions, are — unusually for a 'small scale' sector of industry — numerous in this industry[12]. Then, there are women who perform 'hidden' (in the statistical sense) work in their homes and on the street, unravelling scraps of waste material. An unseen domestic labour force, they are on the periphery of industrial development. But I also encountered women, in a limited number of instances, who had middle-management jobs in the largest knitting firms. There are both children who stay in school until the age of sixteen and children who work anywhere up to twenty hours a day from the age of seven.

Jobs and skills

As Figure 4.2 shows, the main process divisions in the knitting industry are cloth fabrication — the production of tubular lengths of knitted fabric made with cotton hosiery yarn of different counts[13]; finishing processes — bleaching and dyeing and calendering, or steam-heat pressing; and, finally, 'making-up' the garments. The division of labour is most complex in the making-up workshops and factories. Figure 4.6 indicates the main type of job associated with each part of the production process.

But what constitutes skilled work? First, what are the 'objective' sets of conditions necessary for the worker to be able to perform the job adequately or well? This is clearly related to the amount of time it takes to learn how to perform the task, but also the kind of skills the worker may need before s/he can even start. Second, how do the tasks which make up that job compare with other jobs in the same workplace or within the industry; and third, who has the power to make the decisions (and why) about what shall be described or thought of as 'skilled' or 'unskilled'. Skill, in other words, is socially constructed as well as objectively determined[14]. Much of the time the underlying issue for both workers and owners is the rate paid for the job.

Knitting-machine attendants (in charge of the circular knitting machines and responsible for the production of knitted fabric), cutters, and machinists in the making-up units are all regarded as holding skilled jobs, and rates of pay are relatively high[15]. All these workers are assisted by (unskilled) helpers who are, for the most part, children or, in some cases, adolescent 'apprentice' boys. (Boys were sometimes described as 'apprentices'; girls were not.) All these jobs are performed, in the main, by men[16]. The overall gender-division of labour (in cutting, making-up, and fabrication firms) based on the employment figures of firms in my sample were: 51 per cent men, 29 per cent women and 18 per cent children (boys and girls

61

below the age of fourteen)[17]. There are women machinists, and owners claimed there was no difference in the amount earned by men and women performing the same jobs. However, the wage rates of a group of 45 workers (collected during fieldwork) show that women machinists earned between Rs.200 and 500 per month, with the average Rs.250. Men's monthly wages as machinists ranged from Rs.500 to 1000, and averaged Rs.650.

Ironing-masters are also regarded as skilled workers, although they are not paid as much as the categories of workers above; pressers and packers are regarded as semi-skilled. Trimmers and checkers are regarded as semi-skilled, but pay rates differ depending on whether a woman or a child performs the job (these jobs are nearly all performed by women and children).

In terms of job content and overall division of labour, little has changed in the last 35 years. Detailed job descriptions, which are broadly accepted by the Unions, exist in the Madras Productivity Report[18]. Disputes have not been over demands for job re-classification, and, since the industry as a whole is so unregulated, potential areas of conflict such as promotion and upgrading, production standards and manning levels, or personnel transfers are unheard of. Cutting-masters and cutters tie, bundle and hand over the cut pieces to the tailoring section. Machinists clean and look after their machines, and helpers (always children) arrange machined sections of garments for the different machine operations. The amounts paid depend upon the skill category of the job and the age of the person performing it. In this industry, women workers tend to range from young adolescents to those in their early twenties. Probably this largely accounts for the lower wages recorded for women workers in the sample group.

Hierarchies in the division of labour
Hierarchies in the knitting industry range from a complex ranking of jobs and personnel, in the large, usually composite — i.e. fabrication and making-up — knitting firms (for the most part, these cross up to twelve separate units of production), to non-existent, in the very small-scale single-owner workshops with one man and a boy helper. As soon as the number of employees is many more than five or six, there is usually at least one clerical or office worker. Thus a split between 'manual' and 'non-manual' work starts to emerge fairly quickly. In terms of rates and type of pay, this is important. Of the 25 firms in the sample, two small-scale workshops employed only one child helper, but most employed between twenty and hundred workers. In these cases, the main status division was between office staff and workers in the factory. The former are usually paid monthly salaries, and in some case benefits such as ESI (Employee's State Insurance), while the latter are paid piece-rates and in many cases are temporarily employed for a specific job[19]. The salaries of office workers would, however, often be quite a lot less than, say, those of the most able machinists.

62

Within the manual-work category, hierarchies are largely determined by the jobs being performed. Jobs seen (and rewarded) as the most skilled are those of machinists (in the making-up units) and knitting-machine attendants (in the fabrication unit). Working in the bleaching and dyeing factories is different again. Workers in dyeing are regarded as highly skilled and paid accordingly — in some cases as high as Rs.1500 per month (equivalent to the monthly salary paid to a woman designer at Poppies — one of the very few larger firms attempting to create their own designs rather than follow instructions). However, age (and therefore the extent of a particular worker's experience) affects the amount paid.

In many of the making-up units with more than approximately thirty workers, there is also frequently a foreman or supervisor. In some cases, this job was not separated from the production line, and the foreman would also be working as a machinist. However, in other cases — particularly in the larger firms which operated an inside contract system — the 'contractor' becomes much more of a Production Manager. Such people are given a residual payment built into the rate for a particular job. Many workers with (both) kinds of experience have the ambition to start their own business; in one interview an owner said with some irritation: 'It keeps happening. I give someone a responsibility and then they want to go off and set up their own place. This has happened twice.' (Loganathan, Gentex)[20]. But in another case (Jay Jay), an owner who instituted an inside contract system after having dealt directly with his own workforce for a number of years said: 'This system works well. The subcontractors [now five in all] were some of my best and most long-standing workers. I call them 'managers' now and they are very happy!'

Only two of the largest firms in the sample had anything that could be described as approaching a stratum of 'middle management'. In both cases, this was still combined with a division of the enterprise into separate units of production (in one case, ten separately-registered units, all with different names). But in one case the 'central departments' were run by four brothers, described as Financial Controller, Marketing and Administration Manager, Production Manager, and General Manager. The father was also active in the business — one of the long established firms in the industry.

Therefore, two main scenarios emerge. In the first, an owner (or several owners in partnership) perform all managerial functions within their firm, including control of production (and all major decisions connected with production): marketing as well as hiring and firing labour. Such firms will also have a small-scale clerical staff, but may well 'buy in' help in keeping accounts. Much depends upon the size of the firm.

The second main scenario involves additional status tiers within the firm. This may take the form of intermediaries who control both production and labour (but still with little or no overall autonomy). Such people are variously described as 'managers', 'contractors' or 'job-work contractors'. But their functional position is the same. However, there are many instances of extended family involvement in firms. Where this is so, power structures alter, and there may be a number of ostensibly equal owner/managers. It soon became clear while conducting interviews that nevertheless some one person in a partnership situation would be regarded as *primus inter pares*. In two of the very large firms, (Poppies and Yuvraj) a perceptible group of 'middle managers' — in addition to 'contractors' in charge of individual units of production — also exists. Such managerial strategy as exists in respect of labour control is highly variable. In many cases it depends primarily on the personalities of the entrepreneurs involved (more or less authoritarian).

Characteristics of the labour force

The most startling characteristic for a foreign researcher was the existence of so many child workers. Estimates varied from 15 per cent to 25 per cent of the workforce. My own employment figures (which showed 18 per cent of workers in the sample group of firms were children) suggest the lower estimate might be more accurate. But that is still a large number of illegally-employed workers. (The legal minimum age is fourteen.) Most children tend to be eight or nine or older (the youngest child I found was seven), and of the six children interviewed all had spent some time in school. However, compared to the horrendous situation in the nearby matchworks industry in Sivakasi, working conditions for children (indeed for everybody) were better, and the children, on the whole, somewhat older[21]. Although Minimum Wages Legislation based upon recognizably 'welfarist' economic conceptions of the man as the main or sole 'breadwinner' exists, most working-class Indian families do not make that kind of calculation. Children's earning power is seen as a valuable extra resource.

Tiruppur has acted as a magnet, drawing large numbers of (relatively unskilled) workers from the surrounding areas and from further afield within the state of Tamil Nadu, particularly during the last ten years. Estimates for the total workforce (SIHMA) over a 25 year period were: 3000 (1960), 7000 (1970), 20,000 (1980), and 40,000 in 1985[22]. Census figures for non-household industry increased from a total of 35,396 in 1970 to 62,065 in 1980. (This would not include children, which the SIHMA estimate was supposed to do.) Of the 45 workers interviewed, eight men came from Tiruppur; twelve came from villages outside Tiruppur (up to 42 kilometres away), one from Madurai, one from Ramanathapuram, one from Madras, and one from Pollachi. Of the women, seven came from Tiruppur, four from nearby villages, and two from Kerala. Of the children, all five now live in Tiruppur, but four came originally from villages. In these cases, the whole family moved to Tiruppur to work. One already lived in Tiruppur.

All but four of the workers had knitting or related jobs in textiles, such as weaving. Many had no other kinds of job before starting in the knitting

Table 4.2 Current and previous jobs of forty-five workers in the knitting industry

Current job	Previous job(s)
Cutters	cutter
	helper
	machinist
	'all other knitting jobs'
	handloom weaver; casual labourer
	ironing-master
	agricultural labourer
	spinning vessel manufacturer
	weaver
	'other knitting jobs'
	machinist
	spinning
Machinists	none
	helper to tailor, milk vendor, coffee shop worker
	none
	none
	aluminium factory worker, trimmer/checker, helper, office boy
	'contractor'
	tailors helper, packer
	weaver
	trimmer
	none
	none
	none
	helper
	none
	helper, checker
	none
Trimmer/checker	housework
Checkers	none
	packer
	none
	none
	none
	trimmer
Ironing	machinist
	none
	none
Knitters	none
	weaver
Knitter/supervisor	helper in father's tailor shop
Foreman	cutter mainly, but other knitting jobs too
Contractor	'all other jobs in knitting'

Source: Worker questionnaires completed during fieldwork 1986/7.

industry (indicated by 'none' in the table). Unlike seeking work in the large spinning or ginning factories, it is not difficult to obtain a job in the knitting industry in Tiruppur. The majority of workers begin work if not as a child

65

worker, then in early adolescence. They gain skills from 'helping' machinists (in fabrication units or helping sewing machinists), as checkers, or in packing jobs. None of the workers interviewed saw any part of their working lives as including any kind of 'formal' training, with the one possible exception of young boys or adolescents who helped knitting machinists. Many of the owners of the larger firms complained of 'labour shortages' and said that they kept notices advertising jobs outside their enterprises for most of the year. These notices were certainly in evidence during the fieldwork period.

A number of brief accounts (transcribed from interviews) of worker's circumstances follow:

My father was working as a 'peon' in a private bank, and I studied only up to 3rd standard in school. Then I took up a job in a knitting factory as helper to a machinist, in 1953, at the age of ten. [He is now 44]. Then I learnt tailoring and cutting. I have served in all capacities — knitter, cutter, and stitching. I am now working as a foreman in Arjee Knitting Mills, and I look after the production of the other workers. I have six brothers and one sister, and they are all employed in the knitting industry. (Rajendran).

I am living jointly with my three brothers, since I have some hearing problems. [Apparently he was quite deaf until 19 but began to hear at 20. He is now 37.] I joined a firm as helper at the age of ten, and worked for six years there. Then I left to join my brothers who were doing dairy business, and later started a tea shop. Later I came to a factory. I am happy about it now because I want to do something different from my brothers. (Shanmugasundaram).

Murugesan (aged 35) belongs to the Mudaliar caste whose tradition is weaving. He became a handloom weaver. Since the income from this was so little, he took up a job in the postal department as a 'casual worker'. This was only temporary; he then took a job with a knitting company as 'ironing-master'. This he did for four years. While working as an ironing-master, he was also trained in cutting. He then joined another company as a cutter. He stated that 'Talent Tex', the enterprise in which he works, is a making-up unit and a partnership concern. They produce vests and briefs for the Indian market. One of the partners, who came from the north of India, is a partner in two other businesses in addition to this one.

My older brother is working in a factory after his school final. I was working on the land but I do not like village life. I came to Tiruppur to search for a job. My brother introduced me to a cutting master and I just worked with him as a helper and learnt cutting. This is my first firm. (Knit Garments, Krishnan, aged 24)

I was learning a tailoring job and trying for another job in a tailor's shop at Pollachi [a town approximately sixty kilometres away from Tiruppur]. My father is an agricultural labourer and he could not provide me with an education. My mother's sister is in Tiruppur, and asked us to move over to Tiruppur, so our whole family came to work here. (Dharmaraj, male aged 23)

Karuppasamy (aged 22) comes from one of the villages near Tiruppur. He left school at the age of fifteen and went to work as a weaver in a powerloom factory. He worked there for two years, then came to Tiruppur to join a fabrication unit in the knitting industry. He described himself at that time as a 'learner' (apprentice). After two years he had become a trained knitter. He then joined another enterprise as a knitter, where he worked for six months; next he went to work for Srinivasa Knitting, a partnership which has another making up unit at Salem. They fabricate knitted cloth for their own use in the making-up unit, and do job work for others. They have five single jersey-knitting machines. Karuppasamy is one of the workers interviewed who intends to start his own business eventually.

My father is a tea-shop owner. He was not doing well, so I completed my school final so I could earn some money to help support the family (one older sister and two younger sisters). I joined a knitting company called Best Knitting Co. I worked there for two years and I learnt cutting the fabric. After I had learned, I joined Titoni as a cutter, and I have worked here now for one and a half years. (Rajan, aged 22)

My father was a watchman in a village near Pollachi — he didn't get much money. We moved to Tiruppur when some of our neighbours moved there. We wanted to get better job opportunities. My father worked again as a watchman for a year but because he is now very old he cannot continue to do that job. He is at home now. My mother can raise some money [Rs.60 a month] by doing waste-knitting collection and selling it. So she has sent me and my brother to work. My brother is seventeen and he is working in a liquor shop. (Lakshmi, aged 13, working at Titoni)

I came to work in order to help support my family. I lost my father when I was six years old. My elder brother is working in a factory as an ironing man. My elder sister worked here (Knit Images) as a machinist, but she got married and has gone away. I came to work in knitting when I was eleven, and learned to be a helper, and then checking and now I am an overlock stitcher. This is the second place I have worked. (Valarmathi, aged 17)

Nancy Roberts had some training as a child in the knitting industry at Aysha Hosieries in Calicut, Kerala. When she got married, she stopped working. She married a gardener. After a while, she came to Tiruppur at the invitation of a relative who was working here. She and her husband then moved to Tiruppur, leaving their son with her sister. She is now

67

working as a machinist and her husband as a bullock-cart driver. (Nancy Roberts, aged 38, working at Arjee Knitting Mills)

The overall picture which emerged from these comments and during the course of fieldwork in general was that this industry has acted as a focus of opportunity for many people (often without any skills or training at all, although many workers have had some education) in the town itself and in surrounding areas. Because the sector is largely unregulated and the ban on child labour is to all intents and purposes ignored, youngsters can readily obtain jobs as 'helpers' and then quite quickly pick up the skills they need to eventually begin work cutting, ironing or machining.

The conditions of work and struggles over pay and productivity: the emergence of a class for itself?
Working conditions are, on the whole, what one might expect to find in a largely unregulated sector of industrial production in a highly unevenly developed country such as India. By 'unregulated' is meant a sector where production takes place under conditions largely unaffected by relevant legislation. Jobs are, on the whole, poorly remunerated relative to other industrial sectors. Daily wages are nevertheless for the most part above the legal minimum requirement which was Rs.16 per day at the time of fieldwork in 1986 (India has had a 'Minimum Wages Act' since 1948, amended by various State Legislatures). However, the concept of a 'minimum wage' is complex, and such legislation, therefore, is highly problematic to formulate and under certain circumstances virtually impossible to implement. This raises the issues of both enforcement of and compliance with such legislation. Compared to other branches of the textile industry, particularly the mill sector (whether private or nationalized), wage rates in the knitting industry are a pittance, even allowing for some variation within the industry.

Conditions of work are also largely unregulated and are highly variable, ranging from fairly well-ventilated, adequately spatially-organized factories to classical 'sweat-shop' conditions in tiny, dirty, noisy, and cramped rooms. Moreover, even in those enterprises in Tiruppur which are in theory regulated (for example, those registered with the Factories Inspectorate) the labour force is substantially unaffected, certainly with regard to wage rates, and often with regard to overall conditions of work. The CITU (Centre of India Trade Unions, affiliated to the CPI(M)) Secretary (who was the subject of one of several lengthy interviews) reported, with not inconsiderable cynical amusement, that not only was the Factories Inspectorate somewhat understaffed (two people dealt with the whole of Palladam taluk), but also that the degree of co-ordination necessary to achieve any measure of success in attempting to pressure enterprises to conform totally undermines the task in hand. There was not only the Factories

Inspectorate, but also different Inspectorates for Employees State Insurance and for the Provident Fund; in addition, the Tiruppur Municipality had to grant a health and safety licence to which the Electricity Board had to agree. Moreover, 'you can bribe them all, and in many cases for less than the small amount they would be able to levy as a fine' (CITU Interview, December, 1986).

Compared to the powerloom industry (a sector of the textile industry which has rapidly expanded in recent years and is also almost entirely unregulated) both from the point of view of noise pollution in powerloom workshops (which reaches unbearable levels in small spaces crammed full of hundred or more looms) and the very considerable danger of industrial accident, the knitwear industry is pleasant indeed. Knitting machinery is quiet as it revolves; it does not slam back and forth like looms; likewise, sewing machines are not particularly dangerous pieces of equipment.

But, despite these relatively favourable points, men, women, and children work unremittingly long hours. A typical work-week (across all jobs in the industry) would be six days a week — one and a half shifts each day: twelve hours in all. That is a 72 hour working week. There is no over-time pay recognisable as such — 'tea money' of Rs.1–2 for the last half shift will be the only additional payment. Moreover, the new boom in exported goods, which imposes strict constraint on production schedules, can mean that, particularly towards the end of a contract period, working days of twenty hours are not infrequent. Children also work these hours, and many sleep on the premises for a few hours before starting work the next day[23]. The vast majority of workers in all sections of the industry (with workers in the dyeing units the only exception) are paid on a piece-rate basis, have little or no access to either ESI (Employees' State Insurance) or pension funds (Provident Fund (PF)), are not remunerated in case of sickness or industrial accident, and in general take little or no holiday time (since it is unpaid). It is, as the garment industry has tended to be in many countries besides India, a seemingly predictable example of what can happen under conditions of capitalist production in a labour-intensive, poorly-regulated, low-wage industrial sector[24]. Work is (to freely adapt Hobbes' aphorism) nasty, brutish, and long.

However, one of the most interesting findings during fieldwork was that Tiruppur, unlike many other small-scale industrial sectors of industry in India, has a recent history of both active, and to some extent successful, struggle by workers and unions. There have been a number of strikes over a ten-year period, many of which have been related to a report prepared by the Madras Productivity Council in 1972. In this report, job descriptions and work-load specifications were laid down for the industry as a whole. In order for members of the Productivity Council to come to a decision about norms in the knitting industry, time studies were undertaken (Taylor fashion) for various operations across different counts of hosiery goods. These

69

different counts were grouped into three categories[25]. Sizes were grouped into four categories, each with separately assessed work-loads. Work-loads were then set for these four size categories to cover production in dozens per person per shift. These work-loads covered the following job categories: cutting, overlock, chain/chainlock, flatlock; labelling; damage (checkers); ironing; packing and folding. For the knitting-machine attendant the number of machines to be allocated to one attendant was assessed as follows:

Counts of yarn: 20s, 24s and 30s	Numbers of machines per machine attendant
Plain	4
Motta, medium and interlock	5
Fine plain counts	6
Fine counts, interlock	6
Rib	2
Non-sinker body	2

(The number of feeders on the machines should not exceed one hundred)

In essence, the Unions rejected these work-load specifications for two main reasons: first, because it was claimed that their representatives had not been present during these time and motion studies; and second, since the majority of workers are paid by the piece the calculations included only piece-rate systems, where productivity is, of course, high and statutory breaks nil. The matter was then referred to an Industrial Tribunal. The Tribunal found in favour of the MPC and moreover objected to the Union demand for uniform wage rates across the industry (as opposed to variable piece-rated wages):

> It also rejected the plea for uniform wages in such a non-scheduled industry — the smaller ones are likely to be elbowed out if the same standards are made applicable to bigger ones (Financial Express, March 13, 1981).

But, although it rejected that demand, it did accept that wage rates in the industry were extremely low, and proposed a 25 per cent increase in wage rates in return for a 13 per cent increase in productivity.

Underlying these responses is the more general question of what is implied for workers (and capitalists) by time-rate (or piece-rate) systems of payment. In a strict sense, it might be argued that the Unions' response to the Tribunal's acceptance of the norms of the Productivity Council is illogical, since there was no other means by which such norms could have been constructed (although that does not answer the objection that their representatives were not present when these studies were conducted). What is really at issue for the Unions, however, is the broad objection to the piece-rate system as a means of payment:

[. . . what we want] . . . what all the workpeople [and the Union] want here is the piece-rate system scrapped and payments to be made on time-rate basis in all the industrial establishments in the knitting industry . . . (CITU General Secretary, interview, December, 1986).

[In 1984 we] demanded Rs.19 per day to be basic pay for cutters, tailors, machinists, and ironing-masters. The rest [we wanted to get] Rs.12 per day, plus dearness allowances of approximately Rs.45 per month, as well as a ten per cent increase in the piece-rates. But we are working more generally towards the abolition of piece-rates . . . (AITUC General Secretary, interview, December, 1986).

Over hundred years ago, Marx (Capital Vol. 1, 1976) made some acute analytical observations about time- and piece-rated systems of payment (the payment according to the duration of labour or by the amount of its product):

Given the system of piece-wages, it is naturally in the personal interest of the worker that he should strain his labour-power as intensely as possible; this in turn enables the capitalist to raise the normal degree of intensity of labour more easily. Moreover the lengthening of the working day is now in the personal interest of the worker, since with it his daily or weekly wages rise . . . From what has been shown so far, it is apparent that the piece-wage is the form of wage most appropriate to the capitalist mode of production.[26]

A relevant comment in a Business India article (1984) underlines the validity of this analysis:

More than 95 per cent of the workers are employed on piece-rates, which were introduced by the units that proliferated in the seventies. They evoked little resistance from workers whose wages after an intense (typically fourteen-hour) day are much higher [now] than they were under time-rates. K. Selvaraj, a DMK trade unionist in the industry, laments, 'the workers were starstruck by their daily earnings. They didn't sit down and reflect what this meant in the long term; they weren't bothered about the provisions of the Factories Act'.

It is worth noting too that one effect of a piece-rate system is to do away with the necessity for close supervision of workers:

piece-wages make it easier for parasites to interpose themselves between the capitalist and the wage-labourer, thus giving rise to the 'subletting of labour'. The profits of these middlemen come entirely from the difference between the price of labour which the capitalist pays and the

71

part of that price they actually allow the worker to receive. In England, this system is called, characteristically, the 'sweating system'.[26]

The 'inside contract' (job work) system in Tiruppur allows substantial use to be made of just such 'middlemen'.

Thus, many of the actions of the unions and workers have been in protest against norms they have always disputed. Following the initial Industrial Tribunal, a Labour Tribunal court decision was made in 1976 accepting the Madras Productivity Council's original findings. These findings, as the Unions have always claimed, reflected suicidally high work-loads and sought to institutionalize productivity rates which were as high as they were only because workers otherwise could not have made a living wage. Work-loads of 60-80 dozen per day in the machining department were treated as normal and, in short, unions claimed that both the Council and the later tribunal decisions were in support of the owners.

These disagreements finally culminated in a strike in 1981 which lasted 49 days. Payment of ESI and Provident Fund was demanded, plus a decision to agree considering revising the work-load specifications. The suggested specification for machinists was 36 dozen per day, with no piece-rate payment system. This work load was agreed by both Unions and owners, but at that point the State Government intervened and said it would form a tripartite panel to consider the whole case in detail. However, it was also agreed that an interim pay-hike of 25 per cent should be implemented. The panel did not report, and in 1984 a strike (which lasted a total of 127 days) was called in protest at the situation. During that time, the same demands were made by the Unions, and these were then referred to the Labour Court, which was supposed to deliver the results of a Court decision within six months. Meanwhile, another ten per cent hike in wages was agreed, plus dearness allowance, to be paid each month for all workers. At the time of fieldwork, the committee still had not reported, and Unions were again making the same demands, plus another wage increase of 35 per cent for PF and ESI. They were also pressing for all enterprises to keep accurate muster rolls.

These two strikes, 1981 and 1984, could be considered quite successful in some respects. Increases in basic wage rates were twice achieved, as well as widespread payment of dearness allowances — albeit with considerable variation within the industry, with some (larger) enterprises more ready to concede than others. The payment of dearness allowance (an index-linked payment that means small-scale additions to basic rates, rising each year with the cost of living) is quite a victory for piece-rate workers. However, despite these increases, many workers' wages are very low indeed, relative to both minimum wage levels and other workers in the (regulated) mill sector of the textile industry. Neither do these struggles take account of the large percentage of children in the labour force. They continue to provide a

72

pool of exceptionally cheap labour, earning well below legal minimum wage levels. Many employers claimed they paid men and women equally for the same jobs; however, firstly, women were not so easily able to obtain work in the areas considered skilled (machining, ironing and cutting) and, secondly, there is considerable evidence that even if they do these jobs, men still earn higher wages[27].

This section is concluded with an excerpt from The Hindu (July 8, 1984) detailing some aspects of the 1984 strike:

. . . labour-management relations have, of late, been strained. The Tiruppur workers have been on strike since April 20 demanding, among other things, dearness allowance and a hike in wages. The four main unions there — CITU, AITUC, AIADMK, and DMK (whose total active membership, according to a police source, cannot exceed 2000) — contend that their demand for dearness allowance is perfectly justified, because the Government has introduced it in several small-scale factories. But an order directing the managements to pay an interim dearness allowance of Rs.46 until the Special Industrial Tribunal, Madras, gave its ruling on the dispute was stayed by the Madras High Court on a representation by the owners. It may be recalled here that the Industrial Tribunal, Madras, had said earlier that the industry would be crippled if it was forced to pay dearness allowance. The owners say that nothing could be more true than this. As many as thousand factories employ not more than fifteen workers each; strictly speaking, it is not even a small-scale industry, but a cottage industry. Stiff competition from the hosiery centres in Calcutta and Ludhiana has not only reduced the margin of profit for the Tiruppur vest to about 1.5 per cent, but has also curtailed its sales. The owners, however, say they are not averse to raising the wages. Another bone of contention between the workers and the managements relates to the work-load. After a detailed study, the Madras Productivity Council said that workers could easily cut or stitch forty dozens of a portion of the vest in eight hours. The Industrial Tribunal, Madras, approved of this finding. But the unions are not agreeable to a work load of more than 25 dozens. The unions also argue that workers are not given time off even on national holidays. They do not enjoy any accident benefits. Recently a nineteen year old youth was killed in a factory accident and no compensation was given to his family.

While the strike continues, the Tamil Nadu Government are reportedly losing Rs.80 000 daily in sales tax. The entire workforce is poorer by Rs.14 lakhs for every day it sits idle. The owners have already lost Rs.10 crores and export orders, also running into crores of rupees have been cancelled. The occupancy rate in the town's twelve hotels is down by at least fifty per cent. The daily sales in one popular and large restaurant has declined by Rs.3000 and many small-scale eating houses and tea shops have closed down. An auto-driver cannot make more than Rs.10, compared to Rs.35 he used to average every day. [Everyone] has been hit.'

Tiruppur's industrial reality exhibits highly contradictory tendencies. On the one hand, job-work forms of organizing production enable large numbers of small-scale capitalists to come into existence, and with this the perpetuation of a 'petit bourgeois' consciousness. On the other, an increasingly sophisticated 'class consciousness' has given rise to a determined struggle for improvement. It is the latter that is both surprising and unusual in a workforce perpetually fragmented through spatial separation exacerbated by job working and internal splitting of firms.

Conclusion

The forms of labour organization in Tiruppur have a number of advantages from the employers' point of view — notably, that by allowing them to claim the spurious (in many cases) status of 'SSIs', they evade a whole range of legal responsibilities to workers (welfare/insurance payments and so on). Such forms also allow them to evade the problems of direct control over a large concentrated work-force and, therefore, the dangers of increased worker solidarity and enhanced capacity for effective trade union organization. Many employers explicitly acknowledge these as dangers they wish to avoid.

Whilst this is so, job work, by allowing the fragmentation of production structures — both spatially and organizationally — makes it impossible for capitalists to enjoy the degree of control over the labour process which facilitates Braverman-type 'de-skilling' processes. Indeed, the process of expansion of the Tiruppur knitwear industry can also be seen as a generalized process of skill acquisition. Workers tend to acquire a range of different skills, in different workshops (since there has been a shortage of labour, due to the very rapid expansion of the industry). In a number of cases, this has allowed those with any entrepreneurial talent or ambition at all to set up their own small-scale independent businesses. Such people continually swell the ranks of the 'petit bourgeoisie'. Moreover, if we agree that jobs may be designated 'skilful' by those who exert control over the labour process, capitalists in Tiruppur attenuate this power by relying on job work. In the same way, they also attenuate opportunities to intensify work through the detailed attention to task specialization and rationalization in combination with more sophisticated (i.e. productive) machinery. The overall tendency has been to rely, rather, on extending the length of the working day. In a Marxian analysis, this represents the extraction of 'absolute' surplus value rather than the extraction of 'relative' surplus value. To some extent, however, as we have seen, paying piece-rates serves to intensify work in any case.

74

Whether or not the de-skilling hypothesis has universal validity, even as a description of advanced forms of capitalist production, its relevance is questionable in a case such as the one considered here. Moreover, the as yet unsophisticated technologies in use serve to perpetuate labour-intensive techniques throughout the industry. Whether or not that will continue to be the case is a matter for speculation. If the Government were to lift its 'small-scale' status designation, would this then result in many more vertically-integrated large factories — perhaps producing entirely for export markets? Would this then mean increased tendencies to seek to impose Taylor-type regulation to drastically improve productivity, accompanied by the division and subdivision of tasks within those factories? Would previously heterogeneously-trained workers become solely trained as highly-productive machinists or cutters (equipped with suitably sophisticated machinery to aid them)? And does such a scenario take account, among other things, of the many petty producers supplying local markets? Tiruppur's complex reality does not readily lend itself now, or probably in the future, to any single hypothesis.

PART II

Gender aspects and policy experience in small-scale industries

5 Gender aspects of industrialization in India and Mexico

ISA BAUD

Industrialization within developing countries has been characterized by the emergence of several forms of production. Large scale factory production is only one form; a form, moreover, which creates employment for only a small percentage of those who work in non-agricultural sectors. Small scale and artisanal forms of production are widespread, and they play an essential role in the total economy. The existence of what has been called a multi-structured economy has important implications for the extent of employment created and its characteristics.

Given the diversity of the industrialization process taking place in developing countries, it is very difficult to predict how different groups of participants will be affected. That some groups will derive more benefits than others is to be expected, as is shown by historical experience. I am particularly concerned with changes occurring in women's employment during the current industrialization process, as we know that in the past women have often been adversely affected by the impact of economic development on their employment opportunities (Boserup, 1970; Beneria and Sen, 1981). More specifically, this study deals with how women's employment varies within large, small-scale and artisanal forms of production, and, to a lesser extent, the implications this has for women's bargaining power within the family-based household.

In order to examine changes in women's employment, I felt it was necessary to pose several questions:

(1) what are the relationships between large, small-scale and artisanal units, and to what extent does each employ women?
(2) what is the extent of labour market segmentation, and by what channels do women gain access to employment in the various forms of production?
(3) what is the nature of the work performed by women within each form of production; what degree of marginalization do they face, due to technological and organizational innovations in production units?
(4) what are the implications of women's employment and income earning for female bargaining power within the household?

Choices and limitations
Before considering the research questions, I will briefly describe to you the choices made for this particular study, its limitations, and the methodology used.

First, I have limited my attention to the category of 'newly-industrializing countries' in which industrial production contributes substantially to the national product, absorbs a relatively large share of employment, and plays an increasing role in world trade. From eight possible countries, I selected two of the four countries which had the highest share of manufacturing value added in 1980 — India and Mexico (the other two possibilities were Brazil and Argentina).

Second, the main category from which sub-sectors were selected was agro-industries. This type of industry still remains one of the more important industrial sectors in developing countries, representing 34 per cent of total manufacturing output and 64 per cent of employment in 1979 (UNIDO, 1985). In addition, these industries are a major employer of women. Case studies have shown that women are an important part of the industrial work-force in such industries (the most well-documented sector is textiles/clothing; figures for women in food processing are scarce). In India, almost three-quarters of women's industrial employment in 1982 was in these industries.

Third, I confined my attention to women production workers. This means that women entrepreneurs, secretarial staff, and technical personnel are not included. This subgroup was chosen because women production workers, in general, have no 'choice' but to work to ensure their own and their children's survival, in contrast to middle-class women, for whom work may also include a certain amount of self-realization.

The research methodology rests on the use of case studies. I preferred case studies because of the greater depth and quality of the material they provide in comparison with surveys. A disadvantage is, of course, that generalizations from such studies are much more limited than those from surveys. However, at this stage, it is more important to extend our knowledge of the factors influencing women's employment patterns than to attempt to measure the extent to which certain patterns occur.

In choosing specific industrial sub-sectors from among those which employed women extensively, I had to select those for which sufficient material on women workers was available. In India, the food-processing industry was selected as a sub-sector because information was available from studies carried out within the IDPAD Programme by Indian colleagues (Banerjee, 1983; Mathew, 1983; Desai and Gopalan, 1983). The sector with the second-highest employment of women in India was the textile/clothing sector; I selected the cotton textile sector and collected information during just over a year of fieldwork in India (within the IDPAD Programme) (see Baud, 1983).

In Mexico, the shoe industry was chosen as a third agro-industrial sector. In one of the three major shoe production centres, an excellent study had been carried out on women's employment. In addition, this was complemented by information from an extensive research programme in the same geographical area on labour markets, industrial firms, and women in the

80

household (Alba Vega and Kruijt, 1988; Hernandez Aguila, 1983; de la Peña and Escobar Latapí, 1986).

Case-study material collected by others provided information on the issues of (1) the extent of women's employment in sub-sector and type of production unit, and (2) changes in women's employment. However, information on the impact of such employment on women's bargaining power within the household was lacking in these case studies. Only the results from my own fieldwork provided information on this point, placing obvious limitations on the conclusions drawn (Baud, 1983).

Forms of Production and their Relationships

To return to the research questions above: the first question has three aspects: first, the relationships between large, small-scale, and artisanal production units, second, their internal characteristics, and third, the manner in which they generally employ women workers. The literature on production units and on women's labour overlap only slightly, so I will discuss them separately.

The development of a multi-structured economy should be seen as part of a historical process; since the Second World War, national planning in many Third World countries has been directed towards import substitution. However, the limitations of that model in terms of employment generation and national income became clear in the early seventies. At the same time, a restructuring of labour-intensive industries occurred in the industrialized countries, with relocation to developing countries. These reacted by making more room for export-oriented industrialization.

This led to certain changes in types of production structures and labour market segmentation. On the one hand, free trade zones were set up, where large-scale factory production took place under stringent conditions imposed by national governments. On the other hand, a great deal of industrial production was subcontracted out to national firms, small-scale modern and traditional producers, and various types of casual workers.

The relationships between large, small-scale, and artisanal production units in developing countries have been considered using the informal-sector approach or that of petty commodity production. Here I will consider only the latter (see Moser, 1978 for criticism of the former). Using the petty commodity production approach, authors emphasize the fact that small-scale forms of production are 'defined in terms of their relationships with the dominant form of production and that they form part of a structure of dominance and dependence existing on a world scale' (Harriss, 1982). Instead of simply accepting this view, it seemed to me more useful to begin by determining the nature of the relationships between production units, including ownership and production, external and internal factors, and to what extent each factor indicated dependence (ibid.).

81

Ownership and production

Forms of production are often defined according to the degree to which ownership and production have been separated. In large-scale capitalist production the separation is complete; in small-scale production the owner generally also participates as manager or producer. In artisanal production, the owner is the main producer (craftsman).

The case studies indicated that the artisanal form of production actually includes two types of production units: domestic outwork and household production. In both cases, the owner of the machines or tools is the producer. However, in domestic outwork a person works at home at disguised wage work, that is, the supply of work comes from subcontracting firms and the finished product is delivered back to the same firm. Household production refers to producers (in the case studies, usually men) working with unpaid family labour. They receive their supply of work from commercial suppliers and sell it to wholesale traders. This distinction is particularly important for women, because in the first instance they work at wage labour, and, in the second, as unpaid family labour.

External factors

A basic external problem faced by all types of production units is scarcity and price fluctuations in the supply of raw materials. The reactions of the different types of production units vary, however. Large-scale units try to increase their control over their sources of supply, and attempt to reduce the price per unit by buying large quantities. Small-scale units get their raw materials from commercial sources or from subcontracting firms. They try to minimize their problems by maintaining close social links with their suppliers. This usually means a fair amount of dependence on a regular supplier.

This type of dependence is even more common among artisanal production units. In domestic outwork, dependence on subcontracting firms is inherent. In household production, the producer can, in principle, buy raw materials from different traders; however, some degree of dependence is often sought to ensure a basic regularity in supply, plus loans to finance such purchases.

A second external relation is that created by the need for sales channels. These are variable: all types of production units sell to wholesalers, among others. In large scale production, these include both domestic and exporting wholesalers; sometimes control is increased by ownership of retail shops.

In small-scale and household production, sales are through wholesale merchants or co-operatives. Such commercial sales channels often provide financing for the producers, creating a relationship of dependency. Domestic outworkers are by definition bound to one sales channel — the subcontracting firm — and are completely dependent.

The basis for the great dependence of small-scale and household production units on the merchants is the fact that they provide working capital. The dependence on commercial capital — as opposed to industrial capital — is extensive and important, and needs to be given more recognition.

Internal factors

Internal factors contribute but little to the dependence between large production units on the one hand, and small-scale and artisanal production units on the other. To begin with, the products made differ: those of large production units are much more standardized and are produced in large quantities. In small-scale and household production, a small range of products, which can vary over a period of time, are made; in domestic outwork, often only part of the production process is completed (shrimp peeling is done this way; subsequent processing occurs in large units).

The technology used varies systematically, and other types of units show little dependence on large capitalist production. Large units exhibit the greatest degree of mechanization and division of functions. The latter is often based on line production. In small-scale production, machines and hand tools are used. The use of second-hand machinery from large units is common, but small smithies making similar machinery form an alternative source. There is less functional specialization, and greater flexibility in division of operations. In artisanal production, hand-tools are the most common, and functional specialization is by age, experience, and gender.

Changes in technology over time can only be traced for large production units, as information on small-scale and artisanal production units is too scattered and sporadic. In large units, increases in mechanization have been found, as well as increases in subcontracting of production (or parts of a production process) outside the unit. Cost factors, limits to technological innovation, and labour relations influence the direction of technological change.

Subcontracting occurs in a greater variety of forms than is assumed in the literature. In the textile industry, large units subcontracted only to small-scale units. In the shrimp-processing industry, large units subcontracted to domestic outworkers. In the shoe industry, small-scale units subcontracted extensively to domestic outworkers.

The final and most important internal factor is the use of labour. In the literature various categories of labour are distinguished, ranging from long-term wage work, short-term wage work, and disguised wage work to dependent producers and truly self-employed (Bromley and Gerry, 1979). Irene Tom (1987) has included another category in which women are extensively represented — unpaid family workers.

In the case studies, I found this continuum a good approximation to the situation observed. However, further differentiation needs to be made within long-term wage work and short-term wage work categories. Within long-term wage work, one finds workers who actually have a relatively stable and secure contract and expect to work in the same unit for a long time, and also those who have not yet gained the status of long-term wage worker, but may expect to obtain it in the future.

Short-term wage workers include workers with even greater variety in their degree of insecurity in income and expectations. It would be preferable to limit short-term wage workers to those whose jobs are not protected by labour legislation, but who actually work a fairly long period in one unit. Those who are recruited on a very short-term basis (daily) or who are not paid fully (apprentices) can be termed casual workers (see also Harriss, 1982).

Women workers

To what extent does each type of production unit recruit women within the various categories of labour? The extent of women's employment generally increases as one moves from large-scale production to smaller units. In large units, they are generally 10–25 per cent of all workers; in small-scale units, their participation varies from 25 to 50 per cent of all workers (this includes various categories of labour). In household production, they may be almost 50 per cent of the work force, mainly as unpaid family workers, and, in domestic outwork, between 50 and 100 per cent of the work force, as disguised wage workers (with children working as unpaid family workers).

Let us examine the categories of labour in more detail. In large-scale production units, women are primarily recruited as long-term wage workers. This applies more to the textile and shoe industries than to the shrimp processing industry (where greater seasonality leads to use of more casual types of labour). In addition, a very small percentage of not yet secure wage workers are found in large-scale production, most of whom are aiming at long-term secure employment. Men are primarily employed as long-term wage workers; however, they include small numbers of less secure apprentices.

In small-scale textile production, women are employed as short-term wage workers and unpaid family labour in equal numbers. Small percentages also work as casual workers and apprentices in these units. For men the situation is somewhat different: they are recruited as short-term wage labour much more often than unpaid family labour. In addition, male apprenticeships are quite common, which is not the case for women. In household production, women are primarily recruited as unpaid family labour. In domestic outwork, both men and women are recruited as disguised wage-workers, and make use of their children as unpaid family labour.

My first conclusion is that in each type of production unit more than one type of labour is used — although the extent varies. The smaller the unit the more casual the labour used, but even large units use labour other than long-term wage labour.

84

Table 5.1 Forms of production and categories of labour

	large-scale	small-scale	artisanal household	artisanal domestic outwork
raw materials supplier	some control over prices/supply	little control over prices/supply/ dependence on traders/sub-contracting firms	little control over prices/supply dependence on: traders	subcontracting firm
sales channels	domestic/ exporting wholesalers	wholesale merchants/co-operatives	wholesale merchants/co-operatives	subcontracting firm
working capital	institutional sources	dependence on private merchant financer	dependence on private merchant financer	in natura dependence on subcontracting firm
technology	machines for each operation	second-hand machines/ hand-tools little dependence on large-scale sources	hand tools little dependence on large-scale sector	hand tools
changes in technology	mechanization within unit/ subcontracting to other units			
ownership/ production separation	separation owner/workers	owner = producer/also other workers	owner = producer/ unpaid family labour	
categories of labour used	long-term wage workers; small and casual workers	short-term wage workers; casual workers; unpaid family labour	producer, unpaid family labour	
women's labour	10–25% of workers; long-term wage workers	25–50% of workers short-term, casual and unpaid family workers	50% unpaid family workers	50–100% disguised wage workers

Second, the extent of women's participation in each type of production unit is greater than is acknowledged by either producers/owners or workers in the production units. The more casual the category of labour, the less explicitly it is acknowledged. Unpaid family labour is the category denied most extensively by everyone concerned.

85

The third conclusion is that, in comparison to men, women within each of the various types of production units are recruited for more casual types of labour. They are also quite explicitly denied access to apprenticeships, a major channel by which they could 'graduate' to more secure and better-paying categories of labour. Table 5.1 summarizes this.

Labour Market Segmentation and Channels of Access

The second question concerns the extent of labour-market segmentation and the differences between men and women workers in gaining access to employment. Two concepts are often used to examine these problems: the reserve army of labour and labour-market segmentation.

The concept of the reserve army of labour identifies various groups of potential workers, who are presently not participating in industrial employment. Three distinctions are usually made: the floating reserve, which consists of that section of the labour force in the capitalist industrial sector which is constantly renewed — basically temporarily unemployed workers. The latent reserve consists of all people previously working in agriculture, but thrown out of it because of capitalization in the sector; Braverman (1974) has also included 'housewives' as a part of this group. The stagnant reserve is the casually and irregularly employed labour force. These forms have usually been discussed within the context of capitalist development in the nineteenth and twentieth century in the USA and Britain; Braverman's classification of women as 'housewives' is much less relevant to a developing country's situation. In addition, women should not be defined a priori as a 'reserve': it makes more sense to find out how and when they are made into a 'reserve'.

The concept of labour market segmentation is more useful, as it indicates the mechanisms by which people gain access to employment. For women this includes two sets of factors: those related to personal and family based household characteristics, and those related to labour mobility and class formation.

Personal factors
Within the first set of factors were women's family relationships, women's ages and levels of education, number and age of children, membership in a community, and channels of access to employment.

A current cross-section of women's access to employment in large-scale industry shows a majority of older women in the textile industry, with few new women gaining access: and a majority of younger women (under 25) in the shoe industry. This situation is linked to changes in the labour process to which I will return in the discussion of the following question.

In small-scale production, there is a concentration of young, unmarried women, in higher percentages than in large-scale production. This is contrary to the expectation that older, married women would be more likely to

86

work in this type of production unit, because here it is easier to combine child care with economic activities. This rather suggests that these women are learning their work on the job in small-scale production, where there is more scope for acquiring skills than in large-scale production.

In domestic outwork, there is a concentration of young, married women. Here the proposition that married women with children will fall outside large-scale production is confirmed. The majority are under 25 years of age, suggesting that they will have young children to care for. In household production, there is a much wider range of women workers in terms of age and marital status. Older women are found in smaller percentages in all types of production units. De La Rocha (1984) suggests that this is due to the increasing contributions of older children to family income.

Although the level of education varies, with women in household production having the lowest levels and women in large-scale production the highest, this does not mean that a higher educational level is sufficient to gain access to a job. Rather, employers in large-scale production units use educational criteria to limit access to jobs that do not in themselves require such education.

Having children makes carrying out a job more difficult regardless of the type of production unit in which women worked. It does not prevent women from staying on their jobs in large-scale production units, where the percentage of women with children under four is substantially higher than in other types of production units (in the shoe industry). This leads me to conclude that it is easier to arrange for child care than to find a job with a regular income.

In India, community membership was found to be an important factor in gaining access to jobs in both large and artisanal production units, but less so in small-scale production. The evidence suggests this occurs when a sector is expanding rapidly, and the labour market is relatively tight.

Labour mobility and class formation

The second set of factors influencing women's access to employment includes brokerage and patronage systems, and the degree of labour mobility. The Indian case studies indicate that brokers operate within each type of production unit; in large units, this includes factory managers and fore(wo)men, and the trade unions, to which women have little access. In domestic outwork, brokers play an essential role in distributing work at the neighbourhood level. In the industries studied, there was little evidence of patronage systems.

Labour mobility is a concept which needs to be differentiated into upward, horizontal, and downward mobility (Breman, 1980). In large-scale production, upward and horizontal mobility are relatively rare. Downward mobility occurs for women over two generations, when daughters of women workers cannot gain access to the types of jobs their mothers had.

87

In small-scale production, horizontal mobility is more extensive for men than for women workers; it is more extensive for both sexes than in large-scale production. It contains elements of necessity (in conflict situations, women often prefer to change units), as well as possible improvements in the work situations. In artisanal production, workers try to get work from several suppliers at the same time — horizontal mobility. This situation is seen as quite threatening.

These results suggest that job security is a more important value than (usually theoretical) upward mobility for both men and women.

Women in the Labour Process

Let us now turn to the question of the nature of the work performed by women and the way their functions change over time. The concept which has been most often used to describe changes in women's employment is that of marginalization. However, several different definitions have been used. These include (1) exclusion from productive employment, (2) concentration outside large scale production jobs, and (3) substitution or segregation (cf. MacEwen Scott, 1986). The concept 'marginalization' has also been used at various levels of analysis, making results difficult to compare. Here I would like to relate the concept more directly to the discussion of the labour process (defined by Schmitz as the combination of material instruments of production, and the social organization of labour (1985)), at the level of the workplace, where the effects of different technologies and labour organization can be measured directly.

In order to do this, a small digression into ideas concerning the effects of technology on the use of labour is necessary to elicit the elements needed for a more precise conceptualization of women's participation in the labour process. Basically, researchers assume one of two positions: either positive effects, in terms of efficiency and increase in wealth, or negative effects, such as the increased subordination of the worker to the machine, de-skilling, and lower wage levels.

Models based on these assumptions have emerged primarily from studies in industrialized countries. Two points relevant to my own study are: first, variations in the use of technology between industries and different labour processes need to be kept in mind, as mechanization and automation have not occurred everywhere to the same degree. In industries not based on craft work, changes in work have occurred in the direction of casualization of work rather than de-skilling (Littler, 1982). Second, the role of trade unions and workers in resisting control over their work has been relatively neglected.

For developing countries, there are few studies on technology and labour utilization, either for employment in general or women's employment specifically. One exception to this is Schmitz's study on Brazilian industries (1985).

Returning to the concept of marginalization, a series of more precise aspects were defined for this study. These aspects are: the division of functions between men and women, skills and acquiring skills, work-loads and wages, job security and mobilization. In addition, women's labour is considered from two perspectives: a current cross-section, describing participation in different forms of production according to the aspects just mentioned; and changes over time, particularly in large-scale production. The trends over time include: (1) marginalization — the situation in which women are relegated to jobs which are fewer in number and pay less than those available previously, (2) segregation — the increasing exclusion of either sex from a particular function, (3) changes in skills (de-skilling and acquisition of new skills), and (4) changes in the categories of labour used (casualization).

Division of functions
The case studies indicated clear variations in the division of functions among the various types of production units. In large-scale production, the production process is split up into many operations, of which the majority are earmarked as unskilled. Women have access to only a limited number of skilled functions; they are mainly confined to unskilled functions. In small-scale production, only major parts of a production process are divided into functions. This implies that work is more varied and requires more and more varied skills. The evidence on women's access to skilled functions is mixed; in the powerloom sector, it was high; in the Mexican shoe industry, it was very low, and gender segregation by function was high.

In household production, the division of functions between men and women is usually stringent and sanctioned by local customs (*jati*). Women mainly carry out subsidiary functions. In domestic outwork, women are dominant in carrying out subcontracted functions. However, in the Mexican shoe industry, highly-skilled domestic outwork was performed primarily by men.

Skills
Skill can be considered to be the actual training needed to carry out a function, or the social definition of a function as 'skilled', determined by employers or trade union negotiations. In large-scale production, training is usually embodied in educational requirements, used to restrict job access (as mentioned previously). On the job training is short and function-specific. Small-scale and household production units are important loci of extensive skills training — in the form of apprenticeships or unpaid family labour. There are clear gender differences, however. Apprenticeships are a male-dominated area, and include all-round artisanal training. Girls learn specific functions, as unpaid family labour. In domestic outwork, women

89

workers must already be skilled in order to gain access to work. Although it is considered unskilled by most employers, it is clearly based on training received within the household in both productive work and/or domestic labour.

Work-loads and wages

Work-loads and wages in large-scale production tend to consist of fixed work-loads for basic wages. Piece-rates are paid in addition for higher production levels. Fringe benefits and social security are added for long-term wage workers. Women usually work eight hours, and are not allowed to work night shifts. Women's work-loads are not readily comparable to those of men, because of differences in the functions carried out and segregation by functions. It is characteristic for women to work hours equal to men, but to have lower wage rates.

In small-scale industry, work-loads may be fixed daily or piece-rates paid per unit of work. Shifts vary from eight to twelve hours. Both men and women work night shifts. There is greater irregularity in the amount of work provided, which makes work-loads more variable than in large-scale production. When segregation of functions occurs, women generally have lower wage levels than men. Only a few workers have fringe benefits.

In artisanal production, the number of hours worked daily varies from four to fourteen. Men and women's working hours are synchronized, and depend on the amount of work available. The use of unpaid family labour is extensive, and shows gender differences: sons have a right to 'pocket money', wives and daughters do not. In domestic outwork, working hours also vary with the supply of work. This implies long hours of overtime in the high season, and unemployment in the slack season. Women receive very low piece-rate wages, and deduction from wages for unacceptable goods is common.

Trade unions and women

In the industries studied, trade unions operate only in large-scale production units. Women receive little help from unions, although they are generally members. Gender-specific issues may be raised by the unions, or by women workers, but are generally given little support by either male workers or union leaders.

Although I did not encounter mobilization of women workers in other types of production units in the sub-sectors studied, there is evidence that this is possible. (See the 1989 paper by M. Chen, based on experiences with the organizations of women in India.)

Change over time

Change over time is most visible within large-scale production units, and in the links between large-scale to small-scale and artisanal production units.

Within small-scale and artisanal units, it was very difficult to trace, as documentation was totally lacking.

Changes in women's employment in large-scale production units is linked to increases in mechanization. Such increase do not have pre-determined effects on the division and contents of functions; in some instances more complex functions have been created (as in the Indian textile industry), so that women are losing the jobs they previously held; in other cases simpler functions have emerged, for which women are specifically recruited (as in the Mexican shoe industry). The latter change has been coupled to women's personal characteristics, with young, unmarried women workers being preferred.

This has meant that segregation of women workers has increased in large-scale industries at the level of functions. It has also meant that in the one industry, women are increasingly marginalized, while in the other they are not. The fact that such trends are influenced heavily by management decisions concerning the nature of 'functions' should be kept in mind.

Changes in the degree of segregation and marginalization of women workers in small-scale and artisanal production unfortunately cannot be traced in the pre-existing case studies used.

Casualization of work is related to changes in the social organization of labour in large-scale production: particularly the extent to which a firm subcontracts out to small-scale or artisanal units. The evidence is clearer from the firm side than from the worker side. This is because increased subcontracting may influence women's work opportunities over generations; i.e. new generations of women may have access only to work that is less secure than that of their mothers. Second, new groups of women workers may carry out more casual forms of work. Therefore, it is likely that the individual woman worker will not be the best unit of analysis for examining casualization. Instead, changes in occupational structure should be considered for women as a group. Table 5.2 indicates such characteristics and changes in women's participation in the labour process.

Women, the Household and Autonomy

The last question concerns the relationship between different types of productive work carried out by women and their position within the family based household. Such a household has been defined as the unit within which reproduction is organized, and in which the 'relations between members are often thought of in kin relations' (Harris, 1981). The household can be seen as a set of exchange relationships, regarding (a) the division of production work and domestic labour among its members, (b) bringing in of income, exchanges and consumption among family members, and (c) decision-making patterns which indicate each person's relative bargaining power.

Table 5.2 Women workers and the labour process

CURRENT SITUATION	large-scale	small-scale	artisanal household	domestic outwork
division of functions	women mainly in unskilled functions	mixed evidence: access to all vs only unskilled and female	strict division/ flexible when nec.	women in unskilled functions dominate workforce
skills	women's functions classified as unskilled	access to skilled functions in growth phase	M/W skilled artisans; women not acknowledged as such	women in 'unskilled' function, which still need experience
workloads/ wages	similar workloads, lower wages than men	similar workload, lower unit wages, less fringe benefits	similar workload, unpaid family labour	long hours, very low unit wages
job security	high, comparable to men	low, less than men, relations to employer important	high, based on family relations	lowest/not comparable with men
mobilization	high, on paper/shop-floor action by women not supported by men	none	not relevant	not relevant

In the literature, a primary distinction is made between female- and male-headed households. Clear differences in the exchange relationships within these two types of households have been documented in Mexico (Chant, 1985). These indicate that the division of labour and income is less burdensome for women in female-headed households, and their say over the use of income is greater (with positive effects on children as well).

Households should also be considered over time, in relation to the family life cycle, for a proper understanding of variations. Expansion, consolidation, and dispersion phases have been identified.

In households using systems of income pooling, women may receive most of the husband's income, a fixed allowance, or a share of the husband's income. The last two systems present women with problems in coping with price increases. Regarding allocation of consumption between family members, there is some evidence that the lower the pooled income of the household, the more important the role played by sex/gender systems in the division of food, health care, and education (Safilios-Rothschild, 1980; Dwyer and Bruce, 1988).

CHANGES OVER TIME	large-scale	small-scale	artisanal household	domestic outwork
Substitution				
segregation	increasing	steady	steady	steady
marginal-ization (by function)	a) when functions become more varied, women marginalized to fewer, less-paid functions b) when functions become simpler, % women increased	no	no	no
Skill changes				
de-skilling	when functions are more varied, women lose access to existing skills			
new skills	when functions are deskilled, women gain access to new skills, more than before			
casual-ization	increasing as subcontracting increases (see text for reasons)	not evident	not evident	

The bargaining power of a woman rests particularly on her participation in household decision-making patterns. This criterion has its limitations: first, only explicitly taken decisions can be traced, not self-imposed decisions, and second, it requires a substantial amount of interpretation by the researcher (White, 1984).

The relationship between productive work and women's positions in the household needs to be looked at in two analytically-distinguishable ways. First, women's employment opportunities are structured by the household and by their personal characteristics. Household composition, religious precepts concerning women, and women's educational levels and marital status are included. Secondly, a woman's employment influences her bargaining power within the household. This is reflected in the division of productive and domestic labour, the pooling and consumption of income, and decision-making patterns. The evidence presented here is based mainly on the results of the case study carried out in the Indian textile industry: the other case studies provided no information on these points.

The influence of women's personal characteristics on their bargaining power varied. Education had little influence, while variations related to marital status were striking. Married women had greater bargaining power than unmarried women. This factor was more important than having children, or even only sons: neither factor had a measurable influence. Caste background also had a measurable influence. In those castes which acknowledged women's economic contributions, women were found to have more bargaining power.

Variations in the balance between domestic and productive labour were important. The heavier the domestic work-burden of the woman, the less bargaining power she had within the household. This applies particularly to married women, who are considered to have primary responsibility for carrying out domestic labour. Women in small-scale and household production spend relatively less time in domestic labour and longer hours in productive work than women in large-scale production.

Variations in pooling and consumption of income were examined. Pooling of income is more common among the families of women working in large-scale production than among the families of women working in small-scale production — the latter gave almost all their income to their parents. In household production, women earned no money.

Consumption of income varied strongly among women working in different forms of production. The main item examined was food consumption. In families where women worked in large-scale production, food expenditure took up a lower percentage of family income than in families of women in small-scale production. For families in household production, food expenditure was the main expense item. The quality of the food also differed; the families of women in large-scale production would eat meat several times per month; in household-production families this occurred a few times per year.

The extent to which a woman's bargaining power was increased by her productive work was the second set of factors considered. A first major difference was found between women who work in various forms of wage labour and those who work as unpaid family members. Women working for wages manifest decidedly greater bargaining power than those whose work is not acknowledged by money.

A second major difference relates to the degree of differentiation between men and women workers in the workplace. It was found that women's bargaining power in the household was positively related to a less rigid gender division of labour in their productive work.

94

A third aspect is related to differences in the wage levels of men and women workers. Comparing women's wages to average levels of wages within production units show that there is a positive correlation between improvements in women's bargaining power and higher wage levels.

Conclusion

Several further areas of research have emerged from this study as a whole. The evidence from the case studies has suggested that for small-scale and artisanal producers, relations with trading capital are at least as important as relations with large-scale industrial capital. This aspect has been relatively neglected in models of petty commodity production, and should be further studied to determine its impact on earnings and investment opportunities for these groups of producers. The case studies also showed that types of subcontracting relationships are much more varied and extensive in nature than is usually assumed. The variety and impact of these links needs further study.

The categories of casual work usually distinguished were found useful, although the neglect of unpaid family labour leads to important underestimates of women's contribution to economic activities. The use of various forms of casual labour is more extensive than classical models of production units would have us believe. Therefore, caution is needed in predicting the impact of change within production units on 'employment'; impact needs to be specified by category of worker. This allows the invisible contribution of women workers to be recognized, so that their interests can be better defended.

Women's access to employment is clearly linked to factors related to their household circumstances as well as to the type of production unit. The extent to which long-term wage work outweighs the disadvantages of inflexible working hours for a large group of women with children is striking; only very young married women are found extensively in domestic outwork. This is rather different from the usual model of the gender division of labour (Heyzer, 1981).

The concept of marginalization previously used to analyse changes in women's participation in productive employment has been replaced here by a model which incorporates a number of specific characteristics of women's work at the level of the workplace, and relates these to changes in the use of technology and organization of work. This approach makes it possible to trace the directions of and the reasons behind transformations in women's productive work, and to discover more effective strategies to counter negative developments.

The extent to which a woman's productive work and income increase the extent of her bargaining power within the household is still a relatively underdeveloped area of empirical research. Although the evidence from

95

this study is of necessity limited, it is clear that aspects of both the existing household situation and the employment situation are factors which influence women's bargaining power. In this area, the methodological problems are also largely unsolved. Further development of a model which incorporates the various relevant aspects and solution of existing methodological difficulties are both important areas for future research. Some work has been done in this area, as illustrated by an issue of *IDS Bulletin* entitled 'Researching the Household: methodological and empirical issues' (1991).

6 Gender inequality — labour market and household influences

INES SMYTH

*And marriage among us — miserable is too feeble an expression for it.
How could it be otherwise, where the laws have made everything for
the man and nothing for the woman? When Law and convention both
are for the man, when everything is allowed to him.*

Raden Adjeng Kartini

This chapter explores the links between women's work and marriage, in
the context of rural Western Java (Indonesia). Recognizing that the structure of the labour market in Java is determined by forces operating outside
both the household and the village, nonetheless, I believe marriage to be
one of the main mechanisms which cause women to be concentrated in
low-paid, household-based activities, and which also determine the benefits
they derive from them.

In addition to the role it plays in differentiating women's work from that
of men, marriage is an important dividing line among women themselves,
as important as that represented by class and ethnic affiliation. For women,
marriage is the initial step towards adulthood, bringing changes in their
behaviour and social position.

The point of departure is Beneria's statement that women's role in production is conditioned by that in reproduction (1978). Her concept of
reproduction includes both the bearing of children and caring for the family, and the perpetuation of all aspects of the social system. In her view,
men's desire to control women's reproductive activities (in order to control
the transmission of wealth to their heirs) conditions their participation in
production by making the household the focal point of their work and
restricting their mobility outside it. Thus for Beneria the constraints on
women's productive activities are a direct consequence of the controls men
exercise over their reproductive capacities.

Beneria's views give important insight into the determinants of women's
work, but also suffer from certain problems. The analysis of reproduction is
carried out at two different levels: a complex level, where she defines
reproduction as '. . . a dynamic process of change linked with the perpetuation of social systems . . .', and a much narrower level — the bearing and
rearing of children — where its influence on women's role in production is
examined. The consequence is that a biological explanation of the processes under observation is seen in the wings; furthermore, the emphasis on
men's desire to control reproduction may easily be interpreted as reflecting
support for a 'conspiracy' theory.

Here an approach is used which may overcome both problems: by focusing on marriage as a social institution as well as a contractual relation between two partners, it takes into consideration a much broader set of social norms, relations and practices.

Furthermore, it sees the relevance of reproduction in a more 'positive' light, in the sense that in the geographical area of this study, the activities commonly embraced by the term (childbearing, child caring, and housekeeping) are highly valued and are considered women's main responsibility and their highest aspiration. Here it is within marriage that women become fully responsible for such activities. Thus views about marriage and practices surrounding it are among the main factors which inform and limit women's capacity to generate earnings through direct production.

As the quotation above and much of the content of this chapter shows, even with a positive evaluation of some of the activities for which women are responsible, they are still limited in their ability to work and live on terms equal to those of men.

It is necessary to state this explicitly because of the tendency, in some of the literature, to portray Indonesian women as enjoying considerable individual freedom and social respect as a direct consequence of their active participation in production. This enthusiasm is to be found in older documents (Subandrio, 1952; Takdir Alisjahabana, 1966) as well as in very recent ones (Papanek and Schwede, 1988). The latter work is of particular interest because it specifically concerns Indonesian women's economic roles and opportunities. The paper contains important statements on the relationship of roles and opportunities to structural and demographic conditions. However, it is overly optimistic regarding the economic strategies open to women. This occurs because, despite passing remarks about the diversity of various ethnic groups, findings concerning Javanese women are applied to all the women in the country (a common ideological transposition in the Indonesian context). 'Indonesian' women are treated as an identifiable, homogeneous category and the wide variations in legislation, religious beliefs, and social norms, as well as in social and ecological, geographical, and economic backgrounds, are underplayed.

In fact, the need to disaggregate the category of 'women' is nowhere so imperative as in the case of Indonesia, where the population is distributed over 992 islands, belongs to 300 ethnic groups, speaks 250 languages, and practices several religions in addition to the dominant Islam (Milone, 1978).

This does not mean that, compared to those living in some other Asian countries, certain women in Indonesia do not enjoy access to a broader range of economic activities and a higher degree of decision-making power in the household. To compare favourably with women in other countries, however, does not eliminate the fact that in their own country women do not enjoy the same opportunities as men. Further, easier access to paid and unpaid work outside the home actually results in a considerable work-burden, for which there is often little remuneration or social recognition. By studying the relation between work and marriage among the women of a particular ethnic group, the need for a much more specific approach to these issues will be emphasized.

The Village of Rankulan

Rankulan is situated about ten kilometre from Tasikmalaya, a medium-sized town in Southwestern Java. It occupies a discrete position, nestling between hills, wet rice fields (*sawah*) and fish ponds. The population is 620 people, in 150 households. The households are grouped in three *Rukun Tetangga* (Neighbours' Associations) of roughly equal size: Rankulan West, Middle, and East.

Houses are of a great variety of ages and types. Brick and stone construction stands side by side with houses with bamboo walls (*bilik*). As in most parts of Java, the population is Muslim, though with varying degrees of devotion and observance. The Mosque and the religious school (*Madrasah*) are the largest religious buildings, with two smaller prayer-houses also serving the needs of the population.

In the village there are no facilities for secular education. Children walk the short distance (½ kilometre) to the primary schools (*Sekolah Dasar*) in nearby settlements, or travel further to attend higher educational institutions in Tasikmalaya. As for education, health facilities are only available outside the village. The most accessible is the '*PUSKESMAS*' (*Pusat Kesehatan Masyarakat*, a Community Health Centre) about four kilometres along the main road. Most people choose to be looked after by the local health practitioners: a masseur, a traditional midwife, and a circumcision expert. A number of the more affluent people are able to pay regular visits to private doctors in Tasikmalaya, or to the two hospitals there.

Land in Rankulan is either bought or inherited, offspring receiving it from both parents in equal parts regardless of sex. However, some practices do result in daughters and sons having unequal access to their parents' land. Rice land (*sawah*) is considered the most important possession. Among the households included in a survey of a sample of the population, 33 per cent had no rice land; of the rest, 10 per cent owned 62 per cent of the total rice land. Other types of land are still more unequally distributed: 80 per cent of the households own no garden land (*kebon*) and 57 per cent own no forest (*hutan*). Despite the more even distribution, ownership of *sawah* is characterized by the very small size of holdings, the average being 0.15 hectare.

Because of the features of land ownership, land provides a considerable contribution to subsistence in only a few cases. Therefore most people must seek paid work; some earnings are available from agriculture, thus men and women work on land owned by others. All agricultural work is gender specific: men are responsible for the preparation of the soil and women for planting, weeding, and harvesting. It is important to note that in many parts of Java the introduction of high yielding varieties of rice, combined with new harvesting practices, have led to a loss of agricultural employment, especially for women (Collier, 1981; Murai, 1980; Stoler, 1980). This is true for Rankulan, but at the same time the majority of women here are still responsible for traditionally female jobs, including harvesting.

Given the uneven distribution of land, and the decline in agricultural employment, most people in Rankulan have been forced to find sources of income in addition to agriculture or entirely outside it. This has also happened in other parts of Java (Collier, 1981; Husken, 1979; White, 1976). The participation of individuals in various activities is regulated by many factors: by the material resources they own; by the opportunities offered by the local economy; by their individual characteristics in terms of education and skills, and, finally, by the social norms which allocate men and women to different and unequally productive areas.

Women's Work

As in all parts of rural Java, men, women, and children of both sexes contribute to the household economy through their work. Most jobs in Rankulan are sex specific: women carpenters are unheard of, and a domestic worker (*pembantu*) is always female. This does not exclude the participation in a given activity of other members of the household, not necessarily of the same sex. But, despite a degree of flexibility, in paid work women and men are segregated into separate productive areas. The main occupations of women in the sample can be grouped as shown in Table 6.1.

Of the 71 adult women in the sample, only one is a waged worker, employed as a teacher in a nearby school. The fifteen labourers are all

Table 6.1 Married women's occupations

Main occupation	Number of women
Housewife	29
Labourer	15
Farmer	12
Handicraft worker	12
Teacher	1
Midwife	1
Trader	1
TOTAL	71

Source: Household Survey 1982 (Smyth).

100

agricultural workers, most of whom receive wages for planting and weeding and are paid in kind for harvesting. Among the others, the craft workers and the farmers receive no individual payment when they are engaged in household based work. In such situations it is difficult to measure their remuneration, since individual and collective needs are satisfied from the income the household as a unit draws from such an occupation (Whitehead, 1981). In general, very few married women in the village are engaged in waged work. Furthermore, average earnings from all the occupations listed are very low.

For unmarried women the situation is different. Those who work are mainly concentrated in basket-making (*anyaman*), and waged work in nearby factories. The factories deserve particular attention, since employment of young females in industrial waged work is a prominent feature of the new international division of labour.

A good deal of research has been dedicated recently to developments in the global economy and the effects on the worldwide gender division of labour. Forty per cent of the industrial work force of Southeast Asia has been reported to be female (Eisold, 1984). Research on the Indonesian case is still limited, but it confirms that young women are cheaper to employ than male workers (Mather, 1983).

In the vicinity of Rankulan there are various small and medium-sized factories, the largest of which employs about 700 people. The physical proximity of the factories to the villages, and the presence of friends and even relatives as workers, makes this a form of employment which is socially acceptable for local young women. The number of female workers from Rankulan varies from eight to fifteen at any given time. According to the girls interviewed, their pay varied from Rp.1300–1500 per week initially, to about Rp.3000 after a couple of years[1]. Few of the girls remain long enough to see much increase in their initial pay or to gain more responsible jobs through seniority. The reasons given for the very high turnover are many. Many said that at some point girls are needed at home, to help with the housework and the care of younger siblings. Others said girls become tired of working long hours for so little money. Marriage is also a frequent reason for leaving factory jobs.

As a result, women's jobs — in comparison to those of men — are much less diversified and more poorly paid. The first characteristic is clear from the survey, which showed six paid occupations for women and eleven for men. In this, the situation seems different from that found by Stoler (1977), who states that 'men . . . have a smaller set of viable alternatives to agricultural labour'. The lower level of diversity seen here also reflects geographical limitations on female occupations. Fewer women than men are employed in places other than their own village or its immediate vicinity. Men of all ages travel daily to their places of work, or migrate for varying periods of time to other cities and even other islands.

101

Women do not have this option; female migration from Rankulan is generally family migration.

Also in comparison to men, women earn less on average. Women's jobs are paid on average Rp.11,721; men's jobs Rp.38,603. Moreover, unlike those of men, many income earning activities open to women are related to tasks they perform in the home: processing and sale of food, paid housework, and so forth. Such tasks undoubtedly require abilities which have been learned in the course of many years.

Nevertheless, involvement in these areas easily precludes the possibility of acquiring additional skills, which would be useful to women in obtaining employment in other sectors of the economy. Moreover, we know that such skills are often attributed to natural inclinations and receive little social recognition (Elson and Pearson, 1981).

Of the activities carried out alongside or instead of agriculture, in Rankulan the most common is the weaving and sale of bamboo goods such as baskets, decorative vases, trays, and lampshades. At the time of this research, 30 per cent of the households in the sample were involved in this sector. For this reason, such activity deserves special attention.

Although the entire region is an important centre for handicrafts, this type of bamboo weaving is exclusively to be found in this village. It is carried out in household-based units, which employ only family labour. Within such production units there is no formal division of labour and, although informants talked about the initial stage of the work (cutting, cleaning, and sawing the bamboo) as men's work, once the producers are in possession of the basic raw materials, there is no fixed gender division of labour. The artisans (*penrajin*) rarely produce goods on their own initiative to sell directly in the market. Normally they receive orders from a local producer, who functions as intermediary (*tengkulak*), or from an outside trader (*bandar*). Design and quantities are specified by the buyer and payment is on delivery.

Earnings from bamboo weaving are low. The literature on the subject testifies that income from non-agricultural rural activities, and especially handicrafts, is normally meagre, generally below wage rates for casual agricultural labourers (Stoler, 1978; White, 1976).

Although it is true, as mentioned, that there is no rigid division of labour in bamboo work, considerable differences exist in the way men and women are involved in this activity and in the benefits they derive from it. Women work longer hours than men and on a more regular basis, since they have more limited earning opportunities outside it. At the same time, their productivity tends to be lower, as they have to interrupt their work frequently to attend to their children or to the needs of the household members.

Qualitatively too, their position is different. Women must depend on male relatives or neighbours at the beginning of the production process

102

for access to the bamboo, because of their real or perceived inferior physical strength. This can mean a delay in starting an order and, consequently, in receiving payment. They also suffer restrictions at the other end of the production process, i.e. in marketing. As will be described below, unmarried women are limited in their movements by dominant norms of conduct, which dictate that they should remain within the confines of the village most of the time. Older married women have more freedom but they are tied to the home by their responsibilities as mothers and housewives. For these reasons, local women sell their goods mostly to village-based intermediaries or to traders with whom they have long-term relations. Because of this, they have little chance to seek higher prices for their goods in outside markets or from different intermediaries. As a consequence, their bamboo earnings tend to be lower than those of men.

Women and Marriage in Rankulan

In Rankulan, being married is considered the proper state for all adults. The feeling is very strong that individuals on their own cannot provide for themselves, hence that it is necessary to join forces with another through marriage. This is reinforced by the teachings of Islam, which considers marriage a duty for all Muslims (Nakamura 1983).

Marriage usually respects village exogamy: incoming spouses are from nearby hamlets and districts, more rarely from further afield. This is a feature also to be found in the rest of rural Western Java (Rusli, 1978). First marriages are commonly arranged by parents, sometimes with the intervention of a close friend or with kin as intermediary. For most informants it was unquestionable that one should follow the parents's guidance in the choice of a spouse. It was acceptable for boys to have a say in the matter, but for a girl, refusal of a proposed party would be seen as a gesture of disobedience, and as such would shame her parents.

When a marriage is not arranged by the family, it is usually the man who takes the initiative. He finds ways to frequent the girl's neighbourhood and befriend her; when the families are alerted, they take over the practical arrangements. This is, of course, provided they have no objection to the choice of girl. Although a woman has ways of showing whether or not she welcomes such attention, the situation is fraught with risks for her, since the boy's courtship can attract gossip and drive the parents to arrange a speedier marriage than desired.

Early age at first marriage for women is common in Rankulan. Among the adults who headed the 77 sample households, the age at first marriage was available for 42 women and 41 men. Among the women, the average age at first marriage was 16; among the men, 25. Ages are distributed as shown in Table 6.2.

Table 6.2 Age at first marriage

Age	Number of women	Per cent	Number of men	Per cent
12–16	30	71.4	3	7.3
17–21	10	23.8	19	46.3
22–26	2	4.8	14	34.2
27			5	12.2
TOTAL	42	100.0	41	100.0

Source: Household Survey 1982.

Thus most women married between the ages of 12 and 16, and most men between 17 and 21.

Here I wish to look at the reasons why women in rural Java are encouraged to marry early, often below the minimum legal age[2]. I do not believe that early age at marriage for women can be attributed to the fact that parents '. . . consider them an economic burden' (Zuidberg, 1975). Girls are a considerable help from a very young age; they can share in the housework and release their mothers for other occupations. I believe the tendency to marry girls early is connected to the fact that for women marriage is perceived as starting the process of maturation, a process completed with the birth of children. For boys this same process starts with circumcision. Thus I would say that girls are married early because a woman's marriage is perceived as starting the process towards adulthood: hence it is desirable that it should accompany the early changes in her body, such as menarche or other visible signs (see also Koentjaraninggrat, 1967).

Another characteristic of marriage here, as in most of Western Java, is the frequency of divorce and re-marriage[3]. The survey showed that men and women divorce with similar frequency. While the first marriage is usually dissolved by mutual agreement, in general it is men who initiate divorces. There is no stigma attached to being a divorced woman (*janda*), but in Rankulan everybody views this as a temporary state, to be rectified by a prompt new marriage. It must also be remembered that although the law requires an estranged husband to provide for his children, this is rarely enforced. This means that divorced women are left to provide for themselves and their children. This and other social pressures make re-marriage a sensible option. In subsequent marriages, woman have a freer choice of partner.

Polygamous marriages are not uncommon in Rankulan: six of the women in the sample were married to polygamous husbands. While the women in question declared themselves satisfied with the situation, many others expressed considerable fear of becoming a second wife (*dimaduin*), since a new, perhaps younger, wife could induce a man to distribute his wealth unfairly.

104

Marriage in Rankulan is nearly universal. Nevertheless, it means different things for men and women. Firstly, the practices described thus far all encourage very early marriages for women. But secondly, specific tasks are considered appropriate for husband and wife within marriage. All informants agree that husband and wife share the same obligation to provide the means to support each other and their dependents. The crucial difference lies in the fact that *before* and *in addition to* this duty, a married woman's responsibility is the procreation of children, their care, and the satisfaction of the immediate physical needs of all household members.

Thus marriage is for a woman both a crucial step in her personal development and the context within which her more fundamental social obligations are performed. Because of this, the period preceding marriage is one in which a girl must learn the skills she will need, and must act in a manner appropriate to her status. As Caplan (1985) remarks for another Muslim region, puberty is the period in which girls are most restricted, for the reasons just mentioned.

In Rankulan, young women seldom venture out after dark unless escorted, but in the daytime they move freely around. The manner of dress is simple but relaxed: only older and devout women cover their heads, and liberties such as short-sleeves and even shorts are permitted. Different rules apply outside the village, where girls' movements are curtailed and controlled, the destination and company they keep are vetted, and dress must be decorous and behaviour guarded.

Two terms express the kind of behaviour young girls should display in public: feeling *malu* (shy, ashamed) and *takut* (afraid). H. Geertz (1961) sees these as states appropriate to all circumstances requiring respectful behaviour. I found, however, that the two terms were used differently for men and women. Children of both sexes are taught to be ashamed of crying in public. But when applied to those who are older, however, the term *malu* is used almost exclusively for the behaviour expected of young women in the presence of strangers or superiors. For people in general, *takut* can express a range of fears: fear of the volcano or of being alone at night[4]. In the case of women, however, it also reflects their apprehension regarding experiences outside their immediate sphere, from big cities to impending marriage.

I do not believe that the controls over girls' lives can be seen as the tools of an Islamic patriarchy led by the local clergy (Mather, 1983). Such restrictions are the consequence of the shared conviction regarding the importance of marriage to all women. Since a woman's skills and her good name are her greatest assets, the years just before marriage are dedicated to preparing her for her duties and protecting her reputation from gossip. This necessitates the imposition of controls on her behaviour and mobility, as described above.

If ideas concerning marriage are important, so is the fact of marriage itself. Many changes take place after marriage. Women's public behaviour alters: quiet and demure girls are not transformed overnight, but with time married women's attitudes in public becomes more expansive and relaxed. Furthermore, they are freer to move around both inside and outside the village.

After marriage, residence is frequently uxorilocal. My survey revealed that, among the 77 sample households, in 11 cases both partners were indigenous to Rankulan (*asli*), and in two cases both were from outside. For the rest, 19 women and 34 men had moved into the village to join their respective spouses. Residence patterns are one of the aspects of marriage which favour women, and this is directly relevant to the issues in question. While this pattern of residence means that women are still partially under the control of their parents, the support of the latter often compensates for this disadvantage. Such support may have many faces. Firstly, the presence of kin and close friends offers the bride a degree of confidence during the first uncertain months after marriage; later it can continue to provide protection against possible neglect from the husband. In practical terms too the woman can call on her family when in need, while shyness would prevent her doing the same with her husband's kin.

Relations between Work and Marriage

The results of the research discussed above demonstrates that people in Rankulan share a view of marriage as the moment at which women begin to grow into social adults. Furthermore, they believe marriage should be women's highest goal and that, within marriage, women are destined above all to be housewives and mothers. The work of a housewife and mother is considered to be skilled and to carry serious responsibilities. Because of this, a woman's earlier life should be largely a preparation. Such views and practices affect female work opportunities through the impact which early marriage has on a woman's education and skills acquisition.

Although in Rankulan similar numbers of girls and boys enter primary school, the number of girls further on in the school career decreases very rapidly. The majority of students attending institutions above the middle level are boys, and the two students presently at university are also male.

Studies which examine fertility trends commonly state that '. . . marriage is delayed with higher education levels' (Smith, 1979). Although it is statistically true that increased years of schooling correspond to later marriages (Hirscham, n.d.), I believe it is possible to reverse this idea. It can just as well be said that it is because women marry early that their qualifications are low, rather then the other way around[5]. It is interesting to note that parents and daughters in Rankulan often express a dislike of having the latter '*duduk di bangku sekolah*' (sit at a school desk) with children, when obviously old enough to be married[6].

106

Of course, there are reasons apart from early marriage that may cause girls to leave school very early, despite the importance everybody attributes to education. One such reason is the scarcity of schools in rural areas, combined with parents' reluctance to allow daughters to leave the village unaccompanied.

I believe it is primarily these restrictions on their mobility and their opportunity to acquire adequate training that limit women's work opportunities, and also that such restrictions can be attributed to marriage-related practices, as discussed above.

After marriage, some of the restrictions suffered by women are gradually lifted; they become freer to move around, to shop and visit friends, and above all to find work. Statistics show that labour-force participation rates of women increase with age, peaking for the 45-54 group (BPS, 1982). In fact, Indonesia differs from other Asian countries in its high labour-force participation of older women (Papanek and Schwede, 1988).

As noted earlier, women are *permitted* to work after marriage by the lessening of restraints which come with marriage. Moreover, they are *forced* to work by circumstances which accompany marriage. In fact, although it is common for newly-married husbands to demand that their wives give up working, this position is soon reversed to meet financial needs. Setting up a separate household, which in Rankulan takes place at the birth of the first or even second child, creates a powerful incentive for women's additional contribution to family budgets.

The frequency of divorces and the incidence of polygamy are other factors which encourage women to be actively involved in production. The instability of unions does not mean that the social and personal importance attributed to marriage is misplaced. Individual marriages may be short-lived, but the married state *per se* is still perceived as 'natural' and advantageous, especially for women. Furthermore, the role future marriage plays in limiting girls' education and work opportunities, viewed in the context of this instability, is not irrational. It is rather the outcome of varied and complex factors. For example, in addition to the factors discussed earlier, where poverty prevents families from providing education for all their children, boys are given priority over girls, since the latter are seen as destined for home responsibilities within marriage, which do not require formal qualifications.

In summary, being married encourages and facilitates women's entry into the labour market. At the same time, being married puts new obstacles in the path of women's productive activities. Rankulan informants unanimously declared that although husband and wife share the same responsibility to support the household through their labour, a woman's primary duty lies in the satisfaction of the physical and emotional needs of its members.

This norm applies to Rankulan women in general. However, the extent to which the presence of children and other dependents tie a specific individual to the home, preventing her from extending or improving her earning efforts, varies from woman to woman and depends on a number of factors, Firstly, household composition: a woman's ability to carry out activities outside the home is predicated on the presence of other household members to whom she is able to delegate her duties. In Rankulan, nuclear families are in the majority (49.4 per cent of the total of the sample households); this may constitute a restriction on the type of work in which married women can engage.

Secondly, the number and age of children: even with help in the home, the presence of very young children may be a temporary obstacle to protracted absences.

Lastly, the nature of the employment available is significant. Work which is far away and has fixed hours may be incompatible with what women perceive as their primary duties. However, when such work pays a regular and relatively large salary, allowances are made. In Rankulan there are several female teachers and office workers, all with children of different ages. The status and remuneration attached to their jobs make their delegation of their functions as housewives to others acceptable to all.

Clearly, despite their increased mobility, married women remain ill-equipped for the labour market by their poor education and limited work experience, in addition to their home ties. Thus their work opportunities are limited to local, home-based activities. These are mostly characterized by informal work organization and flexible hours, but also by low remuneration. An example is bamboo-weaving which, as described earlier, attracts many women on a more regular basis than men.

Although such work is easier to combine with home duties, it should not be seen as especially 'suited' to women or as providing them with particularly high rewards. On the contrary, the combination of the two activities often results in a very long working day. Furthermore, as described earlier, women's productivity and their earnings from bamboo work are lower than those of men, for reasons which again are linked to gender norms and gender relations.

Conclusion

This chapter attempts to demonstrate that many ideas and customs related to marriage have both direct and indirect influences on the way women participate in production. Marriage is the highest goal they are supposed to aspire to, and for which they need to prepare themselves. This generally limits their education and mobility, has consequences for their access to income earning activities. Marriage and the presence of children give women more personal freedom, which creates both advantages and new problems.

7 Women in small-scale industries — some lessons from Africa

MARILYN CARR

With the increasing realization that large-scale, centralized industries and services do not, by themselves, provide a route to sustainable economic development has come an increased interest in the small-scale, decentralized provision of goods and services. Based as it is on the use of local materials and skills to meet local demand, and being sparing in its use of foreign exchange, capital, electricity, and other expensive infrastructural goods, this small scale approach is compatible with the development objectives of many least developed countries.

As more research has been undertaken on small-scale and micro-enterprises, it has become increasingly apparent that large-scale sector enterprise represents only the tip of the iceberg. The bulk of industrial activity seems to take place in enterprises which have fewer than ten workers. For example, the average size of an 'industry' in Sierra Leone is 1.9 persons. Thus, it is totally misleading to think of manufacturing activity in terms of large factories. In reality, most manufacturing is carried out in very small enterprises indeed.

With increasing landlessness, and with the inability of the large-scale sector to provide jobs on anything like the scale required, small-scale, often informal-sector activities provide the only means of earning cash for the masses of the very poor. These activities also provide the only source of supplementary income for the great number of farmers in least developed countries who are struggling at subsistence level. Thus, it is hardly surprising that rates of participation in rural off-farm activity have been growing rapidly. For example, in West Africa, the proportion of the rural labour force in off-farm activities rose from 12 per cent in 1950 to 25 per cent in 1980.

As knowledge of the small-scale sector has increased, it has become apparent that women play a major role in it, not just as employees and self-employed part-time workers, but also as entrepreneurs. While there are still relatively few businesswomen at the high end of the small industry scale, their ownership increases dramatically as the size and formality of businesses decreases. They also tend to be more prominent in rural areas where they cater to basic rural needs for foodstuffs, clothing, shelter, basic household durables, and household-related services.

Micro-enterprise is attractive to women because of low barriers to entry and the flexible nature of the work, which makes it easy to combine gainful employment with domestic responsibilities. These very factors, however, also make it difficult for women to expand their enterprises and make a decent living from them.

As recognition of women's major role in the small-scale industry sector has increased, so has recognition of the constraints they face. At the same time, questions are being asked: why do women, who are often the majority of small entrepreneurs, seem to have far less access than men to support services such as credit, training, and technical assistance?

In an attempt to gain a better understanding of women's enterprises in southern African countries, and to determine the extent to which support agencies do or could assist them, a meeting of all small-scale support agencies in the SADCC countries[1] was held in Harare in October 1989 to facilitate an exchange of experiences and to discuss future directions[2]. This paper draws on the substantial country papers which were prepared for that meeting.

Characteristics and Constraints

Country papers confirmed that women's enterprises tend to be confined to the smaller-scale end of the small scale sector. The vast majority are sole proprietors who make little or no use of hired labour; or they are members of income-generating groups, in which they generally work on a part-time basis. Most information on group activities comes from Tanzania, where private enterprise is only now being encouraged. In the other countries, data relate mainly to individual women entrepreneurs.

A common and depressing feature of women's enterprise in all countries is the extent to which they are confined to a limited number of traditional 'women's' activities.

In Zambia, out of 215 women entrepreneurs registered with SIDO, 180 are involved in textiles, knitting, and food processing. In Lesotho, a survey of 500 women entrepreneurs revealed that over 50 per cent are involved in food and textile-related activities. In Zimbabwe, clothing, textiles, crochet, and basket-making account for 75 per cent of women's enterprises. Women clients of SEDOM in Malawi have a high involvement in confectionery, knitting, and clothing. In Botswana, of 432 women registered with the Financial Assistance Programme, 316 were involved in knitting and sewing, and 60 had bakeries.

The situation is similar for income-generating groups. In Tanzania, out of a sample of 500 groups, 44 per cent were found to be engaged in handicrafts and 39 per cent in tailoring. In Zimbabwe, the vast majority of the 48,000 women in income-generating groups organised by the Ministry of Community and Cooperative Development were involved in making school uniforms, baking, or handicrafts.

The reasons given for this lack of diversity are the same in all countries. The activities in which women are involved are based on traditional domestic skills, which are learned at home. Such activities also tend to require little in the way of capital investment for machinery or physical infrastructure, and they may lend themselves to flexible working hours, which fit in well with women's domestic responsibilities. Risks are low, but so are returns; few women make sufficient profit to reinvest in their businesses in an attempt to scale up their level of activity.

A closer look at the position of women in the SADCC countries helps to explain the above phenomenon. Women basically lack access to resources such as credit, training, and information. The unequal distribution of labour within the household also means that, because of domestic responsibilities, women lack time to invest in business activities. In addition, they have a role subordinate to men, which reduces their own sense of self-confidence and assertiveness and produces an environment which is basically hostile towards the woman who wants to succeed in business.

The problem of access to resources is seen as a key constraint for women entrepreneurs in most of the SADCC countries. Credit is a major problem: women usually lack the savings needed to put down the equity payment required to get a loan. Also, they often have no access to land or physical infrastructure, which could be used as a collateral for a loan. The complex forms which have to be filled out are a deterrent for small women entrepreneurs who have had limited access to education; women also often lack the business and marketing skills required to put forward viable business proposals.

As a result, statistics show that women make up only a small proportion of the clients of most credit schemes. In Zimbabwe, only eleven per cent of SEDCO's loans go to women; those that do average US$17,000, which is generally at the high end of the small-scale range. Other statistics from Zimbabwe reveal that the smaller the enterprise, the less likely it is that the woman owner has made use of formal credit; and that as many as forty per cent of enterprises are begun with no start-up capital or credit at all.

In Malawi, INDEFUND — which gives credit to small entrepreneurs requiring sizeable (K30,000–K120,000) loans — has only four women clients out of a total of 79. SEDOM, which gives loans up to a maximum of K75,000 has more women clients. These women do, however, have smaller businesses and smaller loans than do men. Although women represent thirty per cent (660 out of 2200) of SEDOM's clients, they have borrowed only eighteen per cent of the total amount on loan. Similarly, in Botswana, while women are only five per cent of the clients of Tswelelo's macro-loan scheme, they make up sixty per cent of the clients of the micro-loan scheme.

Women's access to credit from commercial banks is even less than their access via small industry support agencies. In Tanzania, for example, only three per cent of the clients of the National Bank of Commerce are women, and a survey of 500 women's groups in the country revealed that only thirteen per cent had received loans; most of these were acquired from sources other than banks.

111

Women's businesses tend to be small and under-capitalized because of the lack of savings and credit to invest in them. The problem is partly one of demand. Women do not ask for loans because often they do not know that they are available or how to apply for them. They lack business and technical skills and therefore tend to set up enterprises which involve small amounts of capital and do not require loans.

At the same time, their demand for training in business and technical skills is low because, again, they often do not know such services exist. Support agencies seem to be less successful in reaching women entrepreneurs with training services and technical assistance, possibly because extension services tend to be staffed predominantly by men. In Malawi, for example, of the total clients of DEMATT, the agency set up specifically to provide technical and business advisory services to small entrepreneurs, only ten per cent are women. Until the creation of a special women's programme in 1988, all DEMATT's extension workers were men.

Even when women are aware of the services available, however, still other factors constrain their demand for credit. Predominant here are their multiple roles and responsibilities, and the lack of time they have available to invest in running a business. Taking out a loan to buy premises and expensive equipment is often too much of a risk for a woman who knows she cannot devote all of her time and energy to ensuring that it is repaid. These same time constraints reduce women's ability to attend the training courses which could improve skills and productivity. Thus, most women take the low-risk, low-return options which allow them the flexibility they need.

The problem is also partly one of supply. Even those women who have the knowledge, ability, and time to engage in larger-scale business activities face difficulties in obtaining loans. In some countries, e.g. Botswana and Lesotho, this is partly due to discriminatory laws, which prevent a married woman from taking out a loan without the permission of her husband or father. In all countries, however, there seems to be a bias against women, with bank managers (predominantly men) giving preference to male clients. In general, the environment of the SADCC countries is hostile to the idea of women in business, and women have to fight much harder to succeed than do men.

Support Services for Women Entrepreneurs

In theory, all policy and assistance measures aimed at supporting small-scale industry and the informal sector should help women as well as male entrepreneurs. The constraints reviewed in the previous section, however, suggest that, in practice, additional measures aimed specifically at women will be needed if women are to benefit to the same extent as men.

For women entrepreneurs, there is obviously a need to review legislation

112

that restricts women's access to credit and property. Banks need to make a concerted effort to employ more female staff at decision-making levels, and to orient all staff towards an appreciation of the value of women clients.

When necessary, special schemes should be introduced which provide credit to women. Small-scale industry support agencies should have more female staff whose job it is to identify potential or existing women entrepreneurs in need of assistance, and to provide on-going advice and assistance to them. Again, special women's units or women's business advisory services may need to be established — preferably within existing support agencies.

More attention obviously needs to be given to the introduction of labour-saving devices that can release women from endless hours of drudgery and enable them to devote more hours to business activities. Facilities for child care would also help in this respect.

Women need greater access to a wider range of technical skills, so they can engage in less traditional and more remunerative businesses. Training to provide such skills should take into account the difficulties faced by women in leaving their families and businesses for even a short period of time. Business training should also be provided in a way which accommodates women's ongoing commitments.

Technology centres should play a bigger role in identifying the technology needs of women's micro-enterprises, and should devote more time and attention to working with women entrepreneurs to developing improved technologies, and to increase the productivity of their businesses. Technology centres can also play an important role in the design and development of labour-saving devices for women.

Finally, at a more fundamental level, there is obviously a need for a change in traditional education and child-rearing patterns, since these currently make it difficult for women to think of entrepreneurship as a viable economic opportunity for themselves. Until the way men and women view women's role in the enterprise sector changes, there will be a need for special entrepreneurial training for women.

These are among the major suggestions from the SADCC countries themselves for addressing the particular needs of women entrepreneurs. Encouragingly, as revealed in the papers prepared for the October 1989 meeting on 'Support to Women Entrepreneurs', some headway has already been made in implementing such measures in the SADCC region.

In recognition of their own poor record in reaching women entrepreneurs, several small-industry support agencies have established special women's desks or programmes to address this problem. In Tanzania, SIDO has established a women's desk, which is involved in surveying the needs of women entrepreneurs and designing programmes to assist them. Since the establishment of the desk, the number of loans approved for women clients has increased — from 35 in the years preceding to 129 in the two years it has been operating. In Zambia, SIDO has a women's desk, which is part of the project department, and seeks to ensure that women's interests are fully integrated into SIDO's programmes. In Malawi, DE-MATT has initiated a Business Advisory Service for Women which will increase the agency's female extension staff from one to eight, and will provide for loans to women.

Other small-industry support agencies are considering establishing special women's programmes, and meanwhile are making greater efforts to reach women entrepreneurs. For example, several agencies now run hire purchase schemes. These remove the need for collateral, since the equipment acquired through the scheme acts as collateral. MUSCCO in Malawi plans to recruit a woman credit specialist in an attempt to increase its female membership (currently 26 per cent). The small-scale industry department of the Ministry of Industry and Technology in Zimbabwe is trying to encourage diversity by giving priority treatment to women in non-traditional trades.

Various non-governmental organizations and financial institutions have also been actively involved in trying to assist women entrepreneurs. National branches of Women's World Banking have now been registered in Malawi, Botswana, Zimbabwe, and Zambia. A special credit fund (the Mudzi Fund), based on the Grameen Bank model and funded by IFAD, is to be established in Malawi.

The National Bank of Commerce in Tanzania has established a women's desk, and UNIFEM has assisted Tanzania in acquiring four million US dollars from DANIDA to establish a special credit scheme for women, to be implemented through the National Bank.

At the technical level, agencies such as RIIC in Botswana have been involved in developing technologies for women's income-generating activities (e.g. food processing and bakery ovens) and to reduce the burden of their domestic responsibilities (e.g. sorghum mills). Various technical training centres are beginning to encourage women to enter non-traditional fields such as mechanics, electrical repair, carpentry, masonry, and metalwork. The number of women on such courses is still small, but at least a start has been made.

The main conclusion of the October Seminar on 'Support to Women Entrepreneurs' was that a concerted effort should be made to identify priority areas for the implementation of national and regional programmes aimed specifically at assisting women entrepreneurs. Recommendations included:

○ all small industry support agencies should be encouraged to establish a special women's programme or desk;
○ a regional credit fund should be established, aimed specifically at the smallest women entrepreneurs in the informal sector;

o an existing technology institution in the region should be assisted to establish a special programme for developing technologies appropriate for women's small enterprises, in response to requests from enterprise-support agencies;

o a programme should be developed to assist women to receive training in non-traditional skills;

o a programme should be established to assist women in moving from the informal to the formal business sector.

Much is already happening, but much more remains to be done. Experience to date shows that women can benefit a great deal from assistance targeted specifically at their business activities, and that even the poorest illiterate woman can improve the tiniest, most marginal business if she is given the right kind of assistance in the right way. Hopefully, a successful implementation of the above recommendations will be a step in the right direction.

8 Women's organizations and subcontracting — a case study from India

MIRA SAVARA

Subcontracting arrangements exist in both traditional and modern industries. They exist in both rural and urban areas. As their labour base they may take the entire family, a subset of the family, or an individual. Work may be carried out in the home or centralized near the home in a workshop.

That the majority of women in subcontracting arrangements are at the lowest level of the hierarchy of subcontracting arrangements has been extensively documented, particularly their concentration as home-based workers. It has often been argued that the development of organizations amongst isolated women workers is an essential step in improving their conditions of work.

One of the policies now being advocated as a means of 'integrating women into development' is the setting up of women's income-generating units. This paper examines the experiences of several such women's organizations, the context of their growth, and the current legal position and policies regarding this sector, and offers suggestions on what may need to be done. The situation and problems differ widely according to the sort of subcontracting involved; here urban examples involving the more modern industries are given.

Experiences of Women's Organizations

Case 1

J.M.M. began by making ready-made clothes and petticoats. When they tried to sell to the shops, they found their prices were too high; nor did they have the variety of colours and sizes shopkeepers wanted. J.M.M. maintained that the contractor could provide the petticoats at the lower rates because he bought cheaper cloth at wholesale rates, the quality of thread used was not as good and he paid seamstresses a lower rate. When they tried alternatives such as marketing directly to slum and middle-class women — thinking that by removing the middleman they would be able to keep prices a bit higher — they found they did not have the variety necessary for direct sales. Nor could they get orders from contractors at a rate which made it beneficial for them to participate.

For some time the women did not do any work. They then obtained a contract from a government organization which wanted envelopes made. J.M.M. gave a quotation of Rs.15 for 1000 packets, with the assumption that the women making the envelopes would be paid Rs.3 for 1000, and could make Rs.6 in four to five hours of work. This included the cost of raw material, i.e. paper, cutting, and gum. The government agency received another quotation of Rs.12. If J.M.M. wanted work, they would have had to agree to the lower rate. The organizers of J.M.M. feel the other contractor could afford to give a lower rate because he had his own printing press and owned a cutting machine, and did not have to travel and hire out these services.

J.M.M. had a meeting of its members to ask if it should take on the work. The women, who were quite desperate for work, agreed to take only Rs.2 per 1000 packets made. J.M.M. had to pay a deposit and agree to a two-year contract to provide a certain number of envelopes each month.

Once they got the work and the women started doing it, they found that the work was more difficult than they had expected. Perhaps because the work was new their productivity was low; women found they could make barely 1000 envelopes a day. It was exhausting, and the payment was only Rs.2. They do not want to continue doing this work, but J.M.M. finds itself in difficulties. They have already given a money deposit, and are now bound to work at the rate agreed.

Case 2
Another organization (UMM) contacted Mavim, a government organiza-tion set up to assist women small-scale producers, asking for ground spices. UMM started production, but only a limited amount was required. They then sought other outlets.

Co-operative shops wanted spices, but UMM found that they could not provide the spices at the prices they would pay. Why was this? According to UMM, they used pure spices and did not adulterate with colours or other material. How other small manufacturers managed to provide spices at lower rates was explained by one of the women members who had worked in a factory, making spices. She said ground rock was kept in piles in this factory, and was regularly mixed with the ground spices. This increased the weight. Then oil and colours were added to give it the desired colour.

When UMM tried to reason with the co-operative shops and other groc-ery shops, explaining that these were the practices of other suppliers and that their material was more expensive because it was pure, shops said that customers buying the spices did not complain; hence they were not inter-ested in stocking the more expensive material.

It is interesting to note that now the women's organizations have to compete with not only small-scale manufacturers, but also multinationals, who have entered the local spice market in India, backing their products with extensive advertising on TV and radio and in magazines.

Currently they make spices only when they manage to get orders; women work at the rate of 1 rupee per hour. They work very little and members meet only irregularly.

117

Case 3

Another experience involved stitching uniforms. The government made a central shed available to SB and gave them a large government contract to make uniforms for all the schools run by the state government. One hundred women got work at piece-rate wages for four months. But when all the uniforms had been made, there was no more work. In the next year they got orders for only half as many uniforms, and at a lower rate. (The other half probably went to a contractor who had offered a lower rate.) The women decided that all one hundred women would share the existing work. However, the real decision was probably not made by the group as a whole. Many women were angered by the lack of work and, instigated by a male union leader, put on a demonstration before the government authorities, asking for more work. In the course of the demonstration, slogans were also raised against the women's organization, saying it was not making sufficient efforts to get work. This organization operates primarily as an income-generating programme, but the women members do not really participate in all levels of decision-making, and are not aware of the problems involved in obtaining the work.

Case 4

MAH/COOP has started several income-generating units — units carrying out stitching, packaging safety-pins, pasting envelopes, producing school notebooks, and operating a canteen — which are envisioned as eventually working on their own as separate co-operative societies, or as one multi-purpose co-operative. MAH/COOP employees are training the women in accounting and sales. However, at present these projects operate under the direction of three Economic Programme Organizers and one Income Generation Co-ordinator from MAH/COOP. Most of the projects are housed in municipal buildings that MAH/COOP has been allowed to use, which are located in the slums.

The stitching unit started in 1984, and has gone through several changes. At first the women sewed the school uniforms that MAH/COOP distributed to foster children. The initial target was 28,000 uniforms. The women were trained in cutting and sewing. The cutting was done at the centre. The women bought sewing machines using bank loans and did the sewing at home, bringing the finished products to the centre, where the quality was checked. The first year an insufficient quantity of uniforms was produced, and MAH/COOP had to buy fifty per cent of the uniforms from outside. In 1985-6 the target was reached. Making school uniforms was seasonal work, so the unit looked for other stitching work. They took in napkin stitching on subcontract from Air India, but the pay was low (Rs.10 for twelve hours) and Air India did not pay on time. The unit has started stitching mosquito nets, using velcro. Originally there were 36 women working; now there are 18.

The notebook unit also started in 1984. MAH/COOP buys the materials — paper covers, straw board, binding cloth and thread — from wholesale distributors once a month. The operations involved are ruling, folding, stitching, cardboard pasting, and cutting. Men do the ruling and cutting; women do the rest of the work, working in a group. The women made books for the MAH/COOP-sponsored children. Since this was only seasonal work, the unit attempted to make notebooks and sell them through the retail shops. However, due to lack of experience (when to buy the paper, etc.), they lost money. They then got an order from Apna Bazaar. According to the supervisor: 'They provided us with one ton of paper. The other expenses were ours. When we gave the quotation, the rates were lower than at the time we got the order. As a result we lost money. They wanted to give us another order but we refused.'

According to the supervisor: 'Women cannot work on the cutting and ruling machine, since the work is too difficult. The person handling the machine must know how to repair it. Women do not have the training.' In the beginning there were eleven women; now there are six.

Approximately forty women work in the safety-pin unit. They package various kinds of pins (screw safety-pins and zero pins), performing operations called bunching and debunching, for GKW, a multinational corporation with its factory in the Ghatkopar industrial estate. GKW supplies the materials, which are stored in the municipal building in which the women work. MAH/COOP supplies a watchman and a supervisor, whose wages are subtracted from the income earned by the workers. The job involves several steps, such as separating pins, making bunches, weighing them, sealing them in plastic bags, putting on labels, and boxing the bags of pins. The women are paid 40ps. per bag; 8ps. are deducted for the cost of the supervisor and the watchman. Even if there is sufficient work, the women make under Rs.250 a month. The supervisor is paid Rs.562.50 a month. In general GKW pays MAH/COOP promptly, but initially there were delays, as MAH/COOP did not understand that separate bills had to be made out for packaging the different types of pins. In the first year there was only enough work for ten to fifteen days a month, but recently there has been enough work to last throughout the month. However, in March 1987 so much material was delivered to the hall that the women had nowhere to sit. There is an attempt to get the women involved in running the unit; once a week the co-ordinator of MAH/COOP and the women get together to discuss the internal problems of the unit, and rates for production. There is also some attempt to develop the accountancy and sales skills of the women. The supervisor says: 'Our aim is not to develop one or two women, but to have all the women develop. This on the job training includes various aspects of management and so forth.'

The Ghatkopar women have experienced several types of problems in working on the various piece-work income-generation projects organized by MAH/COOP. On all of the projects, income is low and there are no benefits. Most of the work is irregular; some of the operations are seasonal (uniform stitching) and the amount of work in others does not always provide enough work for the women. When MAH/COOP attempted to get into manufacturing, a number of difficulties were encountered which threatened the viability of the project (e.g. making notebooks). Inexperience led to mistakes in obtaining sufficient quantities of materials, in marketing goods, and in being able to produce the product at prices competitive with similar products in the market. When MAH/COOP has acted as a middleman, putting out work from large enterprises there have been difficulties in receiving prompt payment (e.g. Air India). In many ways the income-generation projects resemble the other types of work available to women in these slums, which are located near a large industrial estate: e.g. caning chairs for Godrej, making plastic kitchen scrubbers, and assembling electrical sockets. The main difference is that the MAH/COOP workers spend all or part of their work time in groups, while the other workers do their jobs entirely in their homes.

Subcontracting in Perspective

Subcontracting (or ancillarization) is an important feature of the modern industrial manufacturing system in India. According to R. Nagaraj (1984):

> Subcontracting refers to a type of inter-firm relationship where large firms produce manufacture components, sub-assemblies and products from a small number of firms. In some cases, subcontracting is associated with 'job work' where a 'parent' firm provides the necessary raw materials to small firms which return these materials after turning them into the required form (as per technical specification) at a predetermined rate.

Describing the situation in the Indian context, Annavajhula (1988) says:

> Take the case of Philips. It has been the corporate policy of this multi-plant, multinational industry in India, not to go in for vertical integration but to spread manufacturing activity over a variety of items. The company makes certain critical items 'in house', purchases standard items from other industries and subcontracts several specialized/non-critical items to small and medium units (including cottage industries, blind men's associations, charitable organizations, etc.). Recently Philips has stepped up subcontracting more significantly alongside modernization and automation programmes at its plants because of mounting labour militancy at its plants in the form of go slow, work to rule, disruptive walkouts, and solidary strikes as a protest against the company's imposition of productivity loads.

Subcontracting of final assembly seems to be widespread in sectors like radio, television, sets, calculators, and voltage stabilizers. A large number of subcontracting arrangements in India are used both by the government sectors and in the private sector.

State and national governments have actively intervened to promote subcontracting. Since the 1950s, two types of policies have encouraged the growth of subcontracting arrangements. According to Nagaraj (1984):

'positive' measures have encouraged the setting up of smaller units, and 'protective' measures have restricted the areas of operation and growth of large firms. A large number of institutions (Ex. National Small Industries Corporation) have come into existence to implement state policy for small-scale centres. The existence of a fiscal policy which provides for differential excise duties and certain exemptions for the products made in the small-scale sector has certainly aided the growth of small firms. Further, this policy was compatible with the policy of industrial decentralization.

However, studies have shown that small firms set up as independent units rarely remain independent, and a study in the seventies observed that 'small-scale units which start as independent entities after a while end up as dependent on one or two large customers for job work to make ends meet'. (Annavajhula, 1988).

Under the official definition, all enterprises with capital investment below a certain limit are included in the small-scale sector. Over the last three decades this limit has been periodically revised upwards, from Rs.5 lakhs in the early fifties to Rs.20 lakhs in the 1980s. No licence, approval, or sanction is required to set up a small-scale unit. There are no reliable statistics regarding the extent of paid work done at home in India. Much 'home-based work' is a commercialization of tasks which are done in the household (e.g. pounding spices or cooking). Second, since the work is intermittent, not regular, women do not necessarily see themselves as 'workers'; hence an undercount.

However, an attempt to gauge the extent of home-based work in India has been made by Prasad and Prasad (NCI, 1987). According to their analysis, employment in 'household industry' shows a decline from 9.91 million in 1961 to 8.6 million in 1981. A major part of this decline was in rural areas and among the female work-force. They attribute this to the general integration of rural areas into a wider urban-based market; second, artisans, who constitute a sizable proportion of the workforce in household industry, unable to cope with the competition of commodity production in a market economy and displacement of traditional products by modern substitutes, are losing control over their labour power and are forced into wage labour; finally, changes in technology have also played an important role in replacing traditional forms of manufacture by cheaper mechanized goods.

121

They document the industries in which women work in the home. This includes food products, cotton, woollen and silk textiles, handlooms, chikan embroidery, lace making, garments, incense sticks, hair clips, toys, electrical fittings, plastic boxes, papad making, paper bag making, peeling almonds, extracting rubber strands from tyres, block-printing, quilt-making, unwinding wire strands, bending hooks for garments, soldering wires for radios, packaging naphthalene balls, and making brushes. Actually the list could go on; potentially, it includes every product being made.

Government Action and Policy

In the summer of 1988, the problems of informal-sector workers received national attention when two government sponsored reports, *The National Perspective Plan for Women 1988–2000* (NPPW) and *Shram Shakti: The Report of the National Commission on Self-Employed Women and Women in the Informal Sector* were published.

Although the NPPW has a broader focus than *Shram Shakti*, both reports implicitly embody a distinctive approach towards the state's role in women's economic development: a technocratic-institutional approach in the NPPW and an organizational-facilitative approach in Shram Shakti. The NPPW reviews the approaches toward women in the Five Year Plans and government women's programmes, and the situation of women in various sectors such as rural development, employment, and legislation, and suggests 'interlinked and converging strategies towards a holistic development of women by 2000 AD' (Department of Women and Child Development, 1988). Its recommendations include strengthening existing policies and setting up two types of institutions to co-ordinate women's economic programs: Women's Development Corporations at the central and state levels, plus a National Training Institute for Women. It endorses a technically-improved version of the existing top-down approach to women's development, with new women-specific institutions to ensure women get their share of services. For example, the NPPW suggests that the Women's Development Corporations would play a major role in supplying women with credit.

Shram Shakti contains chapters that provide occupational profiles and labour-force analyses of women workers in the informal sector, examines the impact of macro-policies on unprotected women's labour, and discusses factors that impede and facilitate organizing informal-sector women. Its recommendations include expansion of existing labour legislation to cover various groups of informal-sector workers, and the creation of new procedures, offices, and bodies to facilitate organizations of women workers bringing complaints about wages and working conditions to the government. For example, the report calls for separate labour commissioners for unorganized workers in each state, women's organizations and trade unions being vested with the right to bring complaints to a labour court, and the establishment of an Equal Opportunities Commission in the Central Government to investigate charges of discrimination.

Discussion

We can see from the above brief report that, in most cases, units which started their own projects (that is, involving raw material, manufacture, and selling) could not maintain that sort of activity for long. This was largely due to their small size and a lack of adequate knowledge of the changing market. In time, most organizations chose to work at a lower level of risk, taking on work on a contract basis from contractors, government institutions or companies. Under this 'putting-out' system the women's organization basically provided labour and did not have to worry about finding a market.

Another striking common feature is that women got very little work and extremely low wages. Often a second contract from an agency required the same work, but offered lower rates for work. When asked why, the women organizers said that other contractors were offering to do the work at lower piece-work rates; hence if they were to get the contract they had to offer competitive rates. Even in the more democratically-run organizations where women members were consulted before taking on contracts at lower wages rates, one notices that the Mahila Mandals (local women's organizations) seem to have got caught in a vicious circle. Once they had been organized and had taken on some work, it became essential to keep the Mahila Mandals going. Thus most of them were compelled to accept work at lower rates.

If lower rates were not offered the quantity of work was reduced; thus in effect — by the time all the women members shared the existing work — the amount of money each one earned was much less.

In cases where entering such schemes had meant a break with previous contractors, women found the contractors hesitant to give them work again, because they had already found alternative sources of labour. This is one reason women are hesitant to form groups or co-operatives: their own experience has shown that the work is not regular; and even if it begins with higher wages and better raw materials, over time things even out, so that the amount earned about equals what the contractors originally offered. This seems bound to happen, given the fact that the women are not operating in isolation but within a total economic system governed by its own rules. Work is contracted out in order usually to get the lowest possible rates. Whoever offers the lowest price will get the job. It is the unorganized home-based women who generally work at the lowest rates. And it is them whom the contractors contact to determine the lowest piece-rate for such jobs. The Mahila Mandals may offer a better alternative if the

123

wage rates are similar, because of the other organizational support (especially funding from national and international organizations; centralization; the workplace; and better supervision).

Given all this support, higher wage rates may be accepted. But piece-rate wages are never sufficient to cover all these costs. Programmes are funded 'to provide employment' and 'to develop leadership'. This basically covers supervision and other costs, and large companies get their work done cheaply.

It is evident that unless income-generating projects confront the macro-level questions within which they and their products are forced to function, their survival becomes precarious. Examples are: the question of adulteration for the organization making spices; and the question of multinationals entering a potential field of employment for women. Partial subsidization of these projects becomes meaningful, if, in addition to direct effects, they also work to improve the market and to preserve or develop women's employment by affecting policy.

One of the drawbacks, it seems, in this work is that if the organization is not run in a truly democratic manner — so that the women have real membership and control of decision-making — the women will see the Mandal only as means of getting work, and will unite and struggle against the Mandal. We have seen one example, in which an external party succeeded in developing a union among the women and organizing a strike, saying that the organizers had not done enough to get employment for the women. Obviously such an action has a detrimental effect, lessening the credibility of women's organizations and hindering the development of other programmes.

Currently there is no law or legislation which determines how wage rates for piece-work should be calculated. This seems to be the only way in which women's wages could be improved; a law might assure that large organizations (at least) were pressed to pass the equivalent of minimum wages when work is contracted out, and to cover all the costs (e.g. supervision, place).

Since government and public-sector enterprises are the major source of such work, it should be possible to argue for such a provision. This could become possible through joint action and struggle of all those involved in this type of work. It would mean that women working in such organizations did not see the work they are doing as being paid for by some sort of 'charity', but instead see themselves as legitimate workers. We found that this view of women as 'workers' sometimes got quite confused, especially in the Mahila Mandals, who often see this type of organizing, and a struggle for consciousness-raising, as being detrimental to the organization.

To what extent can the labour law and the legal framework assist the various occupational groups we have studied? The variety of laws which apply to workers are quite confusing and complex. Many different laws apply, and many of the major definitions have been subject to litigation, so that the definitions have expanded and changed.

The basic criticism, validly levelled against the labour legislation in the country, is that while there may be scope or need for improving the contents of the law, these laws are ineffective in so far as there is inadequate or more often no enforcement of them. The enforcement machinery is inadequate. The provisions of the law are not clear and precise, making it a battleground for legal interpretation in the hierarchy of tribunals and courts. Penalties are inadequate and participation of the workers in the enforcement of the law is totally absent. The adjudicating machinery and the magistracy are quite often indifferent if not hostile to the aspirations of the working people, and even these authorities are too far removed from the workers and their homes for them to seek recourse to these authorities without considerable loss of time and consequently of wages, even if they summon up enough courage — at the risk of losing their employment — to make complaints against the employer concerned. In the case of women workers in the unorganized sector, these difficulties are even more acute. (*Shram Shakti*, 1987).

There seem to be three options for legal assistance in the occupations we have studied:

1. to extend the existing laws to cover the occupations which are currently not covered;
2. to argue for a new law to cover these occupations (like the Beedi Act);
3. to argue for setting up Boards for the regulation of conditions of work.

For subcontracting and home-based workers, there are two possibilities: extend the existing Act to cover such workers, or enact a new law to cover these workers. There are pro and con arguments for each position.

Those who argue for a new law argue that there are so many problems within the framework of the current Factory Law that a new law, based entirely on the nature of the employee-employer relationship and a different definition of site work, would make it far easier to win cases for such workers. The discussion of a draft of a new piece of legislation at the Conference on Law and Home based Workers in 1987 is outlined below.

The National Commission on Self-Employed Women and Women in the Informal Sector (1988), argues in its recommendations for the setting up of Tripartite Boards:

In deciding on the nature of legislative protection that must be given to home based, piece-rated women workers, the question naturally arose as to whether it is necessary to think in terms of a comprehensive self-contained law on the subject of whether the same result could be achieved by making suitable amendments to existing labour laws. After

125

earnest consideration we came to the conclusion that the best way of helping the home based workers would be to have a new law specific to the needs of home based worker as would give them greater visibility. The vexatious question of employer-employee relationship tests can be avoided altogether and a new method for fixing responsibility by looking at control over the production process and ultimate product can be introduced.

Having decided on a new law, we considered whether the new law could be on the lines of the Bidi and Cigar workers (Conditions of Employment) Act 1966, which, after all, relates to an industry where over 90 percent of the workers are home-based and predominantly women. We took note of the gaps in the implementation of the above law, particularly with respect to women workers; most of them do not even get recognized as workers. In the light of the experience of the working of the law, and at the same time, without denying that the law has over the years in certain cases acted as a rallying point of organizations of workers to be formed or attempted to be formed, we came to the conclusion that the law should provide for Tripartite Boards, on the pattern of Dock Labour Board or Mathadi Boards, for the following reasons.

The commission recommends establishment of Tripartite Boards, for the reason that no law, however well conceived, will be of benefit of women workers unless they have a major hand in the implementation of these laws and this should be achieved only at a Tripartite Board in which workers will have as many representatives as the government and employers to give them knowledge. Women workers will be adequately represented proportionally to their numerical strength. The Tripartite Boards will not only regulate the implementation of legislation, but also contribute in making women workers visible and to bring to focus the contribution they make to the family income and to the economy and above all in empowering them, to understand their rights and to demand them, not merely as beneficiaries under any paternalistic pattern but as partners and participants in a production process. Given the nature of shifting employer–employee relationships and even the denial of such relationship and the consequent difficulty in even getting due wages paid in full and on time, the case for Tripartite Boards needs no argument. There is no other method by which a employer–employee nexus can be established; the Tripartite Board arrangement providing for a corpus of employers and a corpus of employees, instead of an individual employer with his employees. In this type of arrangement, it will also be possible for the Board to take on planning functions in respect of the activity concerned, to encourage promotion of co-operatives wherever feasible with the Board helping the co-operative in the matter of supply of raw materials and marketing.(*Shram Shakti*, 1987).

Those that argue against new legislation argue that there is already suffi-cient national legislation; the problem has been in implementation and in application to the conditions which exist. They argue that resources should be used not to set up more bureaucratic systems (like Boards), whose problems are well known, but to educate workers regarding their rights. A comprehensive addition to the Minimum Wages Act, and the Shops and Establishment Act, could effectively bring most home workers within the purview of the law.

To improve women's position in the various subcontracting arrange-ments, three aspects seem crucial:

1. a legal framework covering the context of their work, via either a new law, or an expansion of existing laws;
2. the development of mass organizations which in addition to looking at grassroots problems also look at general macro-level development issues;
3. technical and economic support to assist developing organizations.

In the absence of a legal framework and the development of mass organiza-tions with technical and economic support, women's organizations working in subcontracting arrangements may act only as a sort of middleman, pro-viding managerial and supervisory skills, and getting grants and subsidies for development of infrastructure, while women workers remain cheap labour for large companies.

PART III

Case study — the footwear industry

9   Recent trends in the world footwear industry

FERENC SCHMEL

An old shoemakers' saying is that their profession had a secure future, since people would always wear footwear. This statement and the fact that the trade can now look back over two thousand years of history bespeak the stability of the shoe industry. On the other hand, we all know that footwear is an integral part of clothing; thus its shape, colour, and structure change in accord with current fashions. Thus, while one may say that the last major change in shoemaking was in the nineteenth century — the introduction of left and right shapes as mirror images — another may vote for the ever changing nature of this sector. This chapter attempts to look a little deeper into this dilemma.

Before going into some detail on employment and technology aspects, it is necessary to look briefly at global consumption, production, and international trade patterns in this industry in recent years.

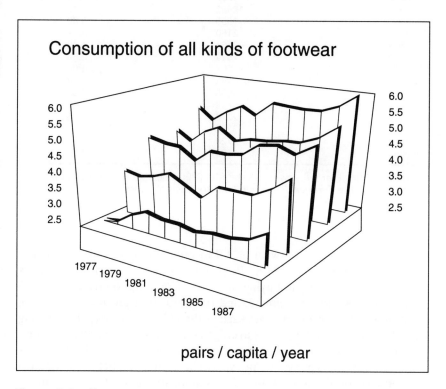

Figure 9.1   *Footwear consumption in selected European countries*

Table 9.1   Consumption of shoes, related to GDP (1986)

Country	GDP consumption per capita (US$)	Pairs per capita
Austria	9485	4.61
Belgium	8739	4.68
Denmark	12117	4.20
France	10214	5.28
Fed. Rep. Germany	11300	4.55
Greece	3748	1.93
Italy	6938	2.94
Netherlands	9647	3.72
Portugal	2256	1.65
Spain	4949	2.69
Sweden	12752	3.35
Switzerland	16412	5.52
United Kingdom	8499	4.85
Bulgaria	3891	3.18
Czechoslovakia	8328	4.97
German Dem. Rep.	10055	5.01
Hungary	6276	3.53
Poland	4853	3.08
Romania	3338	4.31
USSR	6594	4.03
Yugoslavia	5952	3.23
Canada	12582	4.15
USA	17555	5.08
Brazil	2160	3.42
Australia	12164	4.72
New Zealand	7524	2.88
China	257	1.06
Hong Kong	5193	5.34
Japan	9585	4.53
India	258	0.46
South Korea	2274	1.98
Taiwan	3387	1.68
Egypt	729	1.29
Tunisia	1289	1.89

Sources: SATRA, *World Footwear Markets* 1986. European Confederation of the Footwear Industry, *The European Footwear Industry* (several issues).

Consumption

The main function of footwear is still to protect our feet against weather and mechanical damage, but aesthetic considerations (i.e. fashion trends) play an increasing role in buying decisions. Consumption depends mainly on the living standards, climate, and traditions of a given consumer segment. In industrialized countries such as the USA, Germany, United Kingdom, France, and Belgium, the average consumption is over five pairs per capita per year, but in warmer climates (e.g. Italy, Spain, and Portugal) it is less than three pairs per capita per year. The correlation between GDP and consumption of all kinds of footwear is quite strong: $r = 0.775$ (Figure 9.1 and Table 9.1).

Footwear consumption (1984) pairs/capita/year

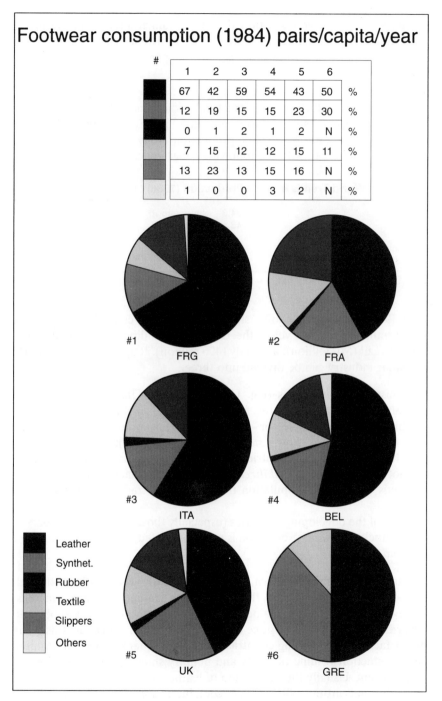

#	1	2	3	4	5	6	
	67	42	59	54	43	50	%
	12	19	15	15	23	30	%
	0	1	2	1	2	N	%
	7	15	12	12	15	11	%
	13	23	13	15	16	N	%
	1	0	0	3	2	N	%

Legend:
- Leather
- Synthet.
- Rubber
- Textile
- Slippers
- Others

#1 FRG
#2 FRA
#3 ITA
#4 BEL
#5 UK
#6 GRE

Figure 9.2   *Footwear consumption by product content*

133

The structure of consumption reflects certain traditions: in Germany, Italy and Belgium, people use more leather footwear, while in France and the UK the share of leather shoes is below 50 per cent (Figure 9.2).

Production

The value of production and structural indicators follow consumption, since fashion articles such as footwear cannot usually be stored longer than one season. The total world shoe production today is approximately nine billion pairs per year, with the following geographical distribution:

Table 9.2   World Trends in Shoe Production (1986) (%)

Europe	34.3	(decreasing)
Asia	43.4	(increasing)
Africa	3.8	
America	17.9	(decreasing)
Australia	0.6	

Source: SATRA.

In 1984, the world's leading shoe manufacturing countries were China (1220 million pairs per year), the USSR (970 million), Taiwan (637 million), Brazil (510 million), and Italy (496 million). It appears that the world footwear industry can be divided into three:

1. industrialized countries (e.g. USA, Germany, UK, France, and even Italy and Spain) where the footwear trade — including the shoe machine manufacturing sector — was and is export oriented, and where the production figures show a *steady decline* (Figure 9.3);
2. other industrialized countries (e.g. Scandinavia and Benelux), where footwear output *has stabilized* at a low level, which could satisfy the needs of the local population if international trade should come to a halt;
3. most of the developing countries (especially those with large numbers of livestock) footwear production is export oriented, and shows an *upward trend.*

In Europe and North America, the majority of footwear is still made with leather uppers. Nevertheless, the share of non-leather footwear is increasing everywhere; this is explained by the penetration of sports shoes into everyday dress, by the low price of textile and rubber footwear (this is the major factor in developing countries), and by frequent changes in fashion. The production volume of safety and military shoes seems to be more or less constant. Usually the proportion of leather footwear for women, men, and children is around 50–30–20 per cent, but in some countries, e.g. Japan and Israel, this is not the case at all (Figure 9.4).

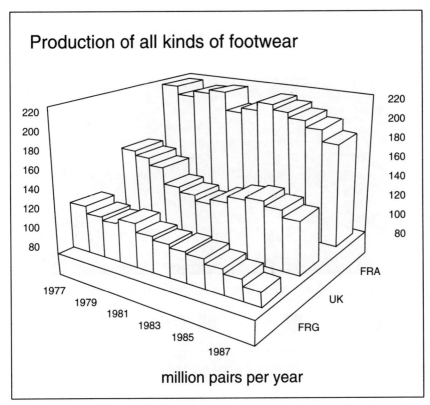

Figure 9.3   *Footwear production in selected European countries (million pairs per annum)*

There are two significant features in the world shoe industry. Countries in which the fine arts developed freely, and which have provided some of history's most outstanding artistic achievements, are today the leaders among fashion industries (the best examples are Italy and France). On the other hand, the case of the most successful exporting countries in the Far East (e.g. Hong Kong, Taiwan, and South Korea) demonstrates that even without significant raw hide and skin resources, shoe production can be developed — if the local supporting sectors, such as chemical and engineering industries, are well developed and the product range is selected accordingly.

International trade
Originally, every community produced shoes and apparel for its domestic market. Industrialization, improved transport, and the general development of international relations did not immediately affect this sector. The

135

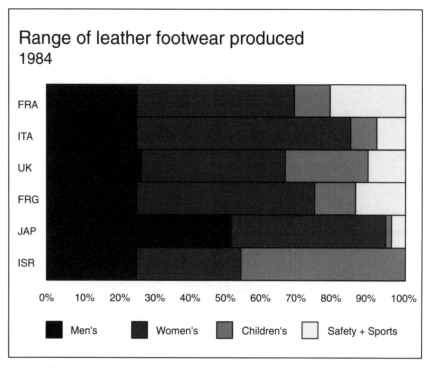

Range of leather footwear produced
1984

FRA
ITA
UK
FRG
JAP
ISR

0%   10%   20%   30%   40%   50%   60%   70%   80%   90%   100%

■ Men's   ■ Women's   ▨ Children's   □ Safety + Sports

Figure 9.4   *Leather footwear production (1984)*

first large-scale export orders were booked during the First World War
— for military boots. The mechanization of manufacturing processes
that took place from the beginning of this century made it possible to
produce surpluses over the local demand; thus foreign trade began. At
that time the larger exporters were those countries where the shoe
industry was already well developed (Germany, France, Czechoslovakia), regardless of local availability of raw hides and skins. Gradually,
industrialization absorbed all of the manpower released from agriculture, and, as the importance of infrastructure increased, the service
sector began to employ more labour. Wages constantly increased in
industry and services, and a higher level of mechanization was achieved
in the so-called drive sectors (e.g. the automobile and engineering industries); at the same time, shoe manufacturing remained a labour-
intensive industry. Telecommunication provided even remote communities with up-to-date information (including fashion trends), tourism
brought people closer. All these factors led to the evolution of the
international trade in footwear.

Seven countries export more than 100 million pairs of shoes yearly (the
world leader is Taiwan, with over 600 million pairs per year). The share of

exports as part of production is increasing, not only in these countries, but also in those where production is steadily declining (Figure 9.5). In the EEC, export channels seem to have stabilized, and the output of the USA, Switzerland, Sweden, and Canada shows positive changes.

Six groups import over 100 million pairs every year: USA (almost one billion pairs), Germany, UK, France, ex-USSR countries, and Hong Kong. The EEC's imports show a more variable picture than its exports: suppliers from the Far East predominate, and their share is rapidly increasing (Figure 9.6).

Some countries rank equally high in both imports and exports. Italy and France are known for up-market, rather expensive fashion (ladies) shoes; their major exports in this area are balanced by importation of cheaper shoes. The Benelux countries and Hong Kong are different: here the volume of exports is several times larger than local production. This phenomena is called re-export, i.e. these countries play the role of world wholesalers.

It is probably well known in Europe and North America that the least expensive footwear (mainly children's and sports shoes, and slippers and

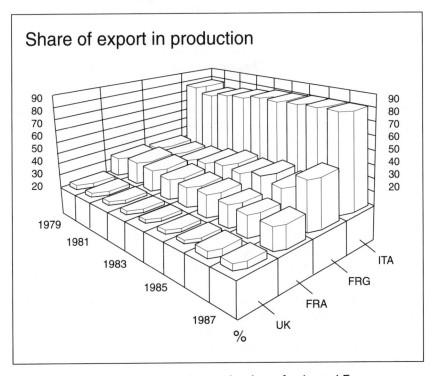

Figure 9.5   *Share of exports in production of selected European countries*

137

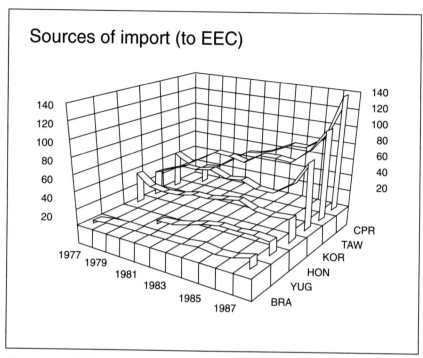

Figure 9.6 *EEC sources of imports (million pairs per annum)*

plastic shoes) are imported from Asian developing countries. Cheaper types of leather footwear come from some East European countries (e.g. Poland, Czechoslovakia, Hungary, and Romania) and Brazil.

Industry Structure

Until the middle of this century, shoe factories were self-sufficient in the manufacture of components such as insoles, unit soles, heels, stiffeners, etc. In the course of the introduction of mechanized technology, the majority of small shoemakers were absorbed by the larger companies. Alongside this concentration, some firms gradually specialized in component manufacture and some shoe factories turned into assembling plants.

Approximately twenty to thirty years ago, international co-operation began between companies in industrialized countries and low labour cost countries. Today, many of the European shoe-producing firms have their uppers made in countries like Portugal, Poland, Morocco, India, the Philippines, and so on. What is new here is the extent of subcontracting: the parent company deals only with product development and marketing, arrangements for appropriate storage and transport facilities, and supervising

138

the movements of materials, components and work-in-progress; all manufacturing activities are undertaken by partner plants.

Three tendencies can be identified with regard to shoe industry structure (Figure 9.7):

1. in countries with *centrally-planned economies*, very high concentration has been achieved since the 1950s by nationalization and introduction of a centralized management and planning system. In certain cases (e.g. the USSR, the German Democratic Republic, Czechoslovakia, and Poland) even tanneries and footwear manufacturing plants were merged into combines, which, despite their lack of viability, have been retained and are in operation today. Here the average firm size is over 1000 employees;
2. in *highly industrialized countries* the sizes of manufacturing units are more evenly distributed. The average size is between 100 and 300 employees per firm;
3. in *lower labour cost European* and most *developing countries* the small scale industry structure dominates.

The footwear trade in Europe and North America experienced a crisis in the 1970s. This period demonstrated clearly that firms could survive — of course not without (sometimes painful) losses — if they:

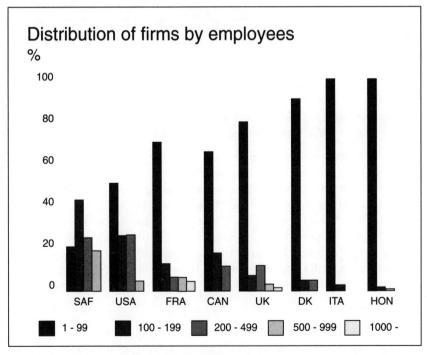

Figure 9.7   *Number of employees per firm (as per cent of all firms)*

139

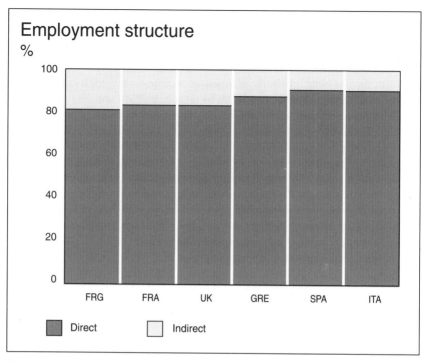

Employment structure

%

Figure 9.8 *Employment structure in selected European countries*

○ had sufficient capital;
○ established and promoted a stable brand identity;
○ launched intensive technical development projects;
○ had several specialized manufacturing units.

There is a preconception concerning the sizes of manufacturing plants. Smaller plants are thought to be more flexible; thus they can respond more quickly to market demands. The crisis mentioned above demonstrated that this is true only in cases of manufacturing plants belonging to large (sometimes multinational) companies. These have many — relatively small, in many respect independently operating — manufacturing plants, but also have a strong financial background. Companies like Clark's, Brown Shoe, Adidas, Puma, Bally, Salamander, and Bata are in that category.

Employment

Worldwide, the footwear industry employs approximately 1.5 million people. The labour-intensive character of this sector is expressed by the high percentage (5 to 25 per cent) of direct-production workers among

140

total employees. There seems to be a linear correlation between the average size of companies and the use of indirect labour: the higher the concentration of the sector, the higher the percentage of people employed in management, production preparation and control, marketing, accounting, transport etc. In the highly industrialized EEC countries about 80-83 per cent of total employees are manual workers, while in Southern European countries their share is above 90 per cent (Figure 9.8). A short visit paid to shoe plants in Italy, Greece, and Spain explains this situation: there the management is a sort of 'one-man show', where decisions are taken, and the majority of administrative and technical functions are performed by the owner (sometimes with the assistance of his family).

Productivity has long been the most reliable parameter to use in assessing the technical level of shoe factories. However, today it is rather misleading to use this indicator to compare various countries, since the industrial structure and statistics differ considerably (i.e. it is unclear whether component manufacturers are included and to what extent international co-operation is used) and the working hours per week are also not the same. One can hardly accept, for instance, that productivity in German shoe factories is only half that of France — even though the available statistical data show 2028 and 4109 pairs per employee per year, respectively.

It is more interesting and informative to analyse trends in productivity. In all EEC countries productivity was increasing until 1987, when it suddenly dropped (Figure 9.9). In that year, many shoe manufacturing plants made firm steps toward process automation, which — in spite of expectations — does not immediately increase productivity. On the contrary, the manufacturing infrastructure (e.g. tooling, programming, maintenance) has to be reinforced, which produces benefits only when automation reaches a certain level.

Historically, the shoe industry employed mostly men. As the priority given to the chemical, metallurgical and engineering industries gradually increased in Europe and North America, and women were released from agriculture, the percentage of male labour started to decrease. Today this sector is known as one in which most employees are women: about 70-85 per cent of all manual workers are women. On the European continent and in the majority of the UK companies some technological operations (e.g. skiving, folding, stitching) are performed only by women. However, there are still some closing rooms at Clark's where some men do stitching. In developing countries it is usually men who work in shoe factories — like everywhere in industry. The exceptions (Iran, India, the Philippines, some African countries) can be explained by social conditions and employment situations in that country.

A deeper analysis made in the 1970s showed that almost half of all manual workers in this industry were unskilled or semi-skilled (Figure

141

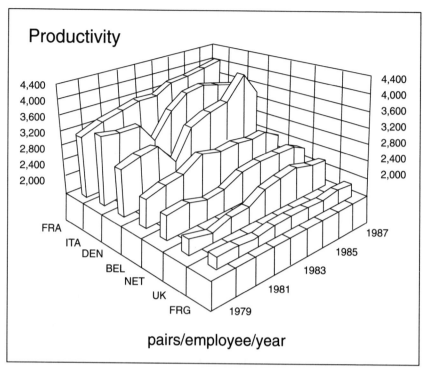

Figure 9.9 *Productivity in selected European countries (pairs per employee per annum*

9.10). Female labour was more often employed in low-grade jobs than in operations requiring more skills. At the same time, they could withstand the monotony at conveyors and in mechanized jobs where simple repetitive movements were required (e.g. feeding machines). One of the reasons for the concentration of women in low-paid jobs lies in the wage system adopted in most of the countries of the world.

The most labour-intensive process in both manual and mechanized shoe technology has long been assembling (making — i.e. lasting, soling, and finishing). This has gradually changed such that the bottlenecks are now usually in the closing room. While earlier the labour content of a pair of shoes did not change very much from one year to the next, fashion and seasonal changes now are important here as well. To resolve the problem of imbalances in capacity requirements, shoe manufacturers use domestic outworkers (mainly women) and co-operation with lower labour cost countries extensively.

The hourly wages paid in the shoe industry in selected countries in 1985 supports the above discussion:

142

Table 9.3   Hourly wages in 1985 (US$)

Europe		America/Australia	
Sweden	5.64	USA	6.06
Netherlands	9.66	Canada	5.76
France	4.34	Australia	6.34
Germany	4.74		
UK	4.19	**Developing countries**	
Italy	5.30	Thailand	2.82
Spain	3.54	South Africa	2.10
Portugal	1.95	India	0.58

Source: SATRA (UK)

As a direct consequence of this situation, there is a great difference in the cost structures of footwear production in industrialized versus low-wage countries. For a pair of shoes made in Europe, labour constitutes nearly fifty per cent of production costs, while this component is well below ten per cent if the same shoe is manufactured in the East or South.

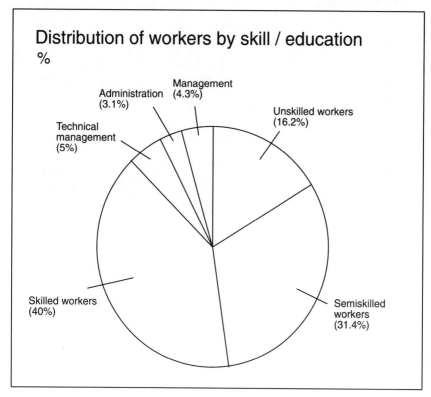

Figure 9.10   *Distribution of workers by skills/education in EEC countries*

Investments

One would think that when production is decreasing an industry would not require substantial investment. Facts do not confirm this hypothesis: although the total output of the nine EEC countries remained practically unchanged between 1977 and 1987, they invested four times more in the footwear sector in 1987 than in 1977. There was no real difference in this respect among countries with falling, stable, or increasing shoe production. The deeper the recession experienced, the more intensive were the investments made in highly industrialized countries. Each pair of shoes produced in the EEC in this period consisted of ECU0.50–0.80 investment costs (Figure 9.11). About thirty per cent of total investments were targeted for extending capacity, nearly fifty per cent for rationalization and twenty per cent to purchase of equipment; approximately one quarter of funds were used for buildings and three-quarters for equipment. Statistics also indicate

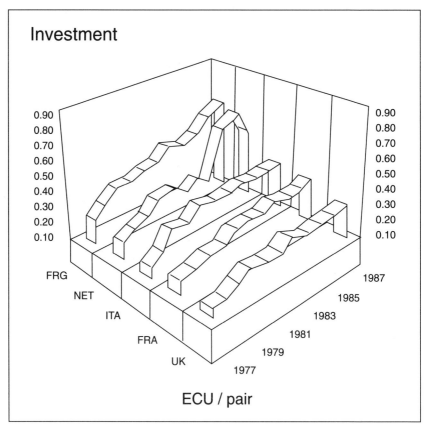

Figure 9.11   *Investment in selected European countries between 1977 and 1987. (ECU per pair per annum)*

that investments most oriented to taking the offensive took place when the EEC shoe industry encountered significant losses on the market.

Generally, shoe production is listed among the light-industry sectors; as such it is not regarded as capital-intensive. This has been true, but now things are changing fast. Manufacturers in industrialized countries have persevered and turned towards automation. Their strategy is based on the following assumptions:

1. the significant markets for footwear will be in countries with high living standards;
2. this market will demand more sophistication with regard to designs, shoe engineering, and quality;
3. acceptable profit margins will be possible only on expensive, high-quality footwear;
4. the decisive factor in competition on the market will be the speed of delivery;
5. automation reduces direct labour costs, but at the same time it requires infrastructure available only in industrialized countries.

Thus, if the production process is automated to the greatest extent possible, shoe factories operating near up-market areas will be in a much better position than their competitors on other continents, since fashion information can be incorporated virtually within hours, and the required ranges may be delivered to the retail shops in a few days. Shoe manufacturers in relatively remote regions such as the Far East and South America will be handicapped by time-consuming and expensive transport. This concept is being published widely under titles and slogans like 'quick response' or 'just in time'. Today shoe firms should prepare a new range for each season, instead of only twice a year, as was done in the past.

Technology

Materials

Apart from some national specialties, shoes have historically been made from leather, i.e. from the tanned skins of animals (primarily mammals). As technical developments provided better living conditions, and protection from the dangers of the surroundings, mortality decreased and the average lifetime became longer. Demand for consumer goods (including footwear) constantly increased. The growth rate of demand was accelerated by industrialization (since new functions such as sport, and working and safety shoes, appeared) and by improved living standards, fashions affordable for more and more people: they could now own several pairs of shoes for similar purposes. The world's animal population has been unable to keep up with these dramatic changes; today its growth rate — in spite of modern husbandry methods — is below the growth rate of the human

145

population. This has led to the replacement of some shoe components traditionally made of genuine leather by substitute (artificial and synthetic) materials. The first replacements were primarily other natural materials, such as wood for heels and textiles for linings. The first real breakthrough was the use of rubber for soles. This was followed by other chemical products such as PVC, poly-urethane (PUR), thermoplastic rubber (TR), and ethyl-vinyl-acetate (EVA).

With the development of the chemical industry, synthetic textiles, poly-ethylene, poly-styrol, alpha-cellulose, and the like were adopted in the construction of certain types of footwear. In the 1970s, a number of por-omerics (synthetic upper materials with ability to breathe) appeared on the market, and a large number of shoe technologists and marketing experts predicted no future for leather. As a matter of fact, by that time only about half of the footwear produced had genuine leather uppers, and the share of artificial/synthetic materials in other components was very close to 100 per cent. But thus far, poromerics (or simulated leather, as a UNIDO study referred to them) have not met the original expectations: their hygienic properties remained far inferior to those of leather, and they are still expensive. Perhaps new research in the field of membrane systems and perhaps some by-products of developments in bio-technology will lead to more encouraging results, but today leather is still the most important basic material in the shoe industry. On the other hand, in the future we will face increasingly serious problems in disposing of production wastes (especially from chrome tanned leather) and used footwear.

Construction

The construction of footwear is determined by a set of rational and irra-tional requirements by custumers. Among the rational elements, we find all the functional capabilities such as the protection of feet from the physical environment, durability and foot comfort. The irrational elements are of mainly aesthetic origin — shape of the toe-part, or heel height. In general, it is safe to say that irrational elements are concentrated in uppers and heels. Both types of elements contribute to the market value of products, and in modern shoemaking it is almost impossible to assign priorities.

Originally, sewing was the only technology available for the assembly of footwear components (real Indian moccasins are good examples). Shoe-makers developed a fairly wide variety in ways of stitching soles to uppers. Even in the middle of our century, velted shoes (Goiser and Good-Year), several different kinds of Veldtschoen, McKay-stitched, California (slip-lasted, Cosy- and Protos-stitched) shoes were produced in mechanized manufacturing units. The chemical industry entirely changed this colorful picture with the introduction of the first good quality (nitrocellulose-based) adhesive for attaching soles, followed by the so-called direct soling meth-ods, such as vulcanizing rubber and injection moulding of polymers. Shoes

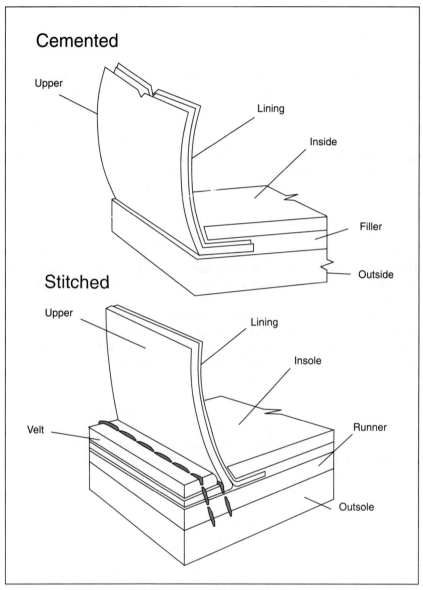

Figure 9.12 *Cross-sections of typical cemented and stitched sole constructions*

became lighter, but more importantly, the construction became simpler, requiring fewer components and operations (Figure 9.12 compares cross-sections of typical cemented and stitched sole constructions). However, in

147

styling uppers, there is a clear tendency for a given shoe style to use a greater variety of components in order to take advantage of specific properties of the variety of materials available.

Fashion

Fashion changes primarily affect the appearance and construction of uppers, sometimes causing drastic fluctuations in requirements for direct (manual) labour for closing. We should, however, realize that fashion does not change randomly or unexpectedly (as is sometimes claimed by entrepreneurs who are unable to meet market demands); instead it is created and impelled by the trade, seeking rapid returns on investments and creating new consumer 'needs'.

Shoe-manufacturing technology has changed significantly in the last twenty years, and can by no means be regarded as oriented to manual skills. Due to the pragmatic approach of the engineering industry, the early mechanical, hydraulic, and pneumatic equipment constructed for this sector tried to imitate the very sophisticated movements of the human hand. These machines are extremely complicated and, therefore, expensive. (To give an example, a heel and waist lasting machine costs approximately US$80–100,000.) The direct soling techniques already mentioned previously simplified the shoe-assembly process considerably, but related additional investments are in the region of several hundred thousand dollars. At the same time, upper-making technology has remained practically unchanged since Elias Howes invented the sewing machine in 1846.

Mechanization diversified footwear technology in two respects. Manufacturing units became specialized for certain assembly methods. While an artisan was able to make a complete pair of shoes, from cutting of components to finishing the complete shoe, the introduction of machines broke down the technological process into shorter operations requiring specific equipment and/or very simple sequences of movements. This differentiation created conditions favorable for using conveyors in workshops, which tied operations together and forced workers to perform at a steady tempo, resulting in a great deal of monotony.

In the late 1970s it became obvious that such a trend could not last, and that revolutionary technological changes were required. The first step was the elimination of conveyors and the introduction of flexible production lines. Meanwhile, the shoe industry has opened its doors wider to experts and ideas originating in other (sub)sectors. A typical example is the evolution of computer-aided design systems (CAD) based on the principle of sheet material handling and its conversion into free-form space object; in this respect there is no significant difference among industries manufacturing aeroplanes, ships, turbines, footwear, or apparel. CAD technology offers new perspectives for process automation by providing an appropriate database for computer-aided manufacture (CAM). Computerized, numer-

148

ically controlled (CNC) water- or laser-jet cutting, mould-making, stitching and roughing machines are common equipment in shoe factories in industrialized countries. Massive research and development projects have been launched to find the most feasible ways of introducing computer-integrated footwear manufacture (CIM).

All these efforts bring this industry closer to capital-intensive technologies and re-integration of operations. The importance of manual skills is disappearing, and the emphasis will be placed on product preparation. The structure of employment is changing: more and better educated people are required in design, tooling, programming, production control, marketing, communication, maintenance, and (quality) management and fewer in the physical transformation of materials into assembled products. However, these developments are not entirely consistent. For example, equipment manufacturers ought to pay more attention to loading and down-loading of automats: it is ridiculous that the most difficult parts of skill-intensive operations are mechanized and/or automated, but operators are still needed for simple (and very boring) operations.

Conclusions

The analysis in the previous sections demonstrates the complexity of the problem in question. The difficulty of describing the prevailing situation in simple and at the same time reliable terms is no doubt evident. The most difficult task in a structural analysis is clustering objects (countries, types of products, technologies, etc.) and making projections on the basis of past trends. In the future, computer technology and development of expert systems should deliver appropriate and objective softwear to help overcome such problems.

The author, therefore, is not in a position to draw conclusions now which can be used as guidelines for policy-making or strategy-planning for the future – especially with respect to women's employment and small-scale industries. Certain views have been adopted by many experts and responsible managers in the trade, but the majority of these are based on fashionable assumptions and slogans, primarily reflect wishes, and/or extrapolate tendencies registered in specific sectors or regions which have almost nothing to do with shoe manufacture.

The following conclusions briefly summarize a shoe technologist's views purely from a technical vantage point, with the intent of challenging other opinions:

1. footwear remains an important accessory to our clothing, and for quite some time we will wear shoes with leather uppers. The reserves in the collection of raw hides and skins seem to be sufficient to cover the surplus demand for leather until suitable substitute materials are invented;

2. developing countries must respond quickly to the challenge of the automation which is taking place in the industrialized world. They should not be afraid to adopt computer technology — at first, for product development, production preparation and control (UNIDO has developed a range of appropriate software for this purpose);

3. the shifting of shoe production from West to East and South is now slowing, and a balance probably will be established by the turn of the century. In the future, the key issue in competition in the future will be marketing power rather than labour costs;

4. shoe manufacture is requiring more and more capital, trained staff and managerial skill. Small-scale industry units in developing and some industrialized countries must establish strong links and enter into co-operation in marketing, technical development and production management; otherwise they will be exposed to the will of the multinational companies;

5. problems of the integration (employment) of women in developing countries can only be solved in conjunction with the general problems prevailing in particular communities and those of local industries.

10 Developments in the Indian leather and leather-products industry

K. SESHAGIRI RAO

The leather industry, including tanning and manufacture of footwear and various leather products, is being treated in India as an engine for development. This is due to its importance as a source of massive employment and of foreign exchange, earned through exports. During the last two decades, exports have recorded phenomenal growth: from a level of Rs.862 million in 1970-71 to Rs.16,084 million in 1988-9. Because of progressive export policies, the share of high value-added leather products in total exports of leather and leather products increased from 12 per cent in 1970-71 to 57 per cent in 1988-9. The industry has been migrating from the traditional rural sector to factories located in urban centres. Several new small-, medium-, and large-scale enterprises have sprung up on the peripheries of urban centres. Both internal and external forces have contributed to the growth of the industry and its export trade. Having a strong raw-materials base, low-cost labour, entrepreneurial skills, and government support, the industry is poised to make further strides; at a global level export opportunities loom large for the products of developing countries. With a view to these growing opportunities, the Government of India has proposed various measures for implementation during the Eighth Plan Period (1990-1 to 1994-5), in order to achieve the export target of Rs.34,516 million by the end of the Eighth Plan (1994-5).

This chapter reviews the progress of the industry and its export during the last two decades, analyses the contributory factors involved and attempts to view the near future.

Factors Contributing to Growth

A host of domestic factors — a strong raw-materials base, low-cost labour, progressive government policies concerning exports and imports as well as in other areas, availability of trained human resources, and others — have contributed to the overall growth of the leather industry and its export trade. At a global level, migration of the leather industry from developed to developing countries and a greater inflow of leather products from low-wage countries to developed countries have created a favourable environment for the promotion of exports from India.

Strong raw materials base
Possessing 194 million cattle, 70 million buffaloes, and 95 million goats, India held 16 per cent, 57 per cent and 20 per cent, respectively, of world

stocks in 1982. India is in first position among major livestock-holding countries. With 48 million sheep, it has 4.2 per cent of the world stock, ranking in sixth position in the sheep population.

Growth trends in livestock reveal that buffaloes recorded an annual increase of 2.1 per cent, and goats, 4 per cent, between 1972 and 1982. This contrasts with 2 per cent for sheep and 9 per cent for cattle, in the same period. These trends in favour of buffaloes and goats are due to the growing economic importance of these species to the farmer: they have higher feed-conversion ratios and greater resistance to disease. Buffaloes have become a major source of milk and goats of meat. The higher reproduction rates among goats in comparison to sheep is another factor in their favour. In view of these factors, buffaloes and goats are promising animals for India in the future.

Working from its pre-eminent position in livestock wealth, in 1986 India produced about 22 million cattle-hides, 16 million buffalo-hides, 76 million goat-skins, and 32 million sheepskins. These provide the basic raw materials for the leather industry. Based on previous trends, both in the number of livestock and the demand for meat, the availability of hides and skins in the near future will be as shown in Table 10.1.

Table 10.1 Estimated Availability of Hides and Skins in India (in millions of pieces)

Category	1987	1990–91	1994–5
Cattle hides	23.62	24.19	25.03
Buffalo hides	18.00	19.08	20.64
Goat skins	77.72	87.40	101.50
Sheep skins	32.80	34.90	37.76

Source: Estimates of the Economic Research Division of CLRI, Madras, India.

About fifty per cent of hides are produced from slaughtered animals; the balance come from fallen animals. Of skins, about ninety per cent are derived from the slaughtered and the balance from fallen animals. According to a recent survey (Central Leather Research Institute, 1987), the country annually loses nine million hides and nine million skins, worth about Rs.330 million at a conservative estimate, due to non-recovery/ neglect of carcasses. Effective measures would make it possible to minimize national losses. During the Eighth Plan period (1990-91 to 1994-5), it is proposed to set up a chain of mini-modern carcass-recovery centres, each to serve for a group of villages. Apart from recovering wealth from waste and mobilizing hides and skins for the leather industry, this programme, when implemented, will ensure an environment free from the stench of dead animals, which are until now left scattered for dogs and vultures. The recovery of these carcasses will provide additional employment and income to traditional artisans. The investment required for each unit is expected to be around Rs.5 million, which should be treated as a social cost.

Imports   With the growth of the tanning industry and the expected growth of demand for leathers, it is now realized that import of hides is inevitable. As such the import policies have been liberalized to allow duty-free imports of hides and even leathers. In 1987-8, the country imported three million hides and two million skins from the USSR, Indonesia, New Zealand and Pakistan to supplement domestic production. The benefits of imports are:

○ after finishing, the grain portion of hides can be either directly exported or retained for production of products for export;
○ splits can be utilized to produce leather products for domestic consumption, thereby releasing finished leather (based on domestic raw materials) for export;
○ a new export trade line in upholstery leather can be developed.

The constraints on import are as follows:

○ installation of heavy-duty machinery and modernization of existing units seem to be necessary to realize the full value of the imported hides;
○ because imports can only be purchase in container-sized lots, each unit must have a great deal of working capital; under the existing rate of bank interest, the additional investment required to acquire imported raw materials may not be within the reach of many small-scale tanners.

Stall-fed animals   To further strengthen the livestock base and meet the growing demand for meat, programmes such as calf rearing and fattening farms and stall-fed goat and sheep farms are in the offing. Such measures, when implemented would, supplement present supplies.

Fur-bearing animal farms   To strengthen the raw materials base, the setting up fur-bearing animal farms in suitable environments has been seen as important. Importation of fur skins for processing and their ultimate conversion into products for re-exports is another measure that can stimulate the growth of fur industry. India has suitable environments for such farms but so far none have been set up other than for rabbits.

Low wages

In addition to the supply of raw materials, the availability of a skilled work force and its low wages do contribute as important factors for the development of the leather industry. The comparative wage levels in selected countries are shown in Table 10.2.

Having a definite advantage in wages, the Indian leather industry has

Table 10.2   Daily wages per worker in the leather industry in various countries (1989)

Country	Daily wage per worker (US$)
India	2
Taiwan	13
S. Korea	15
USA/FRG	50

Source: Seshagiri Rao, 1989.

established an impressive growth. According to the 1981 Census, 1.4 million people were engaged in various activities, from the flaying of carcasses to the production of leather goods. Of this total, fifty per cent were engaged in cottage and small-scale industry. Subsequent to 1981, employment opportunities must have increased considerably, although comprehensive data on employment are not available.

Employment of women   With the accent on the production and export of high value-added leathers and leather products, several clusters of small-scale units have sprung up mainly in the peripheries of urban centres. These have provided ample employment opportunities for women, naturally, following in-plant training at entry level. Wage levels for women are definitely low compared to wage levels for men, although in terms of productivity — especially in the footwear and leather goods sectors — they stand more or less on a par with men. Entrepreneurs find it quite advantageous to employ women, as they do not in general resort to trade union activities and are available at low wages.

Productivity   The average output per worker in the production of finished leather from hides in India works out at 71 square feet per eight-hour day, in contrast to 128 square feet in Brazil, 400 square feet in Italy and 432 square feet in the United States. It may be noted that in comparing productivity levels among countries, other conditions such as level of mechanization, work environment, and management practices would also have to be identical to produce meaningful conclusions. But, in India, conditions comparable to those in developed countries do not exist. It is evident that, in India, entrepreneurs choose a maximum possible utilization of labour inputs and a minimal investment on machinery and equipment (these being relatively scarce and costly); whereas, in developed countries (labour being in short supply and wages high), enterprises are highly capital-intensive, minimizing the use of labour.

In view of the divergent approaches to factor utilization, output per worker is naturally low in India and high in the developed countries. If output is measured in relation to wages paid, however, Indian labour can claim a much higher level of productivity. For example, the wage bill for producing one square feet of leather, works out to Rs.0.42 in India, compared to Rs.1.78 in the USA. Wage factors are to the advantage of India in leather-products sectors. In addition to this wage advantage, Indian entrepreneurs stand to realize substantial savings due to low levels of depreciation and interest, in comparison to their counterparts in developed countries. With regard to footwear and other leather products, which predominantly remain labour-intensive, the competitive position of Indian manufacturers is much stronger than that of their counterparts in developed countries.

Export Policies

India was an exporter of raw hides and skins and low value-added semi-processed leathers until 1970-71. These two categories constituted 86 per cent of total exports in the leather group. Realizing the potential of this industry to generate more employment in the domestic sector and to earn more foreign exchange through export of high value-added finished leathers, the Government of India introduced specific export measures in the early 1970s:

1. a complete ban on exports of raw materials;
2. physical and fiscal restrictions on exports of semi-tanned leathers. Semi-tanned leathers were brought under export-quota regulations, and an export duty of ten per cent on the FOB value was introduced in 1973;
3. the introduction of Cash Compensatory Support (CCS), an air-freight subsidy, a duty drawback, and import replenishment for finished leathers and leather products;
4. institution of import entitlements, using a graded system for finished leathers, footwear, and leather goods, to enable entrepreneurs to import various inputs required for production and export.

In 1975-6, when the incentives were introduced, exports of finished leathers received five per cent CCS on their FOB value, against fifteen per cent for leather footwear and ten per cent for various leather products. Similarly, with a view to reimbursement of various import duties exporters would have paid on various inputs for manufactures, an incentive known as 'duty drawback' was introduced. All types of finished leathers were offered at 3.6 per cent; chrome crust leathers, two per cent; and semi-processed leathers, one per cent, of their FOB values. On leather products, the duty drawback varied from 4.8 to 7.8 per cent of FOB value of exports, depending upon their import content. To ensure timely delivery and to encourage transportation by air, an air freight subsidy was introduced for finished leathers and leather products.

In later years, with attention to the progress of exports of various items, periodic revision of the incentives and disincentives have been effected.

155

Once the transformation of the industry from the production of semi-processed to finished leathers was complete, the Cash Compensatory Support and the air-freight subsidy for finished leather exports were withdrawn. In 1988-9, the export of finished leathers received a duty draw back of seven per cent of FOB value (with a maximum of Rs.1.80 per square feet), and an import replenishment of 6 per cent was maintained. But there was no Cash Compensatory Support nor air-freight subsidy. Incentives for leather products were maintained at a higher level; the aggregate net benefit ranged from 20 to 25 per cent of FOB value, depending upon the type of product (Export incentives for 1988-9 are given in Appendix 10.1).

Liberalization of imports

To encourage the production of finished leather, footwear, leather garments and leather goods for export, import policies were drastically modified:

○ the list of machinery to be imported under OGL was enlarged;
○ import duties on chemicals and machinery were substantially reduced;
○ imports of raw hides, semi-tanned and finished leathers were allowed free of duty under OGL.

Institutional support

Various types of institutional support have also been provided to the leather industry. These include:

1. nine Common Facility Centres set up in the centres where the small-scale units are concentrated to enable small-scale tanners to produce finished leathers. These Centres, set up with Government assistance, offer job-work facilities for such production;
2. various financial institutions providing short-term and long-term loans to set up modern production units and to modernize the existing units;
3. expanded intake into Degree, Diploma, and Certificate courses in tanning, footwear, and leather goods, and the establishment of new training institutions at state level;
4. a Prototype Development and Training Centre set up with Danish aid in Madras, to develop new designs and to promote the indigenous fabrication of suitable machines;
5. reorientation of the programmes of the Central Leather Research Institute, in the context of R & D support, to fill the technological gaps, and transfers of technology to meet the growing needs of the small- and large-scale sectors;
6. introduction of advanced training programmes at post-graduate level in development of footwear design and Computer-Aided Design;
7. an exclusive Export Promotion Agency, known as the Council for Leather Exports, working since 1984 to promote exports through

participation in Trade Fairs, collecting and disseminating market intelligence, organizing meetings of buyers and sellers, and sponsoring visits of delegations and sales teams to importing countries. An International Leather Fair is being held annually in Madras to promote India's leather exports.

As a result of measures undertaken thus far, the leather industry has made remarkable strides in the export sector during the last twenty years. Exports reached Rs.16,084 million in 1988-9, compared to Rs.862 million in 1970-71 (almost twenty times greater in eighteen years).

Favourable international environment
In addition to domestic policies and development measures, the international environment has also substantially contributed to the promotion of India's exports. The world has witnessed a migration of the industry away from traditional strongholds in Europe and North America over the last three decades. After an initial stage in which raw materials were imported from developing countries, developed countries in these two continents started exporting raw materials to countries like Japan, South Korea, Taiwan, and China; and Greece, Spain, and Italy (the relatively low-cost countries in Europe). In 1987-8, the USA retained only 23 per cent of its production of hides for domestic processing; the balance of 77 per cent was exported, mainly to South Korea, Japan, Taiwan, and China.

This reverse trend in raw materials was caused by a growing shortage of labour, coupled with high wages and stringent pollution control procedures adopted in developed countries. Simultaneously, leather and leather products started moving in a big way from low-cost countries into the developed markets. Thus, footwear and other leather products industries in the developed countries suffered not only due to high production costs and a shortage of labour, but also from ever increasing imports from developing countries. All these developments encouraged the growth of the leather industry and trade in countries like India.

Value added during manufacture
If all raw hides and skins produced in India were retained, processed further into different types of leathers, and then converted into consumer products, the net value added to the raw materials would be increased four to six times. This is the sum of 40 per cent in the production of semi-tanned leather, 125 per cent in the finished leather production and up to 500 per cent in the manufacture of export quality consumer products (see Table 10.3).

Therefore, various development policies have been introduced, aimed at discouraging the export of low value-added semi-tanned leathers and encouraging in their place high value-added items. Under this strategy,

157

Table 10.3   Value added to raw materials during manufacture (per cent)

Raw materials	100
Semi-tanned leather	140
Finished leather	225
Shoe uppers	300–350
Leather products	450–600

Source: Estimates of Economic Research Division, CLRI, Madras.

various indigenous inputs (including labour) that could not be exported directly could be exported indirectly, since they were utilized in the production of finished leathers or leather products.

Status of the Tanning and Finishing Sector

In the mid seventies, alongside the introduction of export incentives and liberalization of imports, licensing procedures for setting up medium- and large-scale tanneries converting semi-finished leathers into finished leathers were streamlined. Licences were liberally given to upgrade small-scale semi-tanned leather units into finished-leather production units. Short-term and long-term loans were made available by financial institutions. Fiscal and physical restrictions were put on the export of semi-tanned leathers from mechanized units capable of producing finished leathers. As a result, since 1975, the industry has experienced remarkable growth in numbers of firms and in processing capacities. The major developments are as follows:

o out of the 1008 small-scale tanneries (SSI) and 75 medium- and large-scale tanneries which existed in 1988, 62 per cent of the former and 48 per cent of the latter came into existence after 1975-6, indicating the recent upsurge;

o of the units that came into existence after 1975-6, 81 per cent of the SSI units and 59 per cent of the medium- and large-scale units have built the infrastructure necessary to produce finished leathers;

o job work has emerged as a new phenomenon; this has attracted technocrats who have become individual entrepreneurs;

o with the increased job-work activities, sick units have been revived and the amount of idle capacity has been reduced;

o within the factory sector, SSI units account for 82 per cent and medium- and large-scale units for 16 per cent. Similarly, of a processing capacity of 161 million pieces per year, SSI units make up 79 per cent; the balance is provided by the medium- and large-scale sectors. This shows the growing emergence of the small-scale sector;

o the average capacity utilization in tanneries engaged in the production of finished leather is reported at 70 per cent; in those producing semi-

158

tanned leathers it may vary from 49 to 54 per cent, depending upon the type of raw material;

o the factory sector employs 65,800 persons, of whom 42 per cent are unskilled workers; 28 per cent are skilled; 15 per cent machine operators, and 3 per cent technologists; the balance are administrative staff;

o the distribution of tanneries among the various states is shown in Appendix 10.2.

Effluent treatment plants

With the growing awareness of the potential environmental hazards of tannery effluents, state governments have started introducing regulations regarding pollution treatment at the tannery level. Specific programmes are now being implemented to set up Common Effluent Treatment Plants in localities where there are clusters of tanneries; for new units, unless and until effluent treatment plants are included, fresh licences are not issued. As such, it is now envisaged that existing units all over the country are to be modernized, and that compulsory effluent treatment measures will be introduced. Only in states where raw materials are available and processing units do not exist may new processing units be created, and these must be in the small-scale sector; 'leather complexes' are considered to be a safe system, wherein small-scale tanneries in isolated places can be rehabilitated and treatment plants can be set up. World Bank aid is being sought by the governments of Tamil Nadu and West Bengal to set up separate leather complexes for tanneries and leather products.

Modernization programme

It has been proposed that, during the period of the Eighth Plan, massive numbers of hides and skins be imported into the country to supplement domestic resources. Such imports will naturally have an impact on tanning activities within the country. Imports of heavy-duty machinery to handle imported hides will be inevitable; this will involve further modernization of the tanneries which process the imported materials.

Status of the Footwear Industry

The footwear industry has been scattered over cottage, small-scale, medium- and large-scale sectors. Although in the absence of any systematic study no reliable data are available, very rough estimates indicate that of 350 million pairs of leather footwear produced in the country in 1988-9, 210 million were chappals, 60 million shoes and 80 million sandals and ladies' footwear. During the Eighth Plan period, production is expected to grow from 406 million pairs in 1990-91 to 501 million pairs by 1994-5, of which 26 million and 45 million pairs would be exported. In addition, annual production of non-leather footwear — using plastics, rubber and other materials

159

— is twice the volume of leather footwear. It is estimated that 85 per cent of leather footwear production is concentrated in the cottage sector, with the balance in the factory sector.

Uppers for shoes are an increasingly important item among leather exports. During the Eighth Plan period, the production of uppers is expected to grow from 44 million in 1990-91 to 63 million in 1994-5. To provide reliable estimates of production by sectors and domestic demand for leather and non-leather footwear, a nationwide techno-economic survey will be launched.

As a result of the employment potential and export targets seen to be possible, and the export incentives offered by the government, the footwear industry is developing fast, especially in the factory sector. A good number of export-oriented mechanized units have appeared as adjuncts to finished-leather manufacturing units. International collaborative ventures have also taken shape, and more are in the offing. But it must be confessed that whatever the country makes for export is produced strictly according to the specifications of the buyers, who provide designs, production supervision and guidance. In other words, the industry more or less does job work for others. It depends on the supply of soles and various quality components. There is a growing awareness in the industry that the domestic production of various components, grindery, and machinery is a prerequisite for balanced progress in the footwear industry.

Average productivity in a mechanized footwear factory is around three pairs per day per worker, compared to eight pairs in South Korea and thirteen pairs in Japan. The low output per worker is an indication of the level of mechanization in the production units, rather than the performance of the workers. The concentration of the footwear industry in India is shown in Appendix 10.3.

Leather Products

Although no reliable information on the number of leather products (goods and garments) in different sectors is available, rough estimates indicate there are 2000 units making leather goods and 100 making leather garments in the country. In the leather-goods sector, ladies' handbags (mainly for export) are dominant. Other items include industrial gloves, travel items, wallets, belts, desk-top, and fashion accessories. This industry is spread over small-scale and cottage sectors. Calcutta is the major production centre, followed by Madras and Delhi. About 80–85 per cent of the work force in this sector are women. There is a good domestic market for leather products, in addition to exports. In the mechanized small-scale sector, units oriented to exports are emerging in the peripheries of urban centres. In the absence of locally-available quality components, export-oriented units continue to depend on imports to meet their requirements.

Leather Garments

This is a rather new sector among those contributing to exports. Although these units are by and large in the small-scale sector, they are suitably mechanized and their production is oriented to export markets. A rough assessment of garment production capacity in India is as indicated in Table 10.4.

Table 10.4 Garment production capacity in India per month

Centres	Production capacity
Madras	30000
Bangalore	20000
Delhi	30000
Dewas	10000
Pune and Hyderabad	7000
Bombay	5000
Other places including Kanpur	5000

Source: Agro-Processing: Strategy for Acceleration and Exports, pp. 227. Oxford Publishing, Delhi.

This sector is fairly labour-intensive and depends on quality garment leathers — mainly derived from sheepskins, which are readily available in India. Exports reached Rs.1662 million in 1988-89. The important accessories must be imported. However, this industry shows great promise in view of growing world demand and of India's comfortable position with regard to local availability of both high quality sheepskin leathers and low-cost labour. As for leather goods in general, women workers in leather garment production make up on average approximately 80–85 per cent of the total work force.

Review of Exports

As a result of various promotional policies introduced by the Government of India, exports of leather and allied products have recorded tremendous growth in terms of value. The structure of exports also underwent phenomenal change in favour of leather products, as seen in Table 10.5. Between 1970-71 and 1988-9, total exports increased from Rs.862 million to Rs.16,084 million; an increase of twenty times in a period of eighteen years. In 1970-71, the share of raw and semi-tanned leathers was of the order of 86 per cent, and finished leathers and leather footwear accounted for most of the balance. By 1988-9, low value-added items (e.g. semi-tanned leathers) represented barely 3 per cent, whereas high value-added finished leathers accounted for 40 per cent, and other leather products including footwear components, leather goods, completed shoes and so forth,

161

Table 10.5   Trends in India's structure of exports from 1970–71 to 1988–9 (millions of rupees)

Description	1970–71 (Rs.)	(%)	1975–6 (Rs.)	(%)	1980–81 (Rs.)	(%)	1985–6 (Rs.)	(%)	1988–9 (Rs.)	(%)
Raw hides and skins	38	5	2	Neg	7	Neg	Neg	Neg	Neg	Neg
Semi-tanned leathers	697	81	1437	62	512	13	697	9	450	3
Finished leathers	19	2	548	24	2268	55	3339	43	6499	40
Leather products										
1 leather manufactures	4	Neg	18	1	138	3	203	2	162	1
2 leather goods	9	1	86	4	300	7	865	11	3415	21
3 leather sports goods	2	Neg	24	1	103	3	51	1	NA	–
4 leather footwear	92	11	192	8	337	8	413	5	1302	8
5 footwear components	1	Neg	9	Neg	451	11	2236	29	4256	27
Total of leather products	108	12	2316	100	4116	100	7786	100	16084	100

Note: Neg = Negligible; NA = Not Available.
Source: 1. Monthly Statistics of the Foreign Trade of India, Vol. 1, Exports and Re-exports, March Issue of 1971, 1976, 1981, and 1986 published by the Directorate General of Commercial Intelligence and Statistics, Calcutta-1.
2. 1988–9, Council for Leather Exports, Madras 600 003.
Compiled by: Economics Research Division CLRI, Madras, India.

represented 57 per cent of total exports. Among leather products, footwear components and leather goods made up the major share of overall exports with 27 per cent and 21 per cent, respectively.

Direction of trade

Along with changes in the structure of exports and the volume of merchandise, the direction of trade also changed, as shown in Table 10.6. In 1970-71, 81 per cent of India's exports in leather and leather products were absorbed by ten major countries, of which the USSR accounted for 30 per cent, the UK 19 per cent, the USA 6 per cent, and Italy and France each 5 per cent. In 1988–9, these 10 countries claimed 79 per cent of India's exports. The share of the USSR had come down to 21 per cent and the UK to 11 per cent, whereas West Germany has emerged as an important market, claiming 16 per cent of India's exports. Similarly, the share of the USA has improved from 6 per cent in 1970–71 to 13 per cent in 1988–9.

Place of leather in the country's total exports

Between 1970–71 and 1988–9, as shown in Table 10.7, the share of leather exports consistently improved. Exports of leather and allied products, which were of the order of Rs.862 million, represented 5.7 per cent in the country's total exports in 1970–71. By 1988–9 the share of leather and allied products improved to 7.9 per cent, putting it in fifth rank after textiles, gems and jewellery, engineering and agricultural products. It is expected that the share of leather and allied products will substantially increase in the near future.

162

Table 10.6   Major customers for India's leather products (per cent) (1989)

Countries	1970–71	1975–6	1980–81	1985–6	1988–9
USSR	32	19	25	21	21
United Kingdom	19	15	8	9	11
Italy	5	15	12	9	7
USA	6	13	8	14	13
France	5	8	3	6	4
West Germany	3	5	11	14	16
Belgium	2	1	1	1	NA
Japan	6	8	2	2	2
East Germany	4	2	5	5	4
Netherlands	1	1	2	1	1
TOTAL	81	87	77	82	79
Exports (million rupees)	862	2316	4116	7786	16 084

Compiled by: Economics Research Division, CLRI, Madras.

Table 10.7   India's exports of leather and allied products as a percentage of total exports of all commodities (millions of rupees)

Year	Exports	Total exports	Leather as percentage of total
1970–71	862	15 244	5.7
1975–6	2316	40 259	5.8
1980–81	4116	66 934	6.2
1985–6	7786	110 120	7.1
1988–9	16084	202 810	7.9

Source: Monthly Review of the Foreign Trade of India, Vol. 1, Exports and Re-exports, March Issues 1971–7.
Compiled by: Economics Research Division, CLRI, Madras.

Export targets

The present value of exports of Rs.16,084 million is expected to increase to Rs.34,500 million by 1994–5 (the last year of the Eighth Plan). With the introduction of various development programmes and promotional policies, the structure of exports is expected to undergo further change in favour of full shoes, shoe uppers, leather garments and leather goods, as revealed in Table 10.8. The share of finished leathers will be brought down from 40 per cent in 1988–9 to 22 per cent by 1994–5. The share of shoe uppers is expected to reach 30 per cent, footwear 8 per cent, leather garments 9 per cent, and leather goods 21 per cent of total exports by 1994–5.

Traditional Rural Sector

The traditional cottage units are unorganized, and are found scattered all over the country. During the last fifty years, they have suffered heavily on account of the growing importance of the factory sector (including tanning,

163

Table 10.8 India's exports of leather allied products (millions of rupees)

Items	1988–9 (actual)	Share (%)	1994–95 (Target for last year of Eight Plan)	Share (%)
Semi-finished leathers	450	3	–	–
Finished leathers	6 499	40	7 500	22
Footwear	1 302	8	6 220	18
Shoe uppers	4 256	27	10 258	30
Leather garments	1 915	12	7 320	21
Leather goods	1 915	12	7 320	21
TOTAL	16 084	100	34 516	100

Source: Council of Leather Exports, Madras, India.

footwear, and leather products). Traditionally, the rural sector was the hub of full-time activities: flaying, tanning, and production of leather products. The present situation is discouraging.

With the increasing diversion of old animals for meat purposes, the supply of carcasses to this sector and thereby the availability of hides are being reduced. Even the available raw materials are not all retained for processing in this sector. The top grades are being sold in the mechanized sector, which pays more; only the rejections are retained. The rural tanner has to be content with low-grade material and with reduced production. His end products are naturally of inferior quality and less competitive. In addition to the old traditional techniques of production, the long processing time, and outdated marketing techniques remain unimproved. His end products have a limited market and limited uses. His process and production techniques involve drudgery and result in low yields and low returns. The rural tanner has not been able to withstand the competition from the organised leather sector at different levels. Hence, he has no alternative but to migrate to other activities or to be content with occasional or under employment, resulting in low returns from his traditional profession.

Cottage footwear sector

With the invasion of factory-produced leather and non-leather footwear into rural markets, consumption patterns among the rural population have undergone drastic changes. Footwear from the factory sector in different styles, fashions, and designs, using different raw materials, is fast becoming popular. The traditional footwear artisans, although possessing rich manufacturing skills, are confined to the production of a few types — mainly for men's use — and only meet the needs of a small segment of rural population. Lacking innovation in development of designs to cater to the growing needs of different age groups, and also lacking financial resources to maintain a full-fledged footwear shop, the overall production and

164

marketing activities of the traditional sector have suffered. As a result, heavy migration of rural artisans to urban centres and also to other occupations has taken place. Those who still continue in the rural sector have to be content with occasional self-employment and attending to repair work. Many of the artisans who migrated to urban centres have been helped by various state agencies such as the Leather Development Corporations, which have provided roadside work-shelters, implements, and working capital. States like Karnataka have launched development programmes, both for construction of residential colonies and common work sheds exclusively for rural footwear artisans. Only if these artisans are organized as producers of footwear based on components that can be provided by export-oriented units or by State Leather Development Corporations, can they derive full employment and substantial returns from this activity. These agencies should take the responsibility for providing cut components and designs to the artisans, and then take the responsibility for marketing. However, prospects for revitalizing the rural tanning sector seem very gloomy.

Need for Technical Human Resources

The technical human resources required by the industry include production managers, supervisors, shop-floor workers, machine operators, maintenance staff, designers, pattern-makers, chemists, and analysts. For instance, for closed shoes, a unit with a capacity of 1000 pairs capacity per day requires two production managers, twenty supervisors, two hundred shop-floor workers, fifty machine operators, ten machine-maintenance technicians, and five designers/pattern-makers. Similarly, for tanning, leather garments, and leather-goods production units, the level and type of required skills depend on the scale of the operation and the type and level of production. It is also understood that, if all the leathers produced by that tannery are converted into leather products, employment in the related leather production will be three times that in the tannery.

During the Eighth Plan period, the leather industry is expected to generate an additional 0.17 million jobs of which 0.13 million are for shop-floor jobs, including machine operators, maintenance staff, etc. The necessary training can be provided through in-plant training before absorption. The rest of the jobs will require institutional training in leather technology, footwear, leather goods, and the manufacture and design of leather garments. These jobs are for managers, supervisors and designers. Various institutions in the country provide technical courses at post-graduate, graduate, diploma, and certificate levels. The intake per annum is 350 per year in leather technology; 987 in leather footwear and shoe uppers; and 386 in leather-goods manufacture. It is estimated that, to meet the growing needs of the footwear industry alone, the additional requirements for technical help will have to be met by strengthening existing institutions and also by creating new institutions and new courses. With a view to the employment of women, future training programmes must be oriented to meet their requirements and also to give them opportunities as self-employed entrepreneurs.

To sum up, the Indian leather industry, having established a very good track record in both domestic production and export, is poised to establish new records of growth. A great deal of infrastructure will have to be created, both to modernize existing units and to create new capacities in various sectors.

Major opportunities for joint ventures in the fields of sports shoes, leather shoes, and leather garments are coming. Prospects are also growing for development of machinery and manufacture of grindery and leather goods accessories in collaboration with overseas enterprises. Experience amassed in the leather industry in India can be of use to other developing countries. The Indian leather industry has proven how specific programmes of Government support can lead to progress.

Appendix 10.1 Export incentives for leather and leather products (June, 1989)

Type of Export Product	Cash Compensatory For C&F, CIF, FOB		Duty Drawback (Effective from 1/6/89)	Import Replenishment April 88 to March 91 (1988–9 — 1990–91)
	Air	Sea		
	(per cent)		(per cent of FOB value)	(per cent)
Wet blue hides and skins	Nil	Nil	Nil	Nil
E.I. tanned hides and skins	Nil	Nil	Rs.2.50 per kg	Nil
Chrome tanned, crust leathers other than reptiles	Nil	Nil	Nil	Nil
Finished leather other than reptile leather, for skins and hair-on skins	Nil	Nil	7 Value subject to a maximum of Rs.1.80 per sq.ft.	6
Leather products				
(a) leather garments	18	12	7	15
(b) light leather goods e.g. travel goods, attache cases, briefcases	18	12	4	15
(c) bags, wallets and purses	18	12	8	15
(d) harness and saddlery goods, all sorts	15	8	–	–
(i) harness goods	–	–	8	10
(ii) other	–	–	5	10
(e) leather gloves with or without cotton fabrics	18	12	5	6
(f) industrial leather gloves	18	12	5	6
(g) all leather goods including travel goods not otherwise specified	18	12	4	15
Leather footwear				
(a) leather shoes	22	15	6	20
(b) leather sandals/ slippers/chappels	22	15	4	15
(c) leather uppers including lasted uppers with or without accessories (e.g. insoles, socks, lining, heel covers, and other embellishments)	18	12	7	12.5
(d) soles made of leather and other footwear parts mainly made of leather	22	15	4	12.5

Note: Cash Compensatory Support will be granted for leather footwear, footwear components, and leather goods if at least 60 per cent of the visible area is of leather; for leather garments, the visible surface area should be at least 75 per cent.
Source: Economics Division, Central Leather Research Institute, Adyar, Madras 600 020.

Appendix 10.2 Important centres for leather products in India

State	No. of Tanneries	Tanneries by centre	
Tamil Nadu	577	Madras	(113)
		Vaniyambadi	(101)
		Ranipet	(94)
		Ambur	(74)
		Dindigul	(49)
		Pernambut	(44)
		Erode	(41)
		Irichy	(27)
		Vellore	(15)
		Melvisharam	(13)
		Others	(6)
West Bengal	233	Calcutta	(233)
Uttar Pradesh	147	Kanpur	(133)
		Agra	(10)
		Others	(4)
Andhra Pradesh	23	Warangal	(11)
		Hyderabad	(7)
		Vizianangaram	(3)
		Others	(2)
Maharashtra	30	Bombay	(10)
		Aurangabad	(5)
		Kolhapur	(4)
		Others	(11)
Karnataka	16	Bangalore	(16)
Punjab	11	Janlandhur	(6)
		Kapurthala	(3)
		Others	(2)
Bihar	16	Muzaffarpur	(4)
		Others	(2)
Haryana	6	Jind	(6)
Delhi	5	Delhi	(5)
Gujarat	3	Ankaleshwar	(2)
		Others	(1)
Madhya Pradesh	3	Dewas	(2)
		Others	(4)
Orissa	4	Royagada	(2)
		Others	(2)
Rajasthan	1	Tonk	(1)
Kerala	1	Vanjinad	(1)
Other States	4	–	
TOTAL	1080		

Source: Report on Capacity Utilization and Scope for Modernization in Indian Industry, 1987, CLRI, Madras 600 020, India (unpublished)

Appendix 10.3   Important centres for production of footwear (tentative)

Andhra Pradesh	Hyderabad, Vijayawada, Guntur, Nalgonda, Kajahmundry, Eluru, Ungole, Tirupati, Kirimnagar
Tamil Nadu	Madras neighbourhood (Arandati Nagar), Ranipet, Ambur, Vellore, Coimbatore, Irichy, Vaniyambadi, Dindigul, Karur, Kallupatti, Pallikonda, Madurai
Karnataka	Bangalore, Athni, Nippani, Gadag, Bijapur, Bidar, Hubli, Belgaum, Malavalli
Maharashtra	Bombay, Kolhapur, Solapur, Miraj, Sangli, Satara, Pune, Aurangabad
Uttar Pradesh	Lucknow, Agra, Kanpur, Meerut, Chorakpur, Rai Bereili, Ghaziabad
Delhi	Delhi
West Bengal	Calcutta, Badadiga, Siliguri, Burdwan, Khalimpong
Rajasthan	Jaipur, Bhinmal (Jalore District), Kota, Jodhpur, Alwar, Udaipur, Bikaner, Ajmer, Jhunjhunu, Bharatpur
North-Eastern Region	Shillong, Aizwal
Madhya Pradesh	Bhopal, Gwalior, Indore, Dewas, Jabalpur, Bilaspur, Durg
Punjab	Sangrur, Luidhiana, Bhatinda, Feroxpur, Jalandhar
Haryana	Karnal, Faridabad, Gurgaon
Himachal Pradesh	Chamba, Mandi, Simla
Bihak	Darbhang, Digha (Bata), Biharsharif, Muzafarpur
Jammu and Kashmir	Jammu

Compiled by: Economic Research Division, Central Leather Research Institute, Adyar, Madras, India.

11 Small-scale units in the Agra leather footwear industry

J. GEORGE WAARDENBURG

Anyone who studies leather footwear manufacturing in Agra must be prepared to confront a complete world. This is not merely a collection of tiny, small and medium-sized productive establishments, of smaller and bigger traders, of cost, production, and sales and profit figures, which can be analysed, dissected, and reintegrated by the economist in tables and diagrams. No, it is a complete world of people struggling to survive and to become better off. Notwithstanding their rich traditional skills, and that quite a few now earn a reasonable income in the footwear business, they have a common background: a position at the bottom of the former caste system, since many are Chamars, and their corresponding and so often lamented *mazboori*, the continuous state of misery and unhappiness.

What forges these experiences into one common world with a strong identity of its own is the shared historic consciousness of the highly special nature of shoemaking and working on skins and leather in general. In a purity-directed culture this work may be denigrated, but it nevertheless requires a near-religious dedication and skill. In this world, the work is more than a means of survival or of earning a more or less good living; it is a way of existence that gives identity to the person and to the group. One example may serve as an illustration. Once when talking with a very poor shoemaker, who complained that he was barely able to sustain his family, I asked him why he did not try, like some of his colleagues, to get alternative additional casual work in lean shoemaking periods, e.g. as a rickshaw cyclist. His suddenly clear and proud answer was: 'Sir, if I ever leave my own trade, I will never return to it.'

But let us not romanticize this world; instead we will look at facts. Three-quarters of the artisans, those who do the really skilful manufacturing work, are Chamars. Although it is very low ranking, this is the largest Scheduled Caste in India. In Uttar Pradesh, the state where Agra is located, this group makes up 56.5 per cent of the Scheduled Caste

The research on which this chapter is based[1] focused primarily on employment generating aspects of the part of the leather shoemaking/footwear sector reserved for small-scale production in recognition of its employment potential. This research was carried out within the framework of the Indo-Dutch Program of collaboration in the social sciences on Alternatives in Development (IDPAD). Unless otherwise noted, quantitative data in this paper are derived from the sample of 88 units distributed over different categories used in the 1988 study, as specified in the next section. For the sake of brevity, the technical difficulties of measurement and the statistical analysis of the phenomena are not discussed in this paper.

population. Within this Caste, 54 per cent are tenant cultivators and 20 per cent agricultural labourers; only a few per cent are shoemakers. In rural areas shoemakers have the right as well as the duty to deal with all remains of fallen animals. Among other activities, they are engaged in tanning these hides; thus making leather goods is a natural occupation for urban Chamars. However, although shoemaking is strongly identified with the Chamars, twenty per cent of such artisans come from the weaker Muslim sections, and a few per cent of them are Christians or Buddhists (a way to escape from the caste system). Before the partition in 1947, managing and trading were largely in Muslim hands; since the partition, sikhs or other punjabis from Pakistan have taken over quite a few of these Muslim positions. Even before 1947, some Chamars had reached higher positions, but the attempts of these 'big men' to improve the position of Chamars in general largely failed because of a lack of united action[2]. In recent years, the correspondence between caste position and occupation has gradually begun to blur.

Agra has a centuries-old tradition of shoemaking, especially for men, in connection with both the presence of Moghul courts and later of the British army[3]. Though this tradition was famous in Agra, shoemaking never dominated the Agra economy. Shoemakers traditionally live in *mohallas*, collections of simple houses around a common ground. Therefore, they are barely visible in the streets, let alone to tourists, who fail to visit the medieval inner city of Agra. Further, the concentration of leather footwear manufacturing in the three largest traditional centres, Agra, Calcutta, and Madras, has gradually blurred over the last two decades.

Types of Manufacturing Units

Confronted with either a whole world or a collection of shoemaking units in Agra, one cannot evade the question of how to observe differences and structures within this world or collection, in order to make further analysis and insight possible. First, however, we note the considerable unclarity about just how many manufacturing units exist in Agra. A 1976 Uttar Pradesh Leather Development and Trading Corporation (UPLDMC) survey reports a count of 2701 units, but that 4000 actual units were estimated to exist. A few years later a 1981 UPICO report estimated that 7000 units existed. Anyone who would like to draw conclusions from this difference should notice that a 'unit' is not well defined: quite a few, especially of the tiny units, are out of operation every now and then, and in any case most household units close during many weeks of festivals as well as in the rainy season, during which both working conditions and local demand fall below a feasible minimum. These units often operate at the borderline of subsistence or extinction; thus it is difficult to predict with certainty whether a closed unit will reopen. Therefore it is hard to know whether a

171

'temporarily' closed unit should be counted as existing. Moreover, splitting activities into several units is quite common for several understandable reasons, but when a unit divides, should it be counted as one or more?

Although the task of counting the units presents a rather gloomy picture, fortunately the question of categorizing the units is less bewildering: the question of existence appears to primarily affect one category; those which are tiny and sell locally. In the study, units were classified according to two factors: marketing channels and size, defined in terms of production.

Marketing categories
Following UPLDMC (1970), units were first classified by *marketing categories*; that is, according to the marketing channel through which the majority of production was sold. These categories will be described with special attention to their employment effect per unit of output and per unit of capital. Output figures refer to the year of the sample[4].

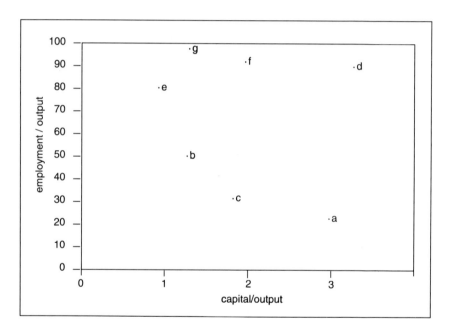

Figure 11.1   *Average employment/output versus capital/output ratio for shoemaking units in Agra (by marketing category)*

Note: The points represent the figures in Appendix 11.2. The letters refer to the categories as given in Table 11.1 and as discussed in the text. Each line corresponds to the employment/capital ratio of one of the categories: a steeper slope indicates a higher ratio and thus a more labour-intensive technology. The further a point is located to the northeast, the more it 'dominates' in terms of efficiency, i.e. it is more efficient without respect to the relative price of labour and capital. For further explanation, see [4].

Exporters An (increasingly) important category is the exporters, predominantly geared to exporting their production. This requires high and constant production quality; often specifications given with the order must be met with precision. Most of these exports go, via the State Trading Corporation (STC), to Eastern Europe in the form of 'uppers'. An upper is the upper part of a shoe, which can easily be mechanically attached to the sole in the buying country. The need to meet special quality standards and specifications induces the use of machinery in these units, which makes the capital output ratio relatively high — around fifty per cent above the sample average. Further, the employment/output ratio only slightly exceeds one-third of the sample average, so the employment/capital ratio is about one- fourth of the sample average. Thus product requirements diminish the employment effect considerably, relative both to output and to the capital used.

Government suppliers A small number of larger units is completely specialized, producing the limited types of footwear demanded by the government (such as for the military and railway). These are large batches of standardized footwear types with low-quality requirements apart from sturdiness, the thickness of the leather used, and the regular and predictable demand. This not only invites the use of machines, but also leads to greater efficiency in their use. This results in both capital/output and employment/output ratios that are about three-quarters of the sample average, and an employment/capital ratio near the sample average. While the employment effect per output is therefore somewhat below average, there is no indication that the technology chosen is unduly capital-intensive.

Ancillaries An increasing phenomenon in small-scale production in many developing countries is ancillarization. In the case of footwear in India as discussed here, this is more precisely called the 'putting-out' system, well-known also from the early industrialization of Europe. In the following section we will see that this is also closely associated with the subcontracting system. The special form this system takes and the reason it occurs in footwear production in India is precisely the reservation of the sector for small-scale production, and the application of the factory act and unionization laws only to medium- and large-size units.

A few large firms of foreign or Indian origin like Bata and Corona — well-known brand names all over India, with a national distribution system that includes a chain of their own shops which are a sign of higher quality/price combinations — have their production carried out by small units. These are normally chosen from among the various categories of small scale producers. It is not clear whether it is careful selection of these units by the national firms or good central quality control that ensures that they meet reasonable domestic quality requirements. However, it is said that the strength of Bata, for example, lies in strict quality control, plus technical education for and

173

inspection of the production processes; while Corona is known for its shrewd sales policy. However that may be, the advantage of such an association for the small units is their assurance of regular demand, even if this is at the cost of considerable outside pressure and without being relieved of the necessity for self-financing. On average they are paid only about three months after their deliveries to the central firm, the argument for this being that three months is the average time shoes have to be kept in stock before being sold. Not only investment capital but also working capital is therefore largely supplied by the small units. The employment/output ratio of these units is similar to that of the exporting units, but the capital/output ratio is equal to the sample average. Thus they produce more efficiently and with some fifty per cent higher employment effect per unit of capital than the exporters, but far below the sample average. This gives the impression that this category is, technologically speaking, rather close to the exporters: they too must meet strict quality standards; however, unlike the exporters, they compete in the national markets, just as the categories described below, and in particular with the following group.

Outside (Agra) or national suppliers   The next category consists of units which market their own products outside Agra, usually through a network of contacts with shops throughout the country. Strangely enough, both their average capital/output ratio and their employment/output ratio are clearly above the sample average, by approximately 50 per cent and 25 per cent respectively. In comparison to the former category, ancillaries, this implies a capital/output ratio that is higher by 50 per cent and an employment/output ratio that is higher by 200 per cent, and therefore also an employment/capital ratio about 100 per cent higher[5]. At first sight it is not clear how these units can survive in competition against the ancillaries. In general, however, their products are priced lower and therefore cater to a somewhat different market. Further, their lower rates of profit may be somewhat compensated by a 'psychic income' resulting from complete independence[6].

UPLDMC, (large and small)   The last three categories, to be called *UP-LDMC, local (large)* and *local (small)*, are presented together, as they can best be understood in connection with and contradistinct to each other.

By far the majority of units sell their low-quality products, in principle, to local traders each day. This business occurs at the end of the afternoon in a place called Hing Ki Mandi, adjacent to the traders' shops[7]. The producers bring what they have produced that day in baskets (*dalias*), and negotiate with the traders. Their position is weak — they must sell, to be able to buy the raw materials for the next day's production. They are normally paid in official or unofficial cheques, which can be cashed only after three months(!), and which must be cashed with the 'money-changers' in this same area, with the loss of the necessary discount. In addition, it is said they are often cheated on the raw material market by incorrect size indications on pieces of leather. The weakness of their bargaining position differs according to the 'name' they have made with traders and the public. Those who have established a name, called *name walas*, produce more or less on order, while the other producers, the *dalia walas* — the 'guys [walas] with a basket' — do not enjoy that fortune. This distinction may to some extent coincide with the distinction made here between large local and small local producers respectively, though the dividing line there is placed at sales of 25 pairs of shoes per day. Technologically, these two categories are very different. While 'large' producers have both a capital/output and an employment/output ratio of roughly ten per cent above the sample averages, values for small producers are roughly thirty per cent lower and seventy per cent higher, respectively, than the sample averages. This implies an employment/capital ratio roughly three times both the sample average and that of the local large units. It looks as if the category of local (small) constitutes, at least technologically, a world of its own — very high employment intensity, but also rather low efficiency — since the capital/output ratio is not correspondingly low.

The UPLDMC has tried to function as a reliable alternative to the wholesale and raw material traders of Hing Ki Mandi *vis-à-vis* small and large local units. Though its overall impact on the market is limited, its clientele display favourable capital/output and employment/output ratios: roughly fifty per cent lower and seven per cent higher than the sample average, respectively. This makes these units absolutely, i.e irrespective of factor prices, more efficient than both local categories. UPLDMC's better marketing assurance and prices may be decisive here, though also careful selection of its clientele may play a role. In any case, the wholesale traders interviewed assured us they have nothing to fear from UPLDMC. And indeed, its share of the market is small.

Table 11.1 presents an overview of the categories of units in our sample and in the UPLDMC survey, giving a quantitative summary of the categories discussed thus far.

Table 11.1 Numbers of marketing units by category: author's sample versus UPLDMC survey

	Sample	UPLDMC survey
(a) Exporters	13	300
(b) Government suppliers	3	9
(c) Ancillaries	17	50
(d) Outside suppliers	9	245
(e) UPLDMC suppliers	12	–
(f) Local suppliers (large)	17	833
(g) Local suppliers (small)	17	1264
TOTAL	88	2701

Viewed qualitatively, from the standpoint of employment creation and technology (as discussed above), exporters and ancillaries may be taken as a related group, and government and national suppliers may be taken together; finally, the last three may be seen as related. However, the recommendation to recognize the still quite separate position of local (small) suppliers must be taken seriously.

Size categories

A second way of distinguishing categories of units is according to size, defined in terms of production: numbers of pairs of shoes[8]. The following six categories are used:

(a)   6–10 pairs
(b)   11–25 pairs
(c)   26–50 pairs
(d)   51–100 pairs
(e)   101–200 pairs
(f)   > 200 pairs

Once again, average capital/output ratios, and employment/output ratios are calculated for each category, as can be seen in Appendix 11.3 and 11.4 and in Figure 11.2.

We will not describe each category as in the previous section, but note that in all but two categories the capital/output ratios differ less than 25 per cent from the sample average[9]. Category C has a 75 per cent higher than average ratio, and category A, 40 per cent lower. There is, however, no systematic increase in the capital/output ratio with size; that of the largest category is the lowest value but one. On the other hand, the employment/ output ratio does decrease regularly with size, and so (more or less) does the employment/capital ratio.

What are the implications of these data? Employment creation per unit of output — and in general also per unit of capital used — decreases with size. But the economies of scale are such that the higher capital/ employment ratios of the larger units do not lead to a higher capital/output ratio. This suggests that quite a few of the larger units are absolutely more efficient in the use of the production factors labour and capital (possibly due not only to technological factors but also to more regular sales). Interestingly the smallest category, A, however, does display both the highest employment per output and the lowest capital use per output, thus being not absolutely inefficient.

There is a relationship between the categorization according to marketing channels and according to size. 'Small locals' are by definition all in the two smallest categories (A and B), but there are also many other units in these categories. And, as noted, the very smallest category (A), has a lower

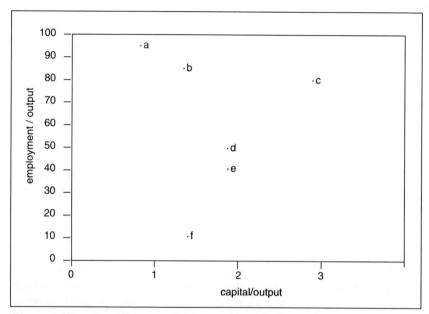

Figure 11.2   *Average employment/output versus capital/output ratios for shoemaking units in Agra, by size category*

Note: Points represent the figures in Appendix 11.4 while capital letters refer to size categories in the text. For further explanation, see the note below Figure 11.1, and the Appendix.

capital use and a higher employment generation than local (small) suppliers: thus the very smallest units are not absolutely inefficient. At the other end of the spectrum, the largest categories, (E) and (F), can by and large be identified with exporters and ancillaries, but also with the government suppliers.

(Sub)contracting Relationships[10]

Subcontracting — the rationale

In conceptualizing (sub)contracting we follow the earlier definition of Chaillou (1977):

> (Sub)contracted work is all the work which requires intervention of an outside person or agency, involving either the description of the product to be made (while making the detailed work description), or the determination of the working methods (while designing the working methods), or the actual work (while making the product or service). This intervention ends with the completion of the work.

The person or agency contracting with a manufacturer is often called a

177

'principal employer', and the contracted manufacturer a 'contractor'. A contractor may then subcontract part of the work to another person or agency, the 'subcontractor'. The distinguishing feature of (sub)contracting is that, while different actors like manufacturers and traders and their corresponding units can be distinguished as separate-acting units instead of being found within one big company, their interrelationships go beyond pure trading of certain goods and services. The independent identity of the manufacturing units and trading units seems to blur; they are interconnected for certain aspects of their activities, as described in the definition above.

The Agra shoe-manufacturing scene is pervaded by such (sub)contracting relationships, both in terms of the relations between units and in terms of actual employment relations of the workers. For some of the marketing categories discussed in the previous section, this is already so by definition, e.g. for (c), where companies like Bata and Corona have ancillaries on a rather permanent basis. However, most other categories are also involved in (sub)contracting in varying degrees and for varying periods of time with the exception of category (d) and the *dalia wala* among the local suppliers in categories (f) and (g). But also one may find 'foremen' with a number of workers under and engaged by them within units. They constitute relatively independent departments, yet operate within the enterprise as a whole, in a pattern of relationships reminiscent of but less permanent than the ancillaries.

Three types of (sub)contracting relations between units can be distinguished:

(a) specialized (sub)contracting, due to the specialized skills and facilities of the (sub)contractor,
(b) capacity (sub)contracting, due to the needs of the principal employer for extra capacity during peak periods,
(c) economic (sub)contracting, due to savings to the principal employer in scarce goods, e.g. management, supervision time, and working capital.

(Sub)contracting can be advantageous for a principal employer, especially in the Indian footwear industry, for several reasons.

First, the general technological-organizational reason is that, as found by McBain (1977), economies of scale in manufacturing of footwear in developing countries may disappear when production reaches even 400 pairs per day[11]. At the same time, the optimum size for marketing footwear may be much larger: in developing countries as well as others, it may be well above 7000 pairs a day, because of brand loyalty and increased efficiency in servicing points of sale[12]. It may be quite advantageous for a wholesaler to contract with a large number of smaller manufacturers, but this still does not explain fully why this could not be fully a market relationship. However, the better the name of the wholesaler or the corresponding

178

shops in the market, the greater their need to demand a good standard of quality from their suppliers. This is even more important for shoes that are largely handmade, where consistency in quality standards or other specifications are difficult to maintain. On the other hand, it is not easy to replace a rejected batch of shoes with another batch having the same specifications in a timely manner. Therefore, it is in the interest of the trader to monitor the manufacturers regularly, and possibly provide some training. This may apply to Bata and Corona, to DST *vis-à-vis* its 'exporting' units, and, to a lesser degree, to UPLDMC *vis-à-vis* its suppliers. Nevertheless, by not fully incorporating the small units into the larger firm, the latter may save management costs as well as capital, because the small units absorb these costs. One may interpret this situation as a reason for economic (sub)contracting.

Second, in India, the reservation of leather footwear manufacturing to small-scale units[13], plus the tax concessions and suspension of application of union laws to them, make small-scale manufacturing in this sector necessary and advantageous. This adds a strong institutional reason to the technological-organizational factors discussed above. However, the technological situation behind this institutional reason should be clear. For a long time, and explicitly since the Industry Policy Resolution of 1956, the Indian government has favoured — alongside emphasis on early development of large-scale basic industrial sectors like steel and machinery — small-scale production in other sectors as appropriate. The labour intensity of production in many small-scale units has been one of the arguments. That the leather-goods sector is considered to be such an appropriate sector has to do also with its limited economies of scale in production. Once such 'appropriateness' has become institutionalized, as discussed earlier in this paragraph, this reservation policy becomes an institutional factor and leads to (sub)contracting of the type which exists to provide extra capacity.

Finally, specialized (sub)contracting also occurs, i.e. with the very small units. The first machine to be purchased in the process of mechanization, the stitching machine, has too large a capacity for a very small unit. In a group of very small units, one owner of such a machine often appears, who does all of the stitching work for the group. The group can then be described as his principal employer, to whom he is a contractor.

Some Observations on (Sub)Contracting in Agra

Contracting occurs in Agra in most of the categories of manufacturing units discussed in the second section. In the category of exporters, the State Trading Company acts as principal employer for units exporting uppers to eastern Europe, both indicating the required designs and helping the units with technical advice. In the category of government suppliers, the

179

Director General Supplies & Disposals (D.G.S. & D.) is the principal employer, specifying the precise design requirements for the shoes. The national organizations Bata and Corona are the principal employers for their manufacturing units; they provide designs, and Bata in particular also provides technical advice and quality control. All these manufacturing units necessarily have some machinery and are partly mechanized; this is needed to meet the quality requirements of their principal employers. The employers in their turn must set these limits to maintain their position with their buyers. This makes access to these marketing relationships difficult for units in other categories: to participate, they would also need the required liquidity, 'relationships', and established trust. Successful 'national suppliers', a category in which no contracting occurs, can be expected to gain some access[14].

As a principal employer, UPLDMC also helps its suppliers with designs, quality raw materials, and occasional technical advice. These appear to be useful to the units. While some of the wholesale traders act more or less as principal employers for some 'large local' units, they do not provide any support — neither technical nor financial. There the contracting relationship hardly appears favourable for those units or for shoe manufacturing as a whole. But, the alternative of being a *dalia wala*, which is always open to all units, is not attractive; and becoming a UPLDMC supplier or a supplier outside Agra is not always a feasible option, because of quality requirements (and, for the outside suppliers, liquidity and relationship requirements). The same requirements stand even more firmly in the way of moving to one of the first three categories.

(Sub)Contracting and Employment Conditions in Agra

The employment situation and labour relations in the Agra small-scale footwear industry can be elucidated by using the concept of contracting. On the one hand, both contracting relationships and labour conditions of manufacturing units differ according to their marketing categories. Therefore, there is at least a certain association between contracting relationships and labour conditions. On the other hand, some of the employment relations are of the contracting type, and should be understood as such. In this subsection we focus on this latter aspect of contracting. Vaid (1966), roughly in line with the ILO, distinguishes three kinds of subcontracting:

(1) labour-only contracting: contractors supply workers to a company, but these workers do not appear on the payroll of that company;
(2) job contracts given to small (ILO) or non-legal (sub)contractors. (Sub)contractors do the work either in their own backyard or on the premises of the company, but their workers' labour conditions are independent of those of the company;

180

(3) job contracts given to large (ILO) or legal (sub)contractors. (Sub)contractors have an obligation to provide the same labour conditions as the company.

In the Agra footwear sector, we are confronted only with contracting of the second and third types. Moreover, following Vaid, we define 'casual labour' as referring to workers directly employed by a principal employer for a limited period of time, and '(sub)contract labour' as workers employed by a (sub)contractor, as defined earlier in this paper.

For (sub)contract labour[15] three types of payment for labour can be distinguished:

o fixed salaries
o piece-rate systems
o family labour, in which workers do not receive direct payments, but share in the family's consumption opportunities.

In most cases, fixed salaries are only paid to personnel whose production cannot be measured in terms of pieces. Generally, this includes supervisors and designers; but in (semi)mechanized (exporting) units workers or artisans may sometimes be included. (Such supervisors and designers receive their official training at one of the footwear training institutes in Agra. So much preparatory educational level is required here that in practice the traditional shoemakers' families, within which skills are transferred to later generations by on the job training, cannot send their young people to these schools.) Other workers are generally employed on a piece-rate basis, which implies that they do not get paid if there is no work[16]. The poorest units and the corresponding families, which employ mainly family labour, cannot offer their working family members more than 'shared poverty'.

There are three clear types of subcontracting in employment relations:

(a) a contract worker may call in 'helpers' for assistance in his work, (i.e. non-adults (mostly family members or 'neighbours') who get training on the job, as well as adult assistants). All are then subcontract workers, making him a subcontractor[17];
(b) an 'independent worker', whom we defined earlier as owning a machine (usually for stitching) and getting his work from several small units, and who was an example of 'specialized contracting', may have others working for him, just as the contract worker under A;
(c) some specialize in collecting orders for fine hand-stitching work on specially designed, somewhat fancier shoes, and subcontracting these to women at home at a very low piece-rate. This amounts to some Rs.7 per day (approx. US$0.50), which is less than fifty per cent of what the subcontractor receives from the manufacturing unit as payment. A subcontractor of type C is normally a monopsonist with respect to all women in a neighbourhood, or *mohalla*. They receive yearly incomes

181

comparable to those of helpers; this is about one-quarter of other adult subcontract workers' wages, or some fifteen per cent of those of artisans (workers) or ten per cent of those of supervisors and designers. This low payment corresponds partly to the fact that the subcontractors provide work for little more than half of the available days. It is said that in turn manufacturers employ a larger number of such subcontractors or distributors than necessary, in order to 'keep them quiet'[18].

Observations on the Effects of (Sub)Contracting

In the literature, evaluations of (sub)contracting lead some authors to generally positive conclusions, and other authors to generally negative conclusions[19;20]. Arguments in favour of either point of view can be derived from the Agra situation, depending also on one's analysis of who bears the costs and who gets the benefits.

Contracting, or ancillarization, in the case of the large national companies like Bata or Corona, provides an opportunity for local units to produce indirectly for the national market. For example, D.G.S. & D. provides such an opportunity for its units, and D.S.T. does so for exporting units. These units need not worry about selling in the (inter)national market, nor about the technical or fashion requirements imposed by these markets. Since such local units are in general more labour intensive than large national factories would be, this may also help to create employment in this sector. Moreover, the national organizations, with their centralized technical expertise, may be in a position to help the units with appropriate technological upgrading. This would enhance both international competitiveness and the supply of reasonably competitive quality footwear to the national market.

However, it is not clear to what extent these favourable features should be ascribed to contracting, since they follow from the government's reservation policy, to which the contracting system is a response. Furthermore, figures are not available on the extent to which workers' income reflects earnings, or on the wage levels in the manufacturing units, in comparison to the earnings of principal employers and contractors. In the early eighties, however, research in Agra by the 'Rotterdam team' has shown that Bata and Corona unit managers had many complaints about worker attitudes and behaviour; sometimes they found it difficult to keep them attached to their units. Exporting units, to the contrary, reported few complaints (or none) about their workers. This may indicate that their workers constituted a somewhat advantaged group, with fewer traditionally skilled workers, but better payment conditions, while the former group may be somewhat squeezed, given the relatively high profit rate in these units mentioned earlier.

Doubts about the distribution of benefits of contracting are considerably stronger in the case of the 'local large' units, and also for *name walas*, vis-à-vis the wholesalers on Hing Ki Mandi. Here the units themselves appear to be, relative to the cases mentioned above, in a far weaker position; one might suspect that workers in these units are no better off than their bosses. However, here, even more than above, one may wonder whether this can be attributed to contracting: the non-contracting units — the 'small local' ones or the *dalia walas* — are worse off, and their (mostly family) workers are also most probably more badly paid.

Leest (1984) noted the apparent contradiction between a relative shortage of contract workers and a less than full use of their labour. He sought an explanation in their attachment to manufacturing units which did not have enough work for them, due to the system of advance payments. At the same time, he suggested, following McGee (1971), the possibility or even likelihood of an involuntary process, in which the degree of 'poverty sharing' is increased, as Joshi and Joshi (1970) call it. As one of the mechanisms here he mentioned the helper system: this eases access to a low productivity, low paid form of employment, in which the training component may serve as a sort of disguise. In any case, as discussed earlier, the adult assistants also receive low pay, while their subcontractors earn far more than fellow artisans who work without helpers or assistants. Moreover, educational access to better-paying jobs (and therefore to opportunities for permanent upward mobility) are practically non-existent for these traditional families. The need to clarify these issues indicates that a careful social, educational, institutional, and economic analysis will be required to understand the static and dynamic intricacies of these employment relations.

Some positive elements can be seen in (sub)contracting with independent workers cum machinery — this serves as an opportunity to introduce low-level technical change, and thus to upgrade average labour productivity at the less productive end of the production system without completely destroying the employment opportunities there — but Leest (1984) is quite negative about middlemen's subcontracts with women for hand-stitching work. The middlemen are themselves not paid too much by their bosses, since this might attract too many middlemen (this would make it harder to 'keep them quiet'). However, they exploit their local monopsony position with respect to the women not only by paying low wages, but also by their disproportionate gains from the women's productive efforts. All this occurs outside the reach of labour laws and union power. While contracting provides the 'form' for this (to say the least) grossly unequal system, one can again question whether it is also its 'cause'. And here to an even greater degree, these observations call for further, precise empirical work, and for critical analysis of their wider ramifications.

183

Conclusion

These sketchy notes on experiences in the world of the Agra leather foot-wear industry can suggest only a fraction of its intricacy. But they may give enough glimpses to suggest the complexities involved. While it should be noted that these sketches are based on observations which date from the first half of the eighties, a drastic decrease in this world's complexity is not to be expected.

The development of the leather footwear industry in Agra concerns several tens of thousands of people. A considerable part of them, in par-ticular the adult assistants and women, are very low paid, as are the minors who act as helpers. The minors do receive some training, though this does not provide access to higher-paying jobs. Even if the industry as a whole were to increase production (and, correspondingly, earnings with regard to the domestic market, plus technological upgrading and more competitive production for the world market), it is questionable to what extent such development would percolate down to the lower strata of the Agra leather footwear world: the smallest production units and of the lowest paid work-ers, including unpaid family members. That is, one can question to what extent these groups are in a position to benefit from any development within the industry. They cater to a low-quality product market, where the threat of competition for parts — PVC soles, or complete footwear made of non-leather materials — may be at its strongest, even stronger than that generated by growth in the footwear market in general. But also they lack the education needed to escape from the institutional arrangements which appear to be associated with their impoverished situation.

This last statement indicates a serious policy dilemma. Further education for these lowly-paid groups may create opportunities for some of them in better-paid jobs in the Agra leather footwear industry, but may lead many to leave this traditional industry. It may also induce modernizing technical changes, decreasing its employment potential. In both cases, employment opportunities existing or arising elsewhere become an important element in the assessment of developments in the industry, at least if people are central to the assessment.

Assessment with regard to the position of women may require a special analysis including other than economic aspects, because for them the odds in this industry are also shaped by other than economic aspects. However, in modernized units outside the traditional atmosphere, their opportunities may be similar to those in other modern industries (small- or large-scale). Moreover, for both women and men, further analysis of opportunities in the lower strata of this industry should take seriously the whole traditional world within which they live, with its values, patterns, and institutions — far away from any awareness of government policies. Its stagnation and partial breakdown, but also its dynamics and opportunities for self-

184

organization must be taken into account. Thus the end of this paper brings us once again to our starting-point.

Appendix 11.1 Average and standard deviation of capital and number of workers per unit* of production per day for the marketing categories

Category	Capital		Employment		Number of Observations			Employment/ Capital
	Av.	SD	Av.	SD	Valid	Msg.†	Total	Ratio
(a) Export	4.14	2.56	37.7	25.1	8	5	13	9.1
(b) Government supplies	1.37	0.40	41.5	34.9	2**	1	3	30.3
(c) Ancillary	3.18	3.62	39.5	17.5	15	2	17	12.4
(d) Outside	1.83	1.50	67.0	25.4	7	2	9	30.6
(e) UPLDMC	0.94	0.21	66.2	41.6	12	0	12	70.4
(f) Local (large)	1.44	1.24	57.0	22.9	14	3	17	39.6
(g) Local (small)	1.26	1.09	109.9	57.9	14	3	17	87.2
TOTAL	2.02	2.28	63.4	42.4	72	16	88	

* 'Unit' is average production value per day: Rs.5,184.79.
† Within the total sample of 88 units some did not provide answers to the relevant questions or were removed by the 'skipping' procedure mentioned in the text.
** This amount is so small that data for this category should be interpreted with care.

Appendix 11.2 Average and standard deviation of capital and number of workers per unit* of production per year for the marketing categories

Category	Capital		Employment		Number of Observations			Employment/ Capital
	Av.	SD	Av.	SD	Valid	Msg.†	Total	Ratio
(a) Export	2.97	1.30	26.46	14.62	8	5	13	8.9
(b) Government supplies	1.46	0.84	47.56	48.68	2**	1	3	32.7
(c) Ancillary	1.97	1.38	28.09	17.18	15	2	17	14.3
(d) Outside	3.11	4.00	93.88	59.83	7	2	9	30.0
(e) UPLDMC	1.01	0.81	78.23	63.18	12	0	12	77.5
(f) Local (large)	2.18	2.27	83.00	34.76	14	3	17	38.1
(g) Local (small)	1.27	1.03	129.37	70.16	14	3	17	101.9
TOTAL	1.94	1.90	73.58	59.48	72	16	88	

* 'Unit' is average production value per year: Rs.966,814.
† See Appendix 11.1.
** See Appendix 11.1.

Appendix 11.3 Average and standard deviation of capital and number of workers per unit* of production per day for size categories

Size Category Production	Capital Av.	SD	Employment Av.	SD	Number of Observations Valid	Msg.†	Total
F >200	1.55	1.44	9.67	2.46	3	2	5
E 101–200	2.13	1.47	39.34	17.05	13	2	15
D 51–100	4.41	4.27	42.10	19.42	12	4	16
C 26– 50	1.50	1.25	56.76	30.54	11	3	14
B 11– 25	1.38	1.09	73.24	27.24	26	3	29
A 6– 10	1.09	0.84	141.16	64.97	7	2	9
TOTAL	2.02	2.28	63.37	42.42	72	16	88

* 'Unit' is average production value per day: Rs.5,184.79.
† See Appendix 11.1.

Appendix 11.4 Average and standard deviation of capital and number of workers per unit* of production per year for size categories

Size Category Production	Capital Av.	SD	Employment Av.	SD	Number of Observations Valid	Msg.†	Total
F >200	1.38	1.30	15.81	14.64	3	2	5
E 101–200	1.62	1.31	30.40	16.02	13	2	15
D 51–100	1.62	3.00	42.90	40.97	12	4	16
C 26– 50	3.45	2.54	83.57	72.89	11	3	14
B 11– 25	1.61	1.13	87.56	31.53	26	3	29
A 6– 10	1.14	0.77	103.49	84.57	7	2	9
TOTAL	1.94	1.99	73.58	59.48	72	16	88

* 'Unit' is average yearly production: Rs.966,814.
† See Appendix 11.1.

12 Women outworkers in the Neapolitan leather trade

VICTORIA GODDARD

In this chapter the relationship between households and the leather trade in Naples will be analysed. I begin by considering the role of women in the relations of co-operation within and between households, and how this contributes to the provision of outworkers to industry. A brief description of the specializations of women in the leather trade is followed by consideration of the conditions of outworkers in the trade. The question of the relationship between skills, education, and women's self-esteem is an important one, as is the question of the differential conditions affecting women and men who seek to establish autonomous units of production. However, these topics are only touched upon briefly; they are dealt with in greater detail elsewhere (Goddard, 1981; Goddard, 1988).

The Social Relations of Survival and the Household

The city of Naples is characterized by the importance of small units of production. In this respect, and in relation to the high levels of unemployment and underemployment, Naples reflects Italy's path of development. These conditions are associated with a bourgeoisie which is largely involved in unproductive activities, such as speculation in the building trade, and which relies heavily on the exploitation of cheap labour (Donolo, 1972).

It could be argued that, just as the bourgeoisie is 'unproductive', much of the working class is not directly involved in the production of commodities. The presence of a few large-scale enterprises cannot absorb the labour of the working-class population of the city. Unemployment is and has been a crucial factor in working-class life. Given the inadequacy of social services, individuals must find some channel for obtaining a livelihood. This may be an illegal or even dishonest channel; the options are limited.

But in addition to these activities there are also those which, although they too have been located within the 'informal sector', are clearly linked to the 'formal' economy: these are the small artisanal units, small sweat-shops often producing for large companies or large markets, with individual workers sewing bags, shoes, or gloves that may end up in an expensive shop in New York. These activities are linked to the wider economic activity of the city and the country as a whole through various forms of sub-contracting. The economic life of these Neapolitans has been described as the *economia del vicolo*; the economy of the alley (Allum, 1975). This descriptive term attempts to portray the survival of a fairly large number of people on perhaps a single income, which is redistributed in the immediate neighbourhood.

But this term fails to bring out the fact that in most cases the *vicolo* is not really cut off from the rest of the economic world; instead it is inserted into it in very specific ways: the inhabitants of the *vicolo* do not produce only for local consumption, they are often involved in production for larger markets, even for export. Thus, neither the *vicolo* nor the neighbourhood are the significant units. The activities that take place here are linked not only to the overall urban situation but also to national and international processes.

The Household

In the difficult economic circumstances which prevail in the city of Naples, households show considerable flexibility in arranging residence and commensality. Pooling of resources within the household is an important means of ensuring survival. The distribution of money and labour is carried out on the basis of an ideology of reciprocity. One of the most important economic consequences of pooling within households is that even very small monetary incomes become viable.

It is important to situate individuals within the context of the household. The diversification of work activities is a strategic choice which responds to the implementation of potential divisions of labour within the household. These divisions must in turn be seen in the light of significant contradictions between ideal gender roles and the real conditions of survival. Thus the adult man is ideally the breadwinner but an individual's expectations in this respect may be frustrated by the objective conditions of unemployment and precarious forms of employment. On the other hand adult women are defined principally as mothers and housewives yet they may be the sole providers over a long period of time.

These contradictions are dealt with through practice and ideology. In the case of contradictions in the male role, a man may combat the consequences of unemployment by becoming involved in myriad activities, while at the same time asserting his preferential position within the household by maintaining certain 'rituals of respect' and, often, by minimizing the contributions of other members, particularly wives. A possible solution is to set up a small business or workshop, frequently drawing on the labour of the household to do so.

Women reconcile the contradictory demands made on them by resorting to remunerative activities which allow them to stay at home, such as outwork and/or mobilizing a division of labour between the women of the household. Thus an elder daughter may take on the responsibility for household chores and child care, freeing her mother and other siblings for wage labour (or sometimes education). This has implications for training,

188

since particular household arrangements will determine that some daughters will receive training conducive to a relatively secure income while others, who have specialized as housewives, are likely to be forced at some future date into precarious and badly-paid unskilled work. This means that women constitute a particularly heterogeneous category of workers.

The availability of women in the labour market is, clearly, not a consequence of individual choice, but rather the outcome of adaptations to the labour market at the level of the household. Furthermore, women are constrained by gender relations which define certain areas of work as unsuitable for women, while others are considered to be particularly suitable. This is the case of outwork, favoured not only for the reasons described above, but in addition it is seen as safeguarding a woman's reputation (Goddard, 1987). Thus many women are pressured by husbands or boyfriends into opting for outwork.

Co-operation is the basis of the household's survival. But significant inequalities, both in terms of inputs of labour and money and in terms of the distribution of these resources, are built into this co-operation. Women bear the brunt of household labour; frequently they must make a monetary contribution as well. The division of labour among children is often unequal, the young ones benefiting from the sacrifices of older siblings. These inequalities generate conflicts and resentments that may simmer beneath the surface or may explode, causing serious rifts in the household and the family. The vagueness and the ambiguities detected in the statements of many Neapolitans regarding family and kin reflects these conflicts.

The Outworkers of Naples

An outworker, or a domestic industry worker, is defined in the trade union contract of the textile-clothing industry as any person who, within a subordinate relationship, carries out at home or at similar premises, work which is paid for by one or more entrepreneurs, with or without the help of family members or resident dependents but without the employment of wage labour or apprentices, using their own materials, accessories, instruments, or those supplied by the employer.

Outwork operates today in both underdeveloped economies and advanced capitalist societies that have already undergone the process of industrialization as a part of their history. Present-day domestic industry shares many characteristics with the form described for nineteenth century England. The most important point for comparison is the lack of independence of the worker. The worker may own his/her means of production or these may be owned by the employer. Generally raw materials are delivered by the representative(s) of one or more employer-units, who also collect the goods. Characteristically, the domestic unit carries out one phase of production, other phases being allotted to other domestic workers or carried out in the factory. The domestic industry worker has no control over the product; even when machinery is owned by the worker her/himself, s/he does not control the means of production: access to work and to raw materials is entirely mediated by an outside person, whether artisan, factory owner or merchant. The domestic industry worker is a proletarian operating outside the boundaries of the factory, and thus is labelled an 'outworker'.

In Italy outwork is distributed throughout the country, but it is especially important in the industrially developed areas of the north and centre, and in some southern areas, as, for example, Naples. Information on this form of production is lacking; it is 'invisible' in relation to official statistics. Therefore we are forced to rely on rather general inquiries, which of course apply only to specific areas. However, Talamo and De Marco (1975) quote national estimates of 1,100,000 outworkers for 1972; trade unions, on the other hand, estimate there are 1,800,000 workers.

Outwork is prevalent in what are described as 'traditional' industries: clothing, gloves, and shoes. However, it is also present in 'modern' industries. It is valid to argue that domestic industry is not a transitional form of production which gave way to factory production, but rather that it is an alternative form which, given its specific characteristics, may give way to, work in tandem with, or even supersede factory production in certain industries or phases of production at particular conjunctures.

These workers are closely linked not only to small-scale enterprises but, either directly or indirectly, to large enterprises and export markets. Even in the traditional sectors of production, domestic industry is frequently important in export-oriented concerns. In Naples, outwork industry is a common feature of the shoe and glove industries, which are very much geared to exports. In the glove industry, where exports are estimated to reach the value of 15,000 million Italian lire, the industry is suffering from the pressure of competition from Japan. In the textile and clothing industry of Carpi, especially knitted fashions, it is calculated that the total invoiced revenue for 1972 was 200,000 million lire, of which 126,500 million came from exports (about twenty per cent more than in 1971).

Outwork Production in Naples — The Shoe Industry

The shoe industry in Naples includes a number of very different types of production units. Some are large and modern and invest considerable capital in updating machinery. This is the case with the Valentino factory, which produces a high-quality shoe for Rome and other Italian cities, has its own shops in Naples, and also produces for export. At the other end of the scale is the small unit that uses labour-power, generally recruited through kinship, friendship, or neighbourhood ties. Machinery is often antiquated, perhaps bought second-hand from a factory where the owner/

190

boss was previously employed. These small units are unlikely to be able to accumulate enough capital to purchase more than sewing machines. Unequipped to perform a complete cycle of production, they are therefore likely to produce components for other, larger factories; in some cases they may produce a cheap shoe for local markets. Outworkers are used throughout this whole range of productive enterprises.

Although the full range of age-groups is represented in my own work and that of others, it appears that the age-group 'women over 25' predominates, followed by the 'very young' age group (10–15). The greater prevalence of the older age group can be explained in terms of the sexual division of labour, the organization of households, and the principal role allocated to women as housewives and mothers. The prevalence of the younger age group can be explained by the use of apprentices.

The women involved in outwork are poor working-class women. The majority are married or engaged to be married. The activity of the husband/fiancé varies. Menfolk vary from being factory workers (often in the same trade as their wives/fiancées) to being unemployed. Even where the husband is unemployed, he is likely to be involved in some kind of income-generating activity, however sporadic or unsatisfactory this may be. The important difference lies in the regularity and dependability of the man's income. Frequently the outworker's earnings are the only stable income for a household. However, we must also consider the factors of the consumption patterns and levels which a particular couple wishes to achieve: in some cases, the woman's contribution supplements a husband's wage and allows for an improved standard of living.

The sexual division of labour in the shoe industry parallels the situation in the majority of industries. Male tasks are considered to be highly skilled, and are better remunerated than the tasks carried out by women. Typically, male tasks are design, cutting, and pressing. Sewing, unless done by hand, is a female task, as is folding the leather and cleaning the shoe. Nevertheless, the trade is interesting in that it does allow for the development of highly skilled women, both within factories and as outworkers.

The main operations which are allotted to outside workers are the machine-sewing of the top parts of the shoes and the final cleaning of the finished shoe. The first operation is highly skilled, and most of the relatively very highly-paid outworkers belong to this category (*orlatrice*).

The orlatrice

This skill requires a long period of training (3–5 years), which is usually conducted by an outworker, who is likely to be a neighbour of kinswoman; training may continue in a factory or as an outworker.

This appears to be an old trade in Naples, especially in the old city, and in particular in the area known as Sanità. It is widespread nowadays and — presumably as a result of the movement of population from the centre to

191

the suburbs — it is now possible to find *orlatrici* in most working-class areas of the city. In fact the majority of outworkers encountered were *orlatrici*.

The trade is often passed on from mother to daughter; it has been a female trade since the introduction of the sewing machine. It was explained to me that it used to be a male trade when sewing was done by hand (in fact the only hand-sewing encountered was done by a man) and it 'became' female when the machine was introduced. No explanation was offered for this. Perhaps the sewing machine was associated with female work because of the garment industry, which characteristically employs women and where the machine was first introduced. Or perhaps the machines, being possessions of women, remained female property when converted for leather work, and therefore the task was transferred to women. Another possibility, related to the above suggestions, is that because it was associated with women through the garment industry the sewing machine was de-qualified, therefore becoming unsuitable for men (Elson & Pearson, 1978).

These workers show a great deal of pride in their skill and their product. Some may specialize in rare skills. For example, one woman had learnt a double-edge moccasin stitch which made her much sought-after. Many have had factory experience, and most of the better paid *orlatrici* had worked in factories.

Instruments consist of a sewing machine adapted for leather work, which in most cases belongs to the worker. In the case of older workers, their first machine was often a gift from their parents: a kind of dowry (*dote*) given to a young girl at the start of her career. This was important because in the old days workers had to bring their own tools to the factory or workshop. This *dote* later allowed these women to sell their old machines and buy newer, improved models, although most claimed, in retrospect, that the old ones had lasted longer and were far more reliable. Other workers obtain used machines from the factory via discounts from their wages as outworkers or for a net payment. Needless to say, from an entrepreneur's point of view this provides a good opportunity to get rid of worn or old machinery, while at the same time securing a hold on a worker. A third possibility is to purchase a machine on instalments from a shop.

The thread, which must match the leather, is usually supplied by the entrepreneur. Electricity costs and repairs to machinery are, in the vast majority of cases, covered by the worker. A driver, a relative or friend working inside the factory, or the entrepreneur himself may bring the pieces: the ready-cut pieces are delivered; collection of the finished 'upper' usually takes place a week later, as does payment. Payment is on a piece-rate basis per pair (*cottimo*). The rate of pay varies according to the model and generally the difficulty entailed in its preparation, the skill and reputation of the worker, and the financial means of the subcontractor. Generally speaking, outworkers receive a lower rate of pay than do factory workers. However, in this trade there were some very highly-skilled

192

women who received the same rate of pay as if they worked inside the factory.

Most *orlatrici* work with the assistance of apprentices, thus providing for the continuity of the trade and also increasing their own productivity. Apprentices receive very low wages — the general perception of their work is that they gain training in a useful skill, which justifies their low pay. Most women interviewed started training at about the age ten or eleven. Today, many girls start learning from their mothers or from a neighbour in a rather casual way, sitting near the worker, watching her and helping out. About age eleven or twelve they may be apprenticed out to a neighbour or relative on a more rigorous basis. Most complete school, at least up to the primary level. Many young girls thus divide their day between school and training as well as helping out at home, which is expected of most girls. Their training will be more or less arduous according to their teacher — most girls encountered quietly sat at the table concentrating on their work with very little to say, but in one case the apprentice seemed to spend more time playing with the *orlatrice*'s toddler than working on shoes (this activity was probably as useful to the *orlatrice* in question as the girl's leather work). As a girl reaches the age of fourteen to fifteen she is likely to dedicate her time exclusively to the trade, and may enter a workshop or factory where her apprenticeship will be continued (the legal working age in Italy is fifteen).

The *orlatrice*'s job is divided into two tasks: the first is folding and gluing the edges of the pieces of leather, making a hem; the second is the actual sewing of the pieces. The apprentice starts by learning to fold the edges tidily, and then to glue the edges and ensure that they are flattened, using a small hammer. In the first part of the operation young children (usually girls) often join in. After many years of perfecting this skill a girl may start to learn to use the machine. Although small boys may sit around a table where these activities are taking place, I never saw a boy actually doing this work, and no boy is ever apprenticed to this trade. Older men, trained under the less mechanized artisan structure, claim they know the entire process of production, including the work of the *orlatrice*.

Within the context of being a working-class woman in Naples, the trade of the *orlatrice* is considered to be prestigious. It is relatively well-paid and it has the appreciated advantage of allowing a woman to leave the factory and continue working at home. It is therefore considered to be a 'good trade' for a woman, although many *orlatrici* would wish their daughters to leave the ranks of manual labour altogether and become secretaries or teachers, professions which confer higher status and in addition are frequently better paid.

There is little doubt that *orlatrici* constitute the cream of the outworkers (and probably the ones with the greatest potential for organized action), and in fact their skills grant them considerable potential: in some cases *orlatrici* had organized a team of skilled and less skilled women, thus greatly increasing their production capacity, income-generating capacity and status *vis à vis* employers. Although single *orlatrici* often worked for more than one employer, teams were in a better position to do so. Clearly meeting the various requirements and deadlines of several employers requires considerable organizational skills.

The azzecatrice *or* apparecchitrice
The *azzecatrice* is less frequently an outworker than the *orlatrice*. Most seem to work inside the factory. The task of the *azzecatrice* requires a great deal of care and attention. Training, on the other hand, is less demanding than for the *orlatrice*. Generally speaking, apprenticeship takes one to two years, although some women claimed they had taken up to three years to learn the skill. Assistance is not so important here; therefore most *azzecatrici* work without apprentices.

The job of the *azzecatrice* consists of cleaning the shoe, removing traces of glue or paint and any other marks, ironing the leather into shape and packing the shoe in boxes. The equipment needed for this task is simple and inexpensive: some cottonwool, a solvent, and a special 'iron'.

The task is less prestigious and rates of pay are lower than for the *orlatrice*, but, because the task is accomplished more rapidly, a good *azzecatrice* can earn as much in a day as an *orlatrice*. However, the *azzecatrice* is not in a favourable position to set up a team of workers.

The Glove Industry

This industry, like the shoe industry, is a tradition in Naples. According to De Marco and Talamo (1976), 85 per cent of national production is carried out in this city. It is an industry which has experienced relatively little technological change since the introduction of the sewing machine. Much of production is geared to export, and consists of production of leather gloves (some of very fine quality), cloth gloves and ski gloves.

The degree of ancillarization in the trade is very high. Thus factories tend to be mere assembly and packing points, and the majority of units of production are very small units, consisting on an average of thirteen workers, as well as outworkers. Most workers carry out only one or two phases of the process of production. The sector employs a high percentage of female labour (85 per cent, per De Marco and Talamo) and the work of minors (61 per cent, per the same study).

The two 'female' tasks within the trade are sewing the pieces of the glove, a difficult job which requires care and skill; and ironing the finished product, which is in theory an easier task. However, the working conditions place demands on the women's ingenuity and skill. For example, one outworker had only one glove mould, for a size 37 glove, and used this same

194

mould to shape and iron all the sizes. In less skilful hands, this task would have been doomed to failure.

Because of the structure of the industry, very few factory jobs are available. In addition, rates of pay are fairly low, and the glove trade does not offer the same opportunities to women workers as the shoe trade. Nevertheless, the only woman outworker who knew the whole process of production was found in the glove trade.

Working conditions and health

The vast majority of workers carry out their productive activities in the same space that is used for eating, 'living' and often sleeping. For the most unskilled tasks, such as flower-making, the table used for work must be cleared and cleaned for the evening meal (the midday meal, if no adult male is present, may be snatched without much care). For other work involving machinery, e.g. that of the *orlatrici*, some degree of separation is required. This may, however, be minimal, especially in the case of the *bassi*.

The *bassi* of Naples have a bad reputation, and in general this is well deserved. The *bassi* usually consist of a single room into which a small kitchen and toilet have been inserted. In some cases the kitchen and toilet may be more separate, and in a few cases there is a second room (usually built over the main room) which is a bedroom. However, since the average population of each *basso* seems to be approximately four inhabitants, the 'front room' almost invariably doubles as a dining-living-bedroom and, where there is an outworker, as a work-room as well.

It is clear that outworkers and their families living in the *bassi* are those most affected by the inconvenience of work carried out in the home, and by the health hazards involved in many trades. Where leather is worked, dust and dirt are a problem, but the most serious health hazard is represented by the glue used in the leather trade (glue is also used in making flowers, but this seems to be a weaker, probably less dangerous type of glue) (De Marco and Talamo, 1976; Berlinger *et al.*, 1977).

The inhalation of glue fumes causes a disease of the central nervous system, which brings on headaches, dizziness, and paralysis. The number of cases of workers suffering from 'polyneuritis' as a result of using certain glues is rising in Italy. The figures may be misleading, since the disease has been (and often still is) misdiagnosed. Only since the mid-seventies have workers' protests, trade union action, and press reports made the disease a public issue. Contact with such glue and inhalation of the fumes can also provoke abortions and possibly malformations of the foetus in pregnant women, as well as the effects noted on the woman herself.

Most outworkers are by now aware of the dangers of glue, due to the publicity given to the problem in recent years. Those involved in the shoe trade as *orlatrici* may take some minimum precautions, such as keeping the

195

glue pot covered, using a brush rather than a finger to apply the glue, and keeping a door or a window open, in spite of the cold, to increase ventilation. But on the whole they express a fatalistic attitude: they must work, this is their job, the one they know, and they must face the risks. They may comfort themselves by saying that so far they have been all right, and therefore are unlikely to be affected. Some women who were not trained *orlatrici* said they would not wish to become involved in such work, even though it is reasonably paid, because of the dangers of the glue.

On the whole, those outworkers who do not live in the *bassi* have better working conditions, and those living in apartments tended to have a separate space or room to carry out their work. This meant that food did not come into contact with the dust and fumes of the work. However, where there were children, they played in the same room where their mother was working.

Problems of working conditions are not restricted to outworkers. In some factories, in response to pressure from workers or from the media, special extractors have been installed. But even such minimum precautions as providing gloves are ignored in most cases (and it must be said that the workers themselves are often reluctant to hamper their movements by using gloves). Management in most factories makes little attempt to ensure adequate ventilation, or to see that safer — and more expensive — glues are used, etc. The smaller and 'poorer' the unit of production, the greater the danger, since here workers will work in more cramped, less ventilated, and generally more dangerous conditions.

Although cases of disease due to the glue have been reported even from the most modern shoe factories, workers in small, cramped workshops and outworkers' premises are at greater risk. In addition, they do not have a trade union which they can pressure into political or legal action (as occurred with the workers from Valentino) against dangerous conditions or in the battle for compensation if they become ill. Their ailment is likely to pass unnoticed by all but themselves and their families. Furthermore, in the case of the outworker it is not only the worker herself who is at risk but her entire family. Small children play in the same room where their mother or aunt is working; babies are breast-fed near machinery and work instruments. Pregnant women work until the birth of their children. Small children, especially girls, help the adult women — and the stage in which they can help is precisely the stage which requires folding and gluing.

Women's Skills in the Leather Industry

Pride in one's ability is especially important where formal education is lacking. Very few of the women interviewed had gone beyond primary level schooling. Although few women expressed a wish to continue studying, those who had not been able to complete primary schooling or who had not been to school clearly felt this to be an impediment. It is perhaps no coincidence that it was these women who asserted their 'natural intelligence' by referring to their skill at work and the ease with which they had learnt their trade.

Having a skill which permits them to earn a regular income gives these women some degree of confidence. The more skilled women, who tended to be those most able to earn well and regularly, seemed to be the more confident. But in all cases women learned only one aspect of the trade in question — knowledge of the overall process of production was absent. Although there is an important gender-derived difference which has major implications for women's potential as entrepreneurs, nowadays that gap is narrowing, as fewer and fewer men train in the old artisan tradition; instead, they learn one isolated skill on the factory floor. However, it is still true that some men know the entire process of production, and under certain circumstances are able to organize an independent unit of production, whereas women never possess this knowledge. Their attempts at independence result in outworker teams.

It is clear that some women are interested in expanding their activities, and that this is most successfully done by establishing teams. Although the cases encountered were successful and required a great deal of organizational skill, they did not become independent in the same sense as most small artisans or other units — they were simply expanded outwork units. Further expansion is thus limited to multiplying the volume of work in the single task undertaken (Goddard, 1982).

Teams have certain advantages over single workers: their productivity is higher and they are able to work consistently for more than one employer. This means they are in a less vulnerable position *vis-à-vis* a particular entrepreneur. In addition, because they generally are built around a woman with special skills or much experience, it is in the interest of an entrepreneur to secure their work. Because other entrepreneurs are eager to contract for the team's labour, an entrepreneur may well decide it is to his advantage to make the organizer 'legal'. This means she will be covered by state provisions, rates of pay will be in accord with trade contracts, and, in addition, the entrepreneur may cover certain costs, such as electricity.

Knowledge regarding the organization of the trade varies. Some women were able to describe the way their trade works in considerable detail. Also, some knew a good deal about the factories they worked for: name, owners, turnover, markets, etc. However, these were the exceptions; in some cases nothing at all appeared to be known about the employer. Of course many women would be reluctant to reveal a name or any detail regarding their employer, for fear of losing their work, should this be discovered.

Conclusion

The importance of outwork in the Neapolitan context must be understood in relation to the strategies adopted by individual households. For these

197

households, in the absence of an economic structure that guarantees secure and adequately remunerated employment, outwork represents a crucial option. Thus for some households the outworker is the only steady contributor. Alternatively, her income may supplement the inadequate wages of one or more other households members. In yet other cases, the income provided by outwork may enable a household to indulge in extra expenses, such as a car, domestic appliances, or a better standard of living and better educational opportunities for the children.

Relations within the household and the division of labour between household members are important factors in determining the availability of certain kinds of labour-power. Given that women are expected to undertake heavy responsibilities as wives and mothers, their possibilities for generating income are limited. Outwork offers the important advantage of flexibility in a woman's organization of time and energy. The amount of time she can dedicate to outwork will depend on the arrangements that can be made within or between households for the care of children, for cooking, cleaning, shopping, and so forth. Gender relations dictate that these arrangements will be made by women; men will not be included.

Gender relations can also affect the choice between outwork and factory work: men's attitudes to women's work can represent an obstacle to work outside the home or outside a kinship or pseudo-kinship context. Thus, young women who as yet have little or no responsibility for household chores may decide in favour of outwork. Ideological factors, as well as the organization of tasks within the household, are a crucial component of the process whereby women make choices in relation to work (Goddard, 1988).

Training in outwork provides skills which frequently feed into factory work. Although some workers in the shoe trade are trained within a factory, most are trained by outworkers, or sometimes in workshops. This means that the costs of training are often not met by the factories. There is some indication that outworkers provide better training than either a workshop or a factory apprenticeship.

Acquiring skills in a trade provides an alternative to formal education. Given the economic conditions that prevail in Italy, and in Naples in particular, a saleable skill is a valid and sensible alternative. However, the education system is still seen by many as a means of social advancement, and at least some parents attempted to ensure that their children both completed schooling and learnt a trade. Many young couples said they would prefer to limit family size in order to ensure a better future for their children.

In those cases where formal education was lacking, or where schooling had been brief and inadequate with regard to basic skills, achievement in a work situation was important for self-esteem and personal evaluation. In particular, those women who had no schooling assessed their intellectual capabilities positively on the basis of their performance at work. Personal satisfaction and pride also relate to the nature of the product. In cases where the product was ugly or of low quality, women felt depressed about their work, and were more reluctant to work than if they had been working on a better product.

This chapter suggests the ways in which social factors (such as household organisation and neighbourhood relations) and ideological factors (such as gender relation, and definitions of work and skill) are central to economic processes such as the organization of production within the Neapolitan leather trade. For example, kinship and other personal relations and networks are important in the organization of outwork. These relations are a resource in the recruitment of workers, the distribution of work from the factories or workshops to the individual outworkers, and the recruitment of apprentices. The 'economic' behaviour of women workers in particular is determined by 'extra-economic' relations and processes. These determine not only the objective conditions of participation in the economic process, but also the subjective conditions which have an impact on the extent of specific types of labour.

Notes

Chapter 1
1. Streefkerk, 1985; Schmitz, 1982, 1990; Carr, 1984; Holmström, 1984.
2. ILO, 1986; UNDP/UNIDO/Gov. of the Netherlands, 1988; AID, 1983, 1985, 1986; IOV, 1988.
3. Heyzer, 1981; IDS Bulletin, 1981; Singh and Kelles-Viitanen, 1987.
4. Carr, 1984; Baud, 1983; Beneria and Roldan, 1987; Alonso, 1983; Pineda-Ofreneo, 1982.
5. This can be seen from the number of conferences organized by donor agencies recently: The *International Seminar on Women in Micro and Small Scale Enterprise Development* held in Canada in 1987; the international conference on *Policy Approaches toward Technology and Small Enterprise Development* held in 1989 in the Hague (hosted by the Institute of Social Studies, Appropriate Technology International and Queen Elizabeth House, Oxford), and the *Workshop on Small Scale Enterprise Development, in Search of New Dutch Approach* in 1989 (hosted by the Dutch Ministry of Foreign Affairs — Directorate General International Cooperation).
6. Agro-industries are defined as those based on the transformation of agricultural products: textiles, clothing, leather goods and shoes, and food-processing.
7. As an exception, see the chapter on the footwear industry in Mexico in *Forms of Production and Women's Labour* (Baud, 1991).
8. A great deal has been written on the external relations of micro and small-scale enterprises from the point of view of donor agencies (or countries) who give supply side support to such enterprises (cf. Dessing/World Bank, 1990; Levitsky, 1989; Gosses *et al.*, 1989). A certain amount has also been written from a bottom/up approach, particularly with respect to projects for women (Chambers, 1983).
9. A good overview of the literature on small-scale and micro-enterprise from an employment perspective is given in *Labour and Work in Small-Scale Enterprises*, Working paper series no. 79, ISS, by H. Thomas (1990).
10. This project is being carried out by the University of Amsterdam, Department of Human Geography (Isa Baud), and the Central Leather Research Institute in Madras (K.S. Rao), with the help of a nine-member team. Final results are expected in 1992.

Chapter 2
1. The advantages of disequilibrium have been a subject of development thought since Schumpeter first published his *Theory of Economic Development* even before the First World War (1913). Perroux later transformed Schumpeter's dynamic entrepreneur into the heart of his growth-pole approach — 'industrie motrice' in '*Notes sur la Pole de Croissance*' (1955), which in turn was taken up by Hirschman in his system of forward and backward linkages (*The Strategy of Economic Development, 1958*). A useful summary of this line of thought is found in Charles Gore (*Regions in Question*, 1984, Methuen, London, Chapter 3).
2. USAID sponsored research in this field is an ongoing activity at Michigan State University, under the direction of Carl Liedholm. A major publication is: C. Liedholm and D. Mead, *Small Scale Industries in Developing Countries: Em-*

pirical Evidence and Policy Implications, East Lancing, Mich, 1987. USAID also organized an international conference on small enterprise development in Washington DC in June 1988, the proceedings of which have been published in Levitsky, J. (ed.), *Microenterprises in Developing Countries* (1989). World Bank sponsored studies include: Little, I.M.D., Mazumdar, D. and Page, J.: *Small Manufacturing Enterprises: A Comparative Study of India and Other Countries*, OUP, New York, 1987; Cortes, M., Berry, A. and Ishaq, A.: *Success in Small and Medium Scale Enterprises*, OUP, New York, 1987; Suri, K.B. (ed.) *Small Scale Enterprises in Industrial Development*, New Delhi, Sage, 1988).
3. Liedholm and Mead op.cit.; Berry, A.: 'The limited role of rural small scale manufacturing for late-comers: some hypotheses on the Colombian experience', *Journal of Latin American Studies*, Vol.19, pp.295–322.
4. These definitions are used by Liedholm and Mead, op.cit.
5. *Inter alia*, in Seers, D. *The Meaning of Development* in Nancy Bastor [ed.], *Measuring Development*, 1972. These ideas were eloquently presented by Seers at the SID World Conference in New Delhi in 1969.
6. de Soto, H., *El Otro Sendero*, Lima, 1987. This book was a major focal point at the USAID conference in Washington mentioned in note 2. (de Soto, H., *The Other Path*, Perennial Library, 1990).
7. Little *et al.*, Suri (ed.), op.cit.
8. Keddie, Nanjundan and Teszler: UNIDO/RSIE Report on Tanzania, published by ILO.

Chapter 4

1. There is an extensive literature about the labour process, beginning with Braverman's pathbreaking but fundamentalist 1974 study. This includes: Palloix, 1976; Brighton Labour Process Group, 1977; Friedman, 1977, 1985; Coombs, 1978; Burawoy, 1978; Cutler, 1978; Taylor, 1979; Elgar, 1979; Zimbalist, 1979; Littler, 1978, 1982a, 1982b; Stark, 1980; Lee, 1981; Wood, 1983.
2. I have deliberately avoided making reference to a 'materially-poorer' or 'underdeveloped' society. England simply conceals from view much of its currently existing less savoury industrial working conditions and highly exploitative social relations. But they exist — particularly poorly-paid, piece-rated women workers. Visit Leicester or the East End of London garment 'sweat-shops' for instance (see Mitter, 1986). Tiruppur is a monument not to underdevelopment, but to uneven development.
3. Directorate of Industries and Commerce (1980), 'Directory of Tamil Nadu Small Scale Industrial Units for Coimbatore', pp.8-20 and 21-66.
4. I was told that there were at least twenty different foreign buyers in Tiruppur at the time of fieldwork in 1986–7.
5. Separate housing areas for people belonging to 'untouchable' castes.
6. 'Water from the Noyyal is very well-suited for bleaching, and produces a very white cloth useful for the banians' (interview with the owner of General Textiles, 1986).
7. The South Indian Millowners Association (SIMA) keeps detailed statistical records of yarn production in the privately owned mill sector, as does the National Textile Corporation (NTC) for public-sector mills. The point to remember, however, is that the mill sector is responsible for practically all spun yarn, apart from small-scale quantities of hand-spun yarn used for the production of *khadi* (woven cloth made from hand-spun yarn).
8. This is part of state policies aimed at promoting 'small-scale' industrial sectors.

201

9. Petty commodity production has tended to be characterized as a transitional mode between feudal and other non-capitalist (peasant) modes and the capitalist mode of production (in which the capital/wage relation is not clear-cut). In the former, the cyclical nature of the productive forces are characteristic compared to the revolutionary development of the latter: expanded reproduction of capital. Harriss (1982) distinguishes between a traditional petty commodity producer and a 'modern' petty commodity producer in his study of small-scale production in nearby Coimbatore, and, in this sense, the petty producers in Tiruppur are clearly 'modern', in that the industrial activity is recent. But the question of transition is altogether more problematic. For an iconoclastic discussion of petty commodity production see 'Capitalism and petty commodity production' by Henry Bernstein, DPP Working Paper No. 3, 1987.

10. This leasing system, however, was not usual. In all other cases where units of production were similarly separated (with subcontractors in charge), raw materials and machinery simply belonged to the 'parent' firms.

11. He nevertheless sees himself as an 'indirect employer' of labour in those enterprises. (His own labour force totals 115, of which the majority are men (approximately 80). Of these, 15 are office staff, who are paid a monthly salary. All others are on piece-rates, with the exception of those working in the dyeing section.

12. This is very unusual for a 'small-scale' — therefore unregulated — sector of industry. Both the CITU (CPI(M)) affiliated union and the AITUC (CPI) had been — to some extent — successfully active in Tiruppur for many years. The only Communist candidate in the Tamil Nadu State Legislature was elected from Tiruppur.

13. The higher the yarn count, the finer the fabric produced. The most common counts are 20s and 40s. The different kinds of fabric are: single-jersey, double-jersey, rib-knitted; interlock; and a variety of patterned fabric which is known in the west as Aertex (called eyelet in Tiruppur).

14. Littler (1982) calls this a weak version of a social construction hypothesis, by which he means that there is always a way in which seemingly objectively determined characteristics (of a job) conceal, as it were, the way in which decisions about those characteristics and labels such as 'skilled' or 'semi-skilled' come into existence: 'Nearly all skilled jobs have some objective skill content but ... it is strategic position within the production process combined with collective organization which gains the occupation a skill label' (p.9).

15. There are three main kinds of stitching or sewing machine: overlock, chainlock and flatlock. In addition there are separate machines for button-holing (sometimes subcontracted out to workshops), and sewing on buttons and labels. There are also hydraulic presses for flattening the garments before packing.

16. This is a reversal of the gender division of labour in the garment industry in the UK. However, in India this represents a closer link with an artisanal past, when tailors (doing what would be called 'bespoke' tailoring) were always men and small-scale tailors' shops abounded in all urban areas.

17. The gender division of labour for non-household industry in Tiruppur according to census figures in 1971 and 1981 respectively were: 83 per cent men and 16.5 per cent women, and 81 per cent men and 18 per cent women. Thus there was only a slight increase over an approximately fifteen-year period.

18. 'Report on work load studies at banian factories in Tiruppur', Madras Productivity Council, 1972.

19. The only exception was workers in the dyeing plants, who were paid monthly salaries. Their jobs were considered highly skilled and also interesting, because

these workers were using some of the most sophisticated machinery in the industry.

20. Gentex comprised six production units, all registered separately as SSIs with the DIC in Coimbatore, but none under the Factories Inspectorate despite a (probably understated) total of more than 165 employees. Loganathan (the owner) also owned a making-up unit in a village (Pulliampatti) about thirty kilometres from Tiruppur, which only employs women and children (sixty women and forty children). He set up this unit during the strike in 1984. 'It is a good way to get labour even cheaper, because women workers are cheaper than men, and they want work in the villages'. The supervisor/contractor of this unit was one of the people who left to set up his own business.

21. Smitu Kothari (1983) 'There's blood on those matchsticks', July 2, Economic and Political Weekly.

22. The truth is that there is no accurate way to assess the numbers of people employed in this industry. The 1981 Census does not disaggregate the four sectors of construction, trade and commerce, transport, and storage and communications and other services. Thus no comparison with the 1971 figures (except in the aggregate) can be made. The other two main sources of information, the Factories Inspectorate Lists and the registrations with the Directorate of Industries and Commerce (particularly the latter), drastically understate the numbers employed. An indication of the extent of the inaccuracy of the registration is revealed by a comparison of the approximate numbers employed across 69 units of production (all units in my 25 firm sample). These came to 3500, against the officially recorded figures of those employed listed in DIC records in 1985 of 11,073 for 1915 units!

23. During fieldwork I lived with a family who owned a knitting enterprise. The owner had been given an order for a German company (through an agent in Bombay) and had trouble getting the T-shirts dyed the right colour. He ran out of time, and the children working in his workshop (along with all the other workers) worked between eighteen and twenty hours each day for a total of five days to finish packing all the goods. The irony in this case was that in the end he had to air-freight the order, which cost so much that all the profit on this particular deal was wiped out.

24. See Pearson and Elson, 1984; Lamphere, in Zimbalist (ed.), 1979; and Open University Third World Studies Case Study 7, 1983.

25. 20s up to 26s (motta varieties); 26s up to 34s (medium varieties); and 36s and above (fine varieties). Madras Productivity Council, 1972.

26. Marx, K. (1976) *Capital*, Vol.1, Penguin, pp.695–8.

27. Having said that, it is not possible to establish from the data collected whether this is because they work, on the whole, fewer hours than men, receive lower piece-rates or whether their lower wages are due to a combination of both these factors.

Chapter 6

1. In 1982 Rp.1200 had approximately the value of £1.00. It is also relevant to note at the time the price of one kilogram of rice averaged Rp.250.

2. The Marriage Law of 1974 (Ordnance no. 1) sets the minimum age for women at sixteen at sixteen and for men at nineteen.

3. In Indonesia as a whole, the Muslim population has a high divorce rate: 58 per cent.

4. The village is only fifteen kilometres from an active volcano, Mt. Galunggung. This erupted several time in 1982–3, causing a considerable amount of damage and disruption.
5. For a discussion of this point see Manderson (1974:89) and Sisworahardyo (1979:9).
6. See also Djuriah (1981:95).

Chapter 7
1. The SADCC countries include Tanzania, Zambia, Lesotho, Botswana, Malawi, Angola, Mozambique and Zimbabwe.
2. This meeting was organized jointly by SEDCO, Zimbabwe and the United Nations Development Fund for Women (UNIFEM), with funds from the SADCC section of the Canadian High Commission, Zimbabwe.

Chapter 11
1. This research is reported in Waardenburg (1988). It has triggered a number of M.A. thesis studies, notably by Romijn (1982), Leest (1984), van den Honing (1986), Tejani (1987), Horikx (1987), and de Jong (1988). Tables given provide additional data from this study.
2. For related data, see Mukerji (1980) and UPICO (1981); for an anthropological political analysis of the position of the Chamars, see Lynch (1974).
3. See Srivastava (1979) and Dhir (1968).
4. Further figures on the kind of data discussed here are given in Appendixes 11.1, and 11.2; the first table uses the concept of output per day, instead of output per year as used in Table 11.2 and in the above text. In general, one may say that using 'output per day' puts the specific marketing difficulties of certain categories out of sight. For further comparison of these data and further discussion, see Waardenburg (1988). To provide an overview, average values for the indicators employment/output ratio and capital/output ratio from App. 11.2 are plotted in Figure 11.1 for each category.
5. Notice, however, in App. 11.2 the very large fluctuations in the capital/output ratio around the average. This indicates not only variations in product quality, but also the presence of some relatively very capital-intensive units, which actually have low production and efficiency. As the calculation of these averages does not weight the individual figures according to output, somewhat strange outcomes may result.
6. In any case, the large national firms and their ancillaries have their own separate selling networks with better quality guarantees. Romijn (1982) estimates a profit rate of just below twenty per cent for the ancillaries, compared to just above ten per cent for these 'national' units.
7. There are several hundred such traders. Raw material traders and money-changers are also available on the spot in Hing Ki Mandi. This market has been extensively described by Romijn (1982).
8. Note that measuring size in terms of production is different from defining size in terms of number of employees. Note also the difference in measuring production by pairs of shoes instead of by the total production value, even though qualitatively the two measures are more or less the same. In this paper, 'output' always refers to total value of production.

9. Again we limit ourselves to data in which output is measured in terms of production per year, though the categories are defined in terms of the number of pairs produced daily.
10. This section is largely based on the MA thesis of Leest (1984).
11. The level of production above which economies of scale are no longer present depends also on the technology or degree of mechanization of the production process. With the far more mechanized methods used in developed countries this level may be between 1200 and 7000 pairs per day. See McBain (1977).
12. This may be the reason van Heemst (1982) found optimum sizes for footwear units in Ghana to be more than 1000 pairs: they included marketing functions. See also McBain (1977) and Kuyvenhoven (1980).
13. With the exception of exporting units.
14. It should be understood that units are categorized according to their dominant marketing channel. As there may be secondary marketing channels which are hardly less important for a unit than the dominant one, 'mixed' cases exist. 'Supplying the Government' is not involved in such mixed cases, nor do 'small' units have secondary channels. But 'marketing outside Agra' and 'acting as supplier to UPLDMC' are relatively frequent secondary channels, especially for 'exporters' and for 'large local' units.
15. The labour conditions and relations within the units of the categories 'outside suppliers' and 'small local' or *dalia walas* are in many respects not essentially different from those of units in the other marketing categories, and we will not discuss them separately.
16. In such cases, manufacturers keep them attached to their units by paying 'advances' on their future wages.
17. This applies also to workers or artisans in non-contract units.
18. This is mentioned by Leest (1984).
19. See United Nations (1974) and Paine (1971).
20. See Mies (1970), ILO (1974), and Vaid (1966).

References

AID, (1983), *The Evaluation of Small Enterprise Programs and Projects: Issues in Business and Community Development,* (Evaluation Special Study no. 13). AID, Washington, DC.

AID, (1985), *Private Voluntary Organization and the Promotion of Small-scale Enterprise,* (Special Evaluation Study no. 27), Washington DC.

AID, (1986), *Promoting Appropriate Technological Change in Small-scale Enterprises: an evaluation of Appropriate Technology International,* (Special Evaluation Study no. 45), Washington, DC.

Alba Vega, C. and Kruijt, D. (1988), *Los Empresarios y la Industria de Guadalajara,* Colegio de Jalisco, Guadalajara.

Alonso, J., (1981), 'The Domestic Clothing Worker in the Mexican Metropolis and their Relationship to Dependent Capitalism', in J. Nash and M.P. Fernandez-Kelly (eds.), *Women, Men and the International Division of Labour.*

Alchian, A.A. and Woodward, S. (1988), 'The firm is dead; long live the firm. A review of Oliver E. Williamson's The Economic Institutions of Capitalism', *Journal of Economic Literature,* Vol. XXVI, pp.65–79.

Allum, P. (1975), *Potere e Società a Napoli nel Dopoguerra,* Einaudi Editori, Torino.

Annavajhula, J.C.B., (1989), 'Japanese subcontracting systems', *Economic and Political Weekly,* Feb.25, pp.M–15–M–23.

Auciello, K.E., (1975), *Employment Generation through Stimulation of SSI, an International Compilation of SSI Definitions,* Atlanta, Georgia Institute of Technology.

Baker, C.J., (1984), *An Indian Rural Economy 1880–1955. The Tamilnadu Countryside,* Clarendon Press, Oxford.

Banerjee, N., (1990), *Indian Women in a Changing Industrial Scenario,* Sage, New Delhi.

Banerjee, N., (1983), *Role of Women in Export-Oriented Industries: Five Case-studies of West Bengal,* ICCSSR, New Delhi.

Barrett, M., (1980), *Women's Oppression Today,* Verso Ed., London.

Bastor, N., (1972), *Measuring Development,* UNRISD, Geneva.

Baud, I., (1983), *Women's Labor in the Indian Textile Industry,* IRIS Publication, No. 22, IVO, Tilburg.

Baud, I., (1991), *Forms of Production and Women's Labour: Gender Aspects of Industrialization in India and Mexico,* Sage, New Delhi.

Belmonte, T., (1979), *The Broken Fountain,* NY, Columbia University Press.

Beneria, L., (1978), *Reproduction, Production and the Sexual Division of Labour,* ILO/WEP, Geneva.

Beneria, L. and Roldan, M., (1987), *The Crossroads of Class and Gender, Industrial Homework, Subcontracting, and Household Dynamics in Mexico City,* Chicago University Press, Chicago and London.

Beneria, L. and Sen, G., (1981), 'Accumulation, reproduction, and women's role in economic development: Boserup revisited', *Signs*, Vol.7, No.2, pp.279–98.

Berlinguer, G., Cecchini, L. and Terranova, F. (eds.), (1977), *Gli Infortuni sul Lavoro dei Minori*, Roma, Il Pensiero Scientifico.

Bernstein, H., (1987), *Capitalism and petty commodity production*, DPP Working Paper No.3, Open University, Milton Keynes.

Biro Pusat Statistik, (1982), *Ulusan Singkat Hasil Sensus Penduduk 1980*, Jakarta.

Boserup, E., (1970), *Women's Role in Economic Development*, New York, St. Martin's Press.

Braverman, H. (1974), *Labor and Monopoly Capital. The Degradation of Work in the Twentieth Century*, Monthly Review Press, New York and London.

Breman, J., (1985), *Of Peasants, migrants, and Paupers; Rural Labour Circulation and Capitalist Production in West India*. Oxford University Press, Delhi.

Brighton Labour Process Group, (1977), 'The capitalist labour process', *Capital and Class*, Vol.1, pp.3–26.

Bromley, R. and Gerry, C., (1979), *Casual Work and Poverty in Third World Cities*, Wiley and Sons, Chichester.

Buroway, M., (1978), 'Towards a Marxist theory of the labor process: Braverman and beyond', *Politics and Society*, Vol.8, No.3–4, pp.247–312.

Business India, (1984), 'Troubles at Tiruppur: an end to cheap labour', Bombay.

Caplan, P., (1985), *Class and Gender in India: Women and their Organisation in a South Indian City*, Tavistock, London.

Carr, M., (1984), *Blacksmith, Baker, Roofing-sheet Maker: Employment for rural women in developing countries*, Intermediate Technology Publications, London.

Carr, M., (1988), *Sustainable Industrial Development*, Intermediate Technology Publications, London.

Chambers, R. *et al.*, (1990), *To the Hands of the Poor: Water and trees*, Intermediate Technology Publications, London.

Chambers, R., (1984), *Rural Development: Putting the last first*, Longman, Harlow.

Chant, S., (1985), 'Single-parent families: choice or constraint? The formation of female-headed households in Mexican shanty towns', *Development and Change*, Vol.16, pp.635–656.

Chen, M., (1989), 'Women and Entrepreneurship: New Approaches from India', paper presented to workshop on small-scale enterprise development 'In Search of New Dutch Approaches', The Hague.

Collier, W.L., (1981), 'Agricultural Evolution in Java', In G. Hansen (ed.) *Agricultural and Rural Development in Java*, Westview Special Studies in Social Political and Economic Development, Boulder.

Coombs, R., (1978), 'Labour and monopoly capital' (review article), *New Left Review*, 107, Jan.–Feb., pp.79–86.

Cortes, M. *et al.*, (1987), *Success in Small and Medium-scale Enterprises: the evidence from Colombia*, OUP, New York.

Cutler, T, (1978), 'The romance of labour', *Economy and Society*, Vol.7, No.1, pp.74–95.

De Marco, C. and Talamo, M. (1976), *Lavoro Nero, Decentramento Produttivo e Lavoro a Domicilio*, Milano, Mazzotta Ed.

de Soto, H., (1990), *The Other Path: the invisible revolution in the Third World*, Perennial Library, New York.

Desai, N. and Gopalan, P., (1983), *Changes in the Food-Processing Industry from Traditional and Modern Forms and its Impact on Women's Role and Status*, ICSSR, New Delhi.

Dessing, M., (1990), *Support for Microenterprises, Lessons for Sub-Saharan Africa*, World Bank, Washington, DC.

Dhir, S.P., (1968), *A Brief History of Footwear Industry in Agra*, Agra.

Djuaria, M.U., (1981), *Pengaruh Kerabat Terhadap Kawin Muda Masyarakat Sunda*, Universitas Padjadjaran.

Donolo, C., (1972), 'Sviluppo ineguale e disgregazione sociale in Meridione', *Quaderni Piacentini*, No.47.

Dwyer, D. and Bruce, J., (1988), *A Home Divided: Women and income in the third world*, Stanford University Press.

Eisold, E., (1984), *Young Women Workers in Export Industries: The Case of the Semiconductors Industry in South East Asia*, ILO/WEP, Geneva.

Elger, T., (1979), 'Valorisation and de-skilling: a critique of Braverman', *Capital and Class*, Vol.7, pp.58–99.

Elson, D. and Pearson, R., (1981), *The Subordination of Women and the Internationalisation of Capital* in K. Young et al. (ed.), *Of Marriage and the Market*, CSE Press, London.

Everett, J. and Savara, M., (1987), 'Institutional Credit as a Strategy toward Self-reliance for Petty Commodity Producers in India: a critical Evaluation' in A. Singh and A. Kelles-Viitanen (eds) *Invisible Hands, Women in Home-based Production*, Sage, New Delhi.

Friedman, A., (1977), *Industry and Labour*, Macmillan, London.

Friedman, A., (1985), 'Managerial Strategies, Activities, Techniques and Technology: Towards a Complex Theory of the Labour Process', Unpublished draft paper, University of Bristol.

Geertz, H., (1961), *The Javanese Family*, The Free Press of Glencoe.

Goddard, V., (1981), 'The leather trade in the bassi of Naples', *IDS Bulletin, Women and the informal sector*, Vol.12, No.3.

Goddard, V., (1987), 'Honour and shame: the control of women's sexuality in Jamaica', In P. Caplan (ed.), *The Cultural Construction of Sexuality*, Tavistock, London.

Goddard, V., (1988), 'Women and Work: the Case of Neapolitan Outworkers', Unpublished doctoral thesis, University of London.

Gore, C. (1984), *Regions in Question*, Methuen, London and New York.

Gosses, A. *et al.*, (1990), *Small scale Enterprise Development: in search of new Alternatives*, Proceedings of a workshop, the Hague.

Government of India, (1971), *Series 19 Village and Townwise Primary Census*, Coimbatore District.

Government of India, (1988), *National Perspective Plan on Women*, Dept. of Women and Child Development.

Government of India, (1981), *Series 20 Tamil Nadu General Population Tables.*

Griffin, K., (1989), *Alternative Strategies for Economic Development*, Macmillan, London, Chapter 5.

Grown, C. and Sebstadt, J., (1989), 'Introduction: Toward a Wider Perspective on Women's Employment' in *World Development*, Vol.17, No.7, pp.937–52.

Haldi, J. and Whitcomb, D., (1967), 'Economies of scale in industrial plants', *Journal of Political Economy*, Vol.75, pp.373–85.

Harris, O., (1981), 'Households as Natural Units', in K. Young *et al.* (eds), *Of Marriage and the Market*, CSE Books, London.

Harriss, J., (1982), 'Character of an urban economy. Small scale production and labour markets in Coimbatore', *Economic and Political Weekly*, Vol.XVII, Nos.23 and 24, June 5 and 12.

Hernandez A. and Paz, E. de la, (1983), 'Las Adornadoras en Guadalajara, Condiciones de Trabajo y Salud', unpublished BA thesis, University of Guadalajara, Jalisco.

Hirscham, C., (n.d.), 'Premarital Socio-economic Roles and the Timing of Family Formation: Comparative Study of Five Asian Societies', Cornell University, Ithaca.

Hirschman, A.O., (1958), *The Strategy of Economic Development*, Yale University Press, London.

Holmström, M., (1984), *Industry and Inequality: the Social Anthropology of Indian Labour*, Cambridge University Press, Cambridge.

Honing, I. van den, (1986), 'De kleinschalige schoenindustrie – Agra, India: Het kapitaalgebruik en ontwikkelingen in 1980–1984', unpublished MA thesis, EUR Rotterdam.

Horikx, J.M.J., (1987), '*Een onderzoek naar associatie tussen nominale data, toegepast op gegevens uit Kanpur en Agra, India*', unpublished MA thesis, EUR, Rotterdam.

Husken, F., (1979), 'Landlords, sharecroppers and agricultural labourers: changing labour relations in rural Java', *Journal of Contemporary Asia*, Vol.9, No.2.

IDS Bulletin, (1981), 'Women in the Informal Sector', IDS, Sussex.

IDS Bulletin, (1991), 'Researching the Household: methodological and empirical issues', Vol.22, No.1.

IOV, (1988), *Women Entrepreneurs*, Operations Review Unit, the Hague.

Jong, M. de, (1988), *The Interaction between the Indian Government and the Small Scale Footwear Manufacturing Industry in Agra, India*, unpublished MA thesis, EUR, Rotterdam.

Joshi, H. and Joshi, V., (1976), *Surplus Labour and the City: A study of Bombay*, Delhi.

Kartini Raden Adjeng, (1921), *Letters of a Javanese Princess*, Duckworth and Co., London.

Knorringa, P., (1988), 'Subcontracting as a Mechanism of Growth and Dependence: Small Scale and Home Based Producers in India', University of Amsterdam, Dept. of Development Economics, mimeograph.

Koentjaraningrat (1967), 'A Village in South Central Java', in Koentjaraningrat (ed.), *Villages in Java*, Cornell University Press, Ithaca.

Kothari, S., (1982), 'There's blood on those matchsticks', *Economic and Political Weekly*, July 2, pp.1191–1202.

Kuyvenhoven, A., (1980), *Technology, Employment and Basic Needs in Leather Industries in Developing Countries*, Centre for Development, Planning Discussion Paper No. 51, Erasmus University, Rotterdam.

Langlois, R.N., (1988), 'Economic change and the boundaries of the firm', *Journal of Institutional and Theoretical Economics*, Vol.144, pp.635–57.

Lazonick W., (1979), 'Industrial relations and technical change: the case of the self-acting mule', *Cambridge Journal of Economics*, Vol.3, pp.231–62.

Lee, D.J., (1981), 'Skill, craft and class: a theoretical critique and a critical case', *Sociology*, Vol.15, pp.56–78.

Leest, G.A., (1984), *The Trade-, (Sub)Contracting-, and Employment Relations in the Small Scale Footwear Industry of Agra, India*, unpublished MA thesis, EUR, Rotterdam.

Levitsky, J., (1989), *Microenterprises in Developing Countries*, IT Publications, London.

Liedholm, C. and Mead, D., (1987), '*Small scale Industries in Developing Countries: Empirical Evidence and Policy Implications*', MSU Internal Development Paper No.9, MSU, East Lansing.

Little, I.M.D. *et al.*, (1987), *Small Manufacturing Enterprises: A comparative study of India and other countries*, OUP.

Littler, C.R., (1978), 'Understanding Taylorism', *British Journal of Sociology*, Vol.29, No.2, pp.185–202.

Littler, C.R., and Salaman, S., (1982), 'Bravermania and beyond: recent theories of the labour process', *Sociology*, Vol.16, No.4, pp.251–69.

Littler, C.R., (1982), *The Development of the Labour Process in Capitalist Societies*, Heinemann Educational Books, London.

Littler, C., (1982), 'Deskilling and Changing Structures of Control', in S. Wood, *The Degradation of Work*, Hutchinson, London, pp.122–209.

Lynch, O.M., (1974), *The Politics of Untouchability; Social Mobility and Social Change in a City*, National Publishing House, Delhi.

MacEwen Scott, A., (1986), 'Women and industrialisation: examining the "female marginalisation thesis"', *Journal of Development Studies*, Vol.22, No.4, pp.649–70.

Mackie, J.W., (1981), *The chief inspector of factories list as a source of data on the distribution of industry in Tamil Nadu, South India*, SOAS Occasional Paper No.4 (New Series), SOAS, London.

Manderson, L. (eds), (1983), *Women's Work and Women's Roles: Economics and Everyday Life in Indonesia, Malaysia and Singapore*, ANU, Canberra.

Mantoux, P., (1928), *The Industrial Revolution in the Eighteenth Century: An Outline of the Beginning of the Modern Factory in England*, trs. M. Vernon, Cape, London.

Marx, C., (1976), *Capital*, Vol.I, Penguin.

Mather, C., (1983), 'Industrialisation in the Tanggerang Regency of West Java: women workers and the Islamic patriarchy', *Bulletin of Concerned Asian Scholars*, Vol.15, No.2.

Mathew, M., (1983), *Women Workers in Food Processing Industry in Kerala*, ICCSSR, New Delhi.

Mazumdar, D., (1984), *The issue of small scale vs large in the Indian textile industry*, World Bank Working Paper No. 645, The World Bank, Washington DC.

McBain, N.S., (1977), 'Developing country product choice: footwear in Ethiopia', *World Development*, Vol.5, pp.829–38.

McGee, T.G., (1971), *The Urbanization Process in the Third World; Exploration in Search of a Theory*, Bell and Sons, London.

Mead, D.C., (1984), 'Of contracts and subcontracts: small scale firms in vertically dis-integrated production/distribution systems in LDCs', *World Development*, Nov./Dec., pp.1095–1106.

Milone, P., (1978), *A Preliminary Study in Three Countries*, Indonesia Report, International Centre for Research on Women, Washington.

Mitter, S., (1986), 'Industrial restructuring and manufacturing homework: immigrant women in the UK clothing industry', *Capital and Class*, Spring.

Moser, C., (1978), 'Informal Sector of Petty commodity Production: Dualism or Dependence in Urban Development', in *World Development*, No.6, pp.1041–64.

Mukerji, A.B., (1980), *The Chamars of Uttar Pradesh: A Study in Social Geography*, Inter-India, Delhi.

Murai, Y., (1980), 'The Bimas Programme and agricultural labour in Indonesia', *Developing Economies*, Vol.18, No.1.

Murphy, E., (1981), *Unions in Conflict: a Comparative Study of Four South Indian Textile Centres 1918–1939*, Manohar Publications, New Delhi.

Nagaraj, R., (1984), 'Subcontracting in Indian manufacturing industries: analysis, evidence and issues', *Economic and Political Weekly*, Aug., pp.1435–53.

Nakamura, H., (1983), *Divorce in Java*, Gadjah Mada University Press.

Nanjundan, S., (1990), 'Should SSE Policy Be an Integral Part of Overall Development Policy?', in Gosses, A. *et al., Small Scale Enterprise Development in search of new alternatives*, Proceedings of workshop, The Hague.

Open University, (1983), *Clothing the world: first world markets, third world labour*, Case Study No.7, Third World Studies, Open University Press, Milton Keynes.

Ouchi, W.G., (1980), 'Markets, bureaucracies, and clans'. *Administrative Science Quarterly*, Vol.25, pp.129–41.

Palloix, C., (1976), *The labour process: from Fordism to neo-Fordism*, CSE Pamphlet No. 1, London.

Panini, M.N., (1978), 'Networks and styles: a study of Faridabad industrial entrepreneurs'. In S. Saberwal (ed.), *Process and Institution in Urban India: Sociological Studies,* Vikas, New Delhi.

Papanek, H. and Schwede, L., (1988), 'Women are good with money: earning and managing in an Indonesian City', In D. Dwyer and J. Bruce (eds), *A Home Divided*, Stanford University Press, California.

211

Pearson, R. and Elson, D., (1981), 'Nimble fingers make cheap workers: an analysis of women's employment in Third World manufacturing', *Feminist Review*, Vol.7, pp.87–107.

Peattie, L., (1982), 'What is to be done with the 'Informal Sector'? A Case Study of Shoe Manufacturers in Columbia' in H. Safa (ed.) *Towards a Politcal Economy of Urbanization in Third World Countries*, Oxford University Press, Delhi.

Perroux, F., (1953), 'Notes sur la Notion de al Pôle de Croissance', *Economie Appliquée*, Vol.8, Jan.–Jun.

Peña, G. de la, and Escobar Latapí, A. (eds) (1986), *Cambio Regional, Mercado de Trabajo y Via Obrera en Jalisco*, Colegio de Jalisco, Guadalajara.

Pineda-Ofreneo, R., (1982), 'Philippine domestic Outwork:Subcontracting for Export-oriented Industries', in *Journal of contemporary Asia*, Vol.12, No.3.

Pratten, C., Dean, R.M. and Silberston, A., (1965), *The Economies of Large-Scale production in British Industry: An Introductory Study*, Cambridge University Press, Cambridge.

Rao, R. and Husain, S., 'Invisible Hands: Women in Home-based Production in the Garment Export Industry in Delhi' in A. Singh and A. Kelles-Viitanen, *Invisible Hands*, Sage, New Delhi.

Rocha, M. de la, (1986), *Los Recursos de la Pobreza, Familias de Bajos Ingresos de Guadalajara*, Colegio de Jalisco, Guadalajara.

Roelofs, A., (1987), *Productive and Reproductive Roles of female construction labourers in Vellore, Tamil Nadu, India*, Urban Research Working Paper, Free University, Amsterdam.

Romijn, H., (1982), 'Hing Ki Mandi', unpublished Masters thesis, EUR, Rotterdam.

Rusli, S., (1978), 'Internal Rural Migration and Circulation in Indonesia: The Case of West Java', MA thesis, ANU.

Rutten, R., (1990), *'Artisans and Entrepreneurs in the Rural Philippines, Making a Living and Gaining Wealth in Two Commercialized Crafts'*, CASA Monograph No.2, CASA, Amsterdam.

Safilios-Rothschild, C., (1980), *The Role of The Family: A Neglected Aspect of Poverty*, World Bank Staff Working Paper, No.403, Washington DC.

Samuel, R., (1977), 'Workshop of the world: steam power and hand technology in mid-Victorian Britain', *History Workshop Journal*, No.3, Spring, pp.6–72.

Schmitz, H., (1982), *Manufacturing in the Backyard*, Frances Pinter, London.

Schmitz, H., (1985), *Technology and Employment Practices in Developing Countries*, Croom Helm, Beckenham.

Shram Shakti, (1988), Report of the National Commission on Self Employed Women and Women in the Informal Sector, June 1988, New Delhi.

Singh, A., and Kelles-Viitanen, A., (1987), *Invisible Hands: Women in Home-based Production*, Sage, New Delhi.

Smith, P.C., (1979), *Contrasting Marriage Patterns and Fertility in South East Asia: Indonesia and the Philippines Compared*, East-West Population Institute, Honolulu.

Sisworahardyo, (1979), 'Social Welfare Strategies to Enhance Women's Roles in Socio-economic Development and Leadership in Rural Areas', mimeo.

Sreenivasan, K., (1984), *India's Textile Industry*, South India Textile Research Association, Coimbatore.

Srivastava, D.B., (1979), *The Province of Agra, Its History and Administration*, New Delhi.

Stark, D., (1980), 'Class struggle and the transformation of the labor process', *Theory and Society*, Vol.9, No.4, July, pp.89–130.

Stoler, A., (1977), 'Rice Harvesting in Kali Loro: A Study of Class and Labour Relations in Rural Java', *American Ethnologist*, No.4.

Stoler, A., (1978), 'Class Structure and Female Autonomy in Rural Java', *Signs*, Vol.3, No.1.

Streefkerk, H., (1985), *Industrial Transition in rural India: Aritsans, Traders and Tribals in South Gujarat*, Sangam Books, London.

Subandrio, H., (1952), 'The social life of women in Indonesia', *Islamic Review*, Vol.40.

Suri, K.B. (ed.), (1988), *Small Scale Enterprises in Industrial Development*, Sage, New Delhi.

Takdir A., (1966), *Indonesia: Social and Cultural Revolution*, Oxford University Press, Kuala Lumpur.

Taylor, P.S., (1979), 'Labour time, work measurement and the commensuration of labour', *Capital and Class*, Vol.9, autumn, pp.23–37.

Tejani, K., (1987), 'A Study of Leather and Footwear Industry in Eastern Uttar Pradesh – India', unpublished MA thesis, EUR, Rotterdam.

The Hindu, (1984), 'The Strike in Tiruppur', July 8.

Thomas, H., (1990), 'Labour and Work in Small-scale Enterprises', WP Series No.79, ISS, the Hague.

Tom, I., (1987), *De inschakeling van vrouwenarbeid in de zijde industrie in Zuid India: de dynamiek van de informele sektor belicht*, Geografische en Planologische Notitie No.51, Free University, Amsterdam.

UNDP/Neth/ILO/UNIDO, (1988), *Rural Small Industrial Enterprise (RSIE): Lessons from Experience*, Vienna.

UNIDO, (1979a), *Monographs on Appropriate Industrial Technology No. 6*, UNIDO, Vienna, pp.41–61.

UNIDO, (1979b), *World Industry Since 1960: Progress and Prospects*, United Nations, New York.

UNIDO, (1985a), *Mechanisms for Small Scale Industry Development: Ancillarisation – Development of Feeder Industries*, UNIDO, New York.

UNIDO, (1985b), *Women and the Growth of Agro-Industries in Developing Countries*, ID/WG.452/1, Vienna.

UNDP/DGIS/ILO/UNIDO, (1988), *Development of Rural Small Industrial Enterprise*, Vienna.

UPICO, (Uttar Pradesh Industrial Consultants Ltd.), (1981), 'Leather footwear artisans in UP', *Rapport in opdracht van de UPLMDC*, Kanpur.

UPLDMC, (Uttar Pradesh State Leather Development and Marketing Corporation Ltd.), (1976), *Survey of Footwear Industry in Agra*, Agra.

Vaid, K.N., (1966), *Contract Labour in Manufacturing Industries; A Report and an Analysis*, New Delhi.

Waardenburg, J.G., (1988), 'Small Scale Leather Shoe-Manufacturing in Agra: A Case Study in Small Scale Industry in India's Development', In K.B. Suri (ed.), op.cit.

Weijland, H., (1982), *Distributive Forces in Economic Development Processes*, Free University Press, Amsterdam.

White, B., (1984), 'Measuring time allocation, decision-making and agrarian changes affecting rural women: examples from recent research in Indonesia', *IDS Bulletin*, Vol.15, No.1, pp.18–33.

Whitehead, A., (1981), 'I am Hungry Mum: the Politics of Domestic Budgeting', In K. Young *et al.* (eds), *Of Marriage and the Market*, CSE Books.

Williamson, O.E., (1981), 'The economics of organization: the transaction cost approach', *American Journal of Sociology*, Vol.87, No.3, pp.548–77.

Wood, S., (ed.), (1982), *The Degradation of Work*, Hutchinson and Co., London.

Zimbalist, A. (ed.), (1979), *Case Studies on the Labor Process*, Monthly Review Press.

Zuidberg, L.C., (1975), *Marriage, Fertility and Family Planning: The Serpong Project*, University and State University of Leiden.